The Eminent Monk

Kuroda Institute
Studies in East Asian Buddhism

Studies in Ch'an and Hua-yen
Robert M. Gimello and Peter N. Gregory

Dōgen Studies
William R. LaFleur

*The Northern School and the
Formation of Early Ch'an Buddhism*
John R. McRae

Traditions of Meditation in Chinese Buddhism
Peter N. Gregory

*Sudden and Gradual: Approaches to
Enlightenment in Chinese Thought*
Peter N. Gregory

Buddhist Hermeneutics
Donald S. Lopez, Jr.

*Paths to Liberation: The Mārga and Its
Transformations in Buddhist Thought*
Robert E. Buswell, Jr., and Robert M. Gimello

Sōtō Zen in Medieval Japan
William M. Bodiford

*The Scripture on the Ten Kings and
the Making of Purgatory in
Medieval Chinese Buddhism*
Stephen F. Teiser

STUDIES IN EAST ASIAN BUDDHISM 10

The Eminent Monk

Buddhist Ideals in Medieval Chinese Hagiography

John Kieschnick

A KURODA INSTITUTE BOOK

University of Hawai'i Press

Honolulu

97 98 99 00 01 02   5 4 3 2 1

Library of Congress Cataloging-in-Publication Data
Kieschnick, John, 1964–
The eminent monk : Buddhist ideals in Medieval Chinese hagiography
/ John Kieschnick.
p.   cm. — (Studies in East Asian Buddhism ; 10)
"A Kuroda Institute book."
Includes bibliographical references and index.
ISBN 0–8248–1841–5 (pbk. : alk. paper)
1. Monastic and religious life (Buddhism)—China—History.
2. Buddhist monks—China. 3. Priests, Buddhist—China.
4. Religious biography—China—History and criticism.   I. Series:
Studies in East Asian Buddhism ; no. 10.
BQ6160.C6K54   1997
294.3'657'0922—dc21   97–5496
                                                 CIP

The Kuroda Institute for the Study of Buddhism and Human Values
is a nonprofit, educational corporation founded in 1976. One of its primary
objectives is to promote scholarship on the historical, philosophical,
and cultural ramifications of Buddhism. In association with the University
of Hawai'i Press, the Institute also publishes Classics in East Asian
Buddhism, a series devoted to the translation of significant texts in the
East Asian Buddhist tradition.

Book design by Kenneth Miyamoto

Contents

Acknowledgments   vii

Introduction   1
CHAPTER 1: Asceticism   16
CHAPTER 2: Thaumaturgy   67
CHAPTER 3: Scholarship   112
Final Reflections   139

Abbreviations   147
Notes   149
Glossary   187
Works Cited   195
Index   213

Acknowledgments

MY THANKS first to my teachers, Bernard Faure, Carl Bielefeldt, and Albert Dien, for their advice and encouragement when I began this project as a graduate student. Thanks also to classmates Philip Kafalas, Mark Csikszentmihalyi, Robin Wagner, and Keith Knapp who read through drafts of the manuscript at that time and offered many suggestions.

When I was rewriting the dissertation for this book, Alan Cole and Elizabeth Morrison offered generous and insightful comments. I am grateful as well to the readers for the Kuroda Institute, T. Griffith Foulk and Daniel Stevenson, for their detailed advice.

Preliminary research for the book was carried out with support from the Fulbright Foundation and the Center for Chinese Studies in Taipei. A postdoctoral fellowship at the Center for Chinese Studies in Berkeley allowed me to complete the final revisons.

Thanks, finally, to my mother, who taught me my first Chinese character, and my father, who gave me my first Chinese book.

The Eminent Monk

Introduction

THIS BOOK is a study of monastic ideals as revealed in three collections of biographies of monks compiled in China from the sixth to the tenth centuries. Although usually based on historical figures, these accounts of the lives of monks contain much that is fabulous and historically inaccurate—tales of monks who lived for hundreds of years, monks who defeated monsters with esoteric spells, monks able to fly through the air, and so on. In the past, scholars have concentrated on winnowing out such fabulous elements in an attempt to uncover a factual core. While this is often an arduous and complicated task, there is much to be said for this approach, which is crucial if we are to understand what a given monk really said and did at a particular place and time. In this study, however, I have chosen instead to set aside the historicity of the accounts and accept them as representations of the image of the monk, of what monks were *supposed* to be. In other words, this is a study of the monastic imagination.

Let me explain what I mean with an example from one of the three collections I draw on. The *Song Biographies of Eminent Monks* (*Song gaoseng zhuan*), a tenth-century collection of biographies of monks, contains two separate accounts of a meeting between the Chinese monk Daoxuan and the Indian monk Śubhakarasiṃha (Ch. Shanwu-wei), two of the most influential monks of the Tang. One account appears in the biography devoted to Śubhakarasiṃha; the other, in the biography of Daoxuan. According to both accounts, Śubhakarasiṃha had heard of Daoxuan while still in India, and on arriving in China, asked to meet the famous Chinese monk. The emperor then arranged for the two monks to share a room at a monastery in the capital. At this point, the two accounts diverge. According to Daoxuan's biography, Śubhakarasiṃha was impressed by Daoxuan's practice of care-

1

fully wrapping fleas in a strip of silk and placing them gently on the ground after catching them instead of killing the pests. Śubhakara-siṃha's biography, on the other hand, recounts that the two roommates had a falling out. Śubhakarasiṃha, the biography relates, was a crude and unkempt monk. But one night when he reprimanded Daoxuan for killing a single flea, Daoxuan realized that the foreign monk was in fact a holy man. Yet another account of the encounter between these two monks supplies more detail, claiming that Śubhakarasiṃha would come home drunk every night and vomit on the floor. In this account also, Śubhakarasiṃha reprimands Daoxuan for killing a single flea.

If we could accept any of these accounts as reliable, we could learn important information about these influential monks and the society in which they lived. Had Daoxuan really become famous in India? Did Daoxuan, a leading expert on the monastic regulations, in fact kill insects? Did Śubhakarasiṃha actually routinely get drunk? Unfortunately, we are forced to reject all three accounts, for such an encounter between these two men could not have taken place: examination of well-attested dates for the two monks reveals that Daoxuan died a half century before Śubhakarasiṃha arrived in China.

Therefore, if we hope to reconstruct the lives of these monks, and perhaps even uncover something of their psychology, we would do better to peel away the layers of legend that grew up around them and try to uncover a factual core from material that can be reliably dated to an earlier period. After all, Śubhakarasiṃha's contemporaries would have found absurd any reference to a meeting with Daoxuan, a figure they knew to have died some time previous. In this case, this approach works well. Daoxuan's writings contain a number of autobiographical references, none of which makes any reference to a meeting with Śubhakarasiṃha, and which on the contrary date Daoxuan's death to a time before the arrival of Śubhakarasiṃha in China.[1] In short, the earliest accounts of these monks indicate that the story of their meeting given in the *Song Biographies* is a later, historically inaccurate legend.

Nevertheless, in the case of Daoxuan, as in the case of most Chinese monks, attempts to strip stories of legendary materials meet with only limited success. For while the value of dating the various layers of a biography and tracing its development over time is undeniable, the assumption that fabulous elements were added to a more sober, early biography does not always hold true. To see the problem more clearly, let us for a moment move from the Tang to modern times and examine the case of the Chinese monk Xuyun, who lived from 1840 to 1959.

Reconstructing the life of Xuyun is considerably easier than reconstructing the life of a medieval monk. Not only are we separated from Xuyun by only a few decades, but he also left us an autobiography. As

Xuyun is perhaps the most revered figure in modern Chinese Buddhism, many legends circulate about his life. In this case, however, we can set aside these later legends and turn instead to an earlier, more reliable source for the monk: his autobiography, the first lines of which begin with his birth:

> I was born at the headquarters of Quanzhou Prefecture on the last day of the seventh month in the year Gengzi, the twentieth of the Daoguang reign [26 August 1840]. When my mother saw that she had given birth to a fleshy bag, she was frightened, and thinking that there was no hope of bearing child again, she succumbed to her desperation and passed away. The following day an old man selling medicine came to our house and cut open the bag, taking out a male child which was reared by my stepmother.[2]

Later in the autobiography, Xuyun describes his enlightenment, which occurred after a period of illness during a long bout of meditation.

> I opened my eyes and suddenly perceived a great brightness similar to broad daylight wherein everything inside and outside the monastery was discernible to me. Through the wall, I saw the monk in charge of lamps and incense urinating outside, the guest-monk in the latrine, and faraway, boats plying on the river with the trees on both its banks—all were clearly seen: it was just the third watch of the night when this happened. The next morning, I asked the incense-monk and guest-monk about this and both confirmed what I had seen the previous night.[3]

While not doubting Xuyun's sincerity, I have difficulty accepting either his account of his birth or his claim to have seen through a wall. Yet to discount the stories entirely, or, worse, to speculate on possible medical conditions that approximate his miraculous birth, or the "real" experience behind Xuyun's belief that he had seen through a wall, is to abandon the cultural context that makes the stories relevant and to lose an opportunity to see the monk's world as he saw it, rather than as a skewed reflection of our own sensibilities. In other words, these stories illustrate that the themes and limits of Buddhist hagiography were a part of Xuyun's life. And if we do not always have access to the actions behind the legends, we can learn to appreciate the far-reaching consequences of the legends themselves.

The same holds true for medieval accounts of monks. When read carefully, these biographies are of great value for reconstructing the geographic spread of monasticism in China, the relative strength of various doctrinal trends over time, the monastic economy, and so on. But in addition to reading these biographies for accounts of actual monks, we can also read them as an expression of the *idea* of the monk, that is, what people thought monks were and what they thought monks should be.[4] The stories of Daoxuan and Śubhakarasiṃha, for example, tell us that for the writers and presumably the readers of these stories, it was wrong for a monk to kill a flea. Curiously, the biography of Śubhakarasiṃha also suggests that it would somehow have been acceptable for the great monk to routinely become drunk. These are the sorts of questions I address in this book—questions about how monks were expected to behave that often yield striking and unexpected answers.

Not surprisingly, the image of the monk and notions of the ideal monk varied widely from one time to another, from monk to layman, and from one genre of biography to another. In the following chapters I draw on biographies of monks to describe and analyze representations of the monk in medieval China. In particular, I mine the biographies for monastic ideals concerning asceticism, thaumaturgy, and scholarship—three of the most common themes in the hagiography. But before diving into the biographies for evidence of monastic ideals, let us pause to consider the nature of the material and the extent of its influence.

The Biographies of Eminent Monks

This study focuses on three collections of Buddhist hagiography known collectively as the *Biographies of Eminent Monks*. At the beginning of the sixth century, the scholar-monk Huijiao (497–554) drew on literary sources and epigraphy as well as personal interviews to compile a collection of 257 biographies of Chinese monks, which he termed *Biographies of Eminent Monks*.[5] In the preface to his work, Huijiao distinguishes his collection from a previous, no longer extant work entitled *Biographies of Famous Monks* (*Mingseng zhuan*).[6] The *Biographies of Eminent Monks*, Huijiao notes, includes only biographies of monks worthy of admiration. "If men of real achievement conceal their brilliance, then they are eminent but not famous; when men of slight virtue happen to be in accord with their times, then they are famous but not eminent. Those who are famous but not eminent are, of course, not recorded here; those who are eminent but not famous have been fully treated in the present work."[7]

In style and format, Huijiao's work was based on Chinese secular histories and owes comparatively little to Indian forms of hagiography. A typical biography begins by listing the monk's secular surname and place of origin. The biography may give information on the monk's father or other ancestors if they were prominent. The biography then usually goes on to relate the monk's first master, when the monk received full ordination, what books he read, works he wrote or deeds he performed, and so on. The biography often ends with the precise date and circumstances of the monk's death, followed by names of his most prominent disciples. The brief biography of Tanjie[8] is a typical example:

> Shi Tanjie, who also went by the name Huijing, was surnamed Zhuo. A native of Nanyang, he was the younger brother of Zhuo Qian, Magistrate of Jiyang in the Ministry of Outer Troops for the Jin.
>
> [Before he became a monk] Tanjie lived in poverty, devoting himself to study, and delving into the classics. Later, he heard that Yu Fadao would lecture on the *Scripture of Great Light*.[9] He borrowed a robe and, on hearing the lecture, was profoundly enlightened to the principles of Buddhism. He then abandoned the secular life and followed the Way, serving Sire [Dao]an as his master. He mastered the Three Repositories [Skt. *tripiṭaka*] and learned to chant more than five hundred thousand words of the scriptures. He bowed in obeisance to the Buddha five hundred times a day. Jin Prince of Linchuan [Sima Bao] held Tanjie in high esteem.
>
> Later, when Tanjie took seriously ill, he chanted continuously, the name of Maitreya Buddha never leaving his lips. His disciple, Zhisheng, who waited on him in his illness, asked him why he did not want to be reborn in [the Heaven] of Peaceful Repose [i.e., Amitābha's paradise, Skt. *Sukhāvatī*]. Tanjie replied, "Together with the Reverend [Daoan] and eight others, I have vowed to be reborn in Tuṣita [i.e., Maitreya's paradise]. The Reverend, Daoyuan, and the others have already been born there, but I have not. That is why I have this wish."
>
> When he finished speaking, a light shone on his body, and an expression of joy appeared on his face. He then quickly passed away. Tanjie was seventy years old. He was buried to the right of Daoan's grave.

Although Buddhist themes predominate, the style and structure of the biography are squarely in the tradition of secular biography established long before the *Liang Biographies* in the *Shiji* and *Han shu*. The mixture in this biography of precise historical information—such as Tanjie's ancestry and place of origin—with the miraculous light that appeared at his death, is typical of the accounts that appear in the *Biographies*, a characteristic that allows for multiple levels of interpretation, from meticulous comparison of dates and travel routes in different biographies to the sort of broad inquiries into beliefs and representations I will engage in below.

In the seventh century, Daoxuan (596–667) compiled a massive new biographical collection, the *Further Biographies of Eminent Monks* (*Xu gaoseng zhuan*), to cover the lives of monks who had lived since the appearance of Huijiao's work. Like the *Liang Biographies*, this book, containing some 485 biographies, was compiled privately.[10] The genre reached its highest level of prestige in 982, when Zanning (919–1001), one of the most distinguished Buddhist figures of the Northern Song court, received an edict from the emperor commanding him to oversee the compilation of a new edition of the *Biographies*, the *Song Biographies of Eminent Monks* (*Song gaoseng zhuan*), to record the lives of worthy monks who lived during the period between Daoxuan's death and the early years of the Song. The completed manuscript, presented to the throne some six years later, contained more than five hundred biographies, ranging in length from a few lines to biographies of more than a thousand characters.[11] One more version of the *Biographies of Eminent Monks* was compiled in the Ming, but it was not to achieve the prestige of its predecessors.

Motivation

When Huijiao compiled the *Eminent Monks*, he was participating in an established tradition of Chinese monastic biography, as demonstrated by the list of works he gives in the preface to his own work. In fact, the better part of the preface is taken up with a review of previous collections of biographies of monks. It is in the deficiencies of these works that Huijiao finds the major justification for compiling a new collection. Previous accounts, he tells us, "are sometimes too long and sometimes too brief; they differ in what they include and what they omit." They are "confused and difficult to draw upon," and the "literary form is inadequate." Even more than the inferior literary style of previous works, Huijiao lamented the lack of completeness and the danger that the noble deeds of worthy monks would soon pass from memory. Previous works, he writes, "each either strives to exalt a single region without covering both the modern and the ancient or concentrates on single good deeds without touching on other activities [of its subjects]." Others, "out of an aversion to multiplicity and breadth, abridge their data, and remarkable [instances of] exemplary conduct are often omitted or cut short."[12]

Zanning, in his own *Song Biographies*, expressed the same concern for the historical record, writing that, "In his compilation, Huijiao used as his criteria 'real achievement and concealed brilliance.' Daoxuan in his collection continued the tradition of those 'eminent though not famous.' They prevented men who practiced the Way over the span of six hundred years from falling into obscurity."[13] Elsewhere, Zanning related his efforts to the historical enterprise championed by the great Chinese secular historians of antiquity when he wrote, "If [the

Song Biographies] contains admirable and accurate accounts, this is because I have imitated Chen Shou.[14] And if it includes egregious errors and misinterpretations of scripture, then I have done a disservice to Sima Qian."[15]

The concern with comprehensiveness drove Daoxuan and Zanning to find fault even with the preceding works on which their collections were based.[16] Daoxuan complained that Huijiao concentrated on southern monks to the exclusion of monks from the north. Zanning included biographies of several monks from the Sui and Six Dynasties period that Daoxuan had failed to record, explaining their absence from Daoxuan's works with the following sympathetic note:

> The empire is vast, and marvelous occurrences take place daily. It is truly difficult to keep abreast of all of them. It is also true that, for whatever reason, information on some monks was simply not included in the historical record. As the biographer then has nothing on which to base his account, he leaves such monks out. Unable to record the biography himself, he leaves the task for a later scholar to complete.[17]

But if the compilers of the *Eminent Monks* were historians with allegiances to Sima Qian and a dedication to a complete historical record, they were also monks, and as such committed to the propagation of Buddhism. In a letter to an acquaintance, Huijiao justified the *Liang Biographies* with the exclamation, "For spreading the Way and explaining the Teaching, nothing surpasses eminent monks."[18] One of the most vital means for monks to "spread the Way" was through the assistance of powerful rulers; and it is to such figures that the *Biographies* were, in part, directed. Information about the intended audience of the *Biographies* is scarce, but all of the compilers must have realized that their works would be read by politically powerful figures. We know very little about Huijiao's life, or the circumstances under which he compiled his work. We do know, however, that Emperor Liang Yuan Di (508–554), who was a contemporary of Huijiao, possessed a copy of the *Liang Biographies*.[19] And a similar collection, the *Mingseng zhuan*—with which, as we have seen, Huijiao was familiar—was compiled under imperial auspices.

Biographical information on Daoxuan, as well as his voluminous extant writings, give ample testimony to his deep commitment to propagating Buddhism in court circles.[20] His inclusion in the *Further Biographies* of a section devoted to monks who defended Buddhism from its enemies at court further suggests that he hoped his collection of biographies of eminent monks would convince powerful political figures of the merits of Buddhism.

Zanning's ties to the Northern Song court are well documented.[21] Specifically, the *Song Biographies* were compiled under imperial auspices in response to an edict that appointed Zanning to head up a team of scholars to complete a collection of biographies of monks for the emperor's perusal. In a memorial to the emperor, composed on completion of the work, Zanning remarked, "Because the Teaching [of Buddhism] and the [Buddha] Law have nothing on which to rely, they must depend on the might of rulers," a comment that resonates with a famous passage in the biography of Daoan in the *Liang Biographies*: "Without the support of rulers, it is difficult to establish the [Buddha] Law."[22] This, the role of benevolent defender of the Law, was a role the emperor was willing to play. In his response to Zanning's memorial, Emperor Taizong wrote, "The marvelous Way of the single vehicle, the profound gate of the six perfections, produces marvelous men in each generation who propagate the holy teaching. If [their deeds] are not recorded, how can [Buddhism] be proclaimed!"[23] Both Emperor Taizong and Zanning, then, saw the *Biographies* not merely as a record of monks, but more importantly as a means of verifying the virtues of Buddhism and making these virtues widely known.

Finally, the compilers of the *Eminent Monks* hoped that their works would serve as models for the monastic community, that they would be held up as ideals to which ordinary monks should aspire. This is how Daoxuan read the *Liang Biographies* when he wrote that it had "been circulated throughout the empire. Truly, [it provides us with] models to be emulated."[24] In a similar vein, Zanning referred to the monks in his collection as marvelous plants displayed before ordinary grass, and as extraordinary beasts placed before ordinary animals. He then called for the emulation of eminent monks, citing a passage from the *Book of Poetry* that states, "When King Wen is imitated in style and demeanor, the ten thousand states follow his example."[25] And in his preface Zanning called on his readers, when reading the accounts of eminent monks, "to become enlightened, and long to equal them."[26]

Structure

When Huijiao compiled the *Liang Biographies*, he divided the 257 biographies into ten categories: (1) Translators (*yijing*); (2) Exegetes (*yijie*); (3) Divine Wonders (*shenyi*), devoted to wonder-workers; (4) Practitioners of Meditation (*xichan*); (5) Elucidators of the Regulations (*minglü*), devoted to scholars of the Vinaya; (6) Those Who Sacrificed Themselves (*wangshen*),[27] devoted to monks who sacrificed their bodies to feed animals, or as offerings to Buddhas or bodhisattvas; (7) Chanters of Scriptures (*songjing*); (8)Benefactors (*xingfu*), devoted to monks who solicited funds to construct monasteries or for other Buddhist enterprises; (9)Hymnodists (*jingshi*); and (10) Proselytizers (*changdao*). In his preface, Huijiao singles out the translators for special praise, for "the enlightenment of China was wholly dependent on them." He then explains that it is for this reason that he places their biographies at the head of his work. Although this comment indicates that a value judgment was involved in the ordering of the categories, there is no evidence to suggest that Huijiao applied such criteria throughout his classification; despite the order of the chapters, it does not seem, for example, that he considered wonder-workers superior to meditators, or chanters superior to benefactors.

Daoxuan followed Huijiao's schema, with a few important innovations. He subsumed the categories for hymnodists and proselytizers under the heading "Miscellaneous Sermonists" (*zake shengde*), which includes monks skilled in poetry, calligraphy, and other areas not covered by the previous categories.[28] Daoxuan also changed the wording for the thaumaturgy chapter, labeling this section in the *Further Biographies* "Spiritual Resonance" (*gantong*) instead of the "Divine Wonders" of the *Liang Biographies*. I will have more to say about this change below. Perhaps the most significant change Daoxuan made was to establish a new category called "Defenders of the [Buddha] Law" (*hufa*) for monks who defended Buddhism from Daoists and from enemies at court. In the *Song Biographies*, Zanning followed Daoxuan's schema without changes in nomenclature, although the section originally devoted to meditators instead included figures associated with the "Chan school" in the *Song Biographies*, whether or not they were known for meditation.

At the end of each of the ten sections, Huijiao also included a "treatise" (*lun*) in which he discusses the subject of the section and usually summarizes the contributions of the monks in that section. Huijiao also included a short "paean" (*zan*) or poem of praise for each of the first eight categories.[29] Like so much else in the structure of the *Biographies*, these conventions are rooted in the practices of secular historians. Daoxuan followed Huijiao's format of including a treatise at the end of each section.[30] In the *Song Biographies*, Zanning added "addenda" (*xi*) to some of the biographies. These are short comments that discuss aspects of a given biography that Zanning found problematic or interesting. Both the treatises of the three compilers and Zanning's addenda are useful when studying the reflection of monastic ideals in the *Biographies* in that they give us more direct and personal information about how the three compilers understood the accounts they included in their collections.

Sources

Very few of the accounts in the *Biographies* were composed by the compilers of the three collections; most are instead taken directly, word-for-word, or with additions and deletions, from sources available to them.[31] Huijiao describes the process of collecting information for his book as follows:

> I was wont in my leisure time to examine a large number of writings. I made a point of investigating the miscellaneous accounts of several tens of authors together with the chronicles and histories of the Jin, Song, Qi, and Liang dynasties, the heterodox histories of the frontier dynasties of Qin, Zhao, Yan, and Liang, geographical miscellanies, isolated pieces, and fragmentary accounts. In addition I made extensive interrogations of experienced ancients, and I widely questioned those more learned than myself. I collated what was included with what was excluded and found where they agreed and where they differed.[32]

As these comments indicate, Huijiao drew on a wide variety of materials for information on the monks he wrote about. Daoxuan and Zanning also drew on a number of different genres of writing as well as a small number of oral sources for their accounts. The *Eminent Monks* biography of a prominent translator may be based on the account in a bibliography of Buddhist books, which in turn was based on a preface to one of the monk's works. Another biography may be copied directly from a collection of miracle tales compiled by a lay literatus devoted to Buddhism.[33] Another common source for the *Biographies* was stupa inscriptions. On the death of a prominent monk, his disciples would compile a brief account of his life (*xingzhuang*) and then ask, or at times hire, an accomplished local literatus to work this material into an ornate encomium, including elaborate metaphors and complicated allusions. This epitaph was then inscribed in stone at the site of the monk's remains.[34]

From the cases in which the original work or works on which the *Eminent Monks* biography was based survives, we can see that the compilers of the *Eminent Monks* often reworked the original material, combining passages from different sources, or, especially in the case of stupa inscriptions, extracting facts about the monk's life from a more ornate context.[35] Other times, the original work is copied into the *Eminent Monks* word-for-word, usually without attribution.[36]

The biography of Tanjie translated above, for example, was apparently taken from an account in the *Mingseng zhuan*, which survives as one of the extant fragments of that work.[37] The *Mingseng zhuan* version of Tanjie's biography is for the most part the same as the version in the *Liang Biographies*. It gives the same information about Tanjie's family background, the same story of him borrowing a robe to attend a lecture on the *Scripture of Great Light*, his tutelage under Daoan, his commitment to chanting the name of Maitreya, and the marvelous light that shone at his death. Even the wording of much of the two biographies is the same. The *Mingseng zhuan* is slightly longer and gives a number of details omitted in the *Liang Biographies*. For example, it makes it clear that the reason Tanjie had to borrow a robe to attend the Buddhist lecture was because his family was too poor to buy him decent clothing.

In this case we might assume that, despite Huijiao's criticism of the *Mingseng zhuan*, the world-view and motives of Baochang, the monk who composed the *Mingseng zhuan*, and Huijiao were roughly similar. But what of the case of a devotee collecting strange tales demonstrating the divine power of the bodhisattva Guanyin that happen to include information about a monk? Or what of the prominent literatus-official who composed a biography couched in allusions to the classics that he knew would be placed on public display at a local monastery? In the majority of cases in the *Eminent Monks*, we do not know where the biography originated. As I cite biographies from the *Eminent Monks* as illustrations of monastic ideals, the question arises of just whose ideals I am describing: those of a prominent monk, a devout layman, or a polished local official?

In general, my response to the troubling question of the origins of the biographies is that I am trying to describe generally held, slowly changing conceptions of how monks were supposed to behave, and that many of these conceptions were held in common by people of diverse social standing and occupation—a supposition based largely on the relative continuity of themes and standards from one biography to the next despite their diverse origins. Nonetheless, the question of just whose ideals a given biography represents is one that haunts any study of this material and is a question that the discriminating reader will pose relentlessly as he or she reads this book.[38]

Reception

Just as important as authorship of the accounts included in the *Biographies* is the question of readership and how readers responded to these accounts of monks. The three collections of *Biographies of Eminent Monks* have become the standard source for modern scholars interested in biographical information on monks of the period. But how widely were these books read in premodern times? Literary and archaeological evidence suggests that Buddhist books were well distributed already in the Tang. An imperial edict of 714 forbade monks from running shops "within the streets of the city wards" to copy and sell Buddhist books.[39] When visiting a pilgrimage site in 1072, the Japanese pilgrim Jōjin noted that various Buddhist and non-Buddhist texts were on sale on either side of the entranceway to the site, including a copy of a collection of miracle tales concerning the *Lotus Sūtra*.[40] Copies of the *Biographies of Eminent Monks* may well have been distributed in a similar fashion. Further, each of the versions of the *Biographies* quickly found its way into the official Buddhist canon, copies of which were periodically donated to the libraries of prominent monasteries as imperial gifts. And there is ample evidence testifying to the frequent use of monastic libraries by monks and literati alike in the medieval period.[41]

In his preface to the *Further Biographies*, Daoxuan mentions reading the *Liang Biographies* in his days as a student.[42] In another work on the proper treatment of a monk's property upon his death, Daoxuan includes biographies of monks among the common property of the monks of his day.[43] And occasionally we read of monks inspired by the biographies of their predecessors.[44] But the greatest testimony to the popularity of the *Biographies* is the fact that their accounts of monks were copied directly into later collections time and again.[45] In sum, the *Biographies* appear to have been well-distributed and widely read.

Assessments of the merit of the *Biographies of Eminent Monks*, however, are far from uniform. The editors of the eighteenth-century *Siku quanshu zongmu* praised the *Song Biographies* for its inclusion of biographical materials from a wide array of sources and for its elegant writing style.[46] Similarly, nineteenth-century scholar and bibliophile Yang Shoujing praised the *Further Biographies* for its elegance, comparing Daoxuan to great secular historians of the past.[47] Others, however, were less generous. The seventeenth-century monk Jiyin said of the *Song Biographies*, "The literary style is a jumble, and the organization of the book inferior. It is worth perusing, but nothing more."[48] In the same vein, the Yuan monk Purui criticized one of the accounts in the *Song Biographies* as "full of errors and not worth citing."[49]

Most critical of all was the Song monk Huihong who leveled his criticism against all three versions of the *Eminent Monks*. First, in reference to the style of the *Biographies*, he remarked, "Daoxuan was well-versed in the Regulations [the Vinaya], but literary style was not his strong point: his biographies of Chan monks read like residence permits and marriage certificates."[50] Elsewhere, Huihong records the comments of one of his students who, he says, once complained to him, "I have read through the histories of monks from Huijiao to

Daoxuan to Zanning, but these books are most different from the *Records of the Historian*, or the histories of the Han, the Southern and Northern [Dynasties] and the Tang. The style is confused and repetitive." Huihong then notes that the prominent Song writer Huang Tingjian also objected to the disjointed style of the *Biographies* and proposed to rewrite them himself.[51] The basis for Huihong's stylistic complaint is that the compilers of the *Biographies* for the most part simply copied out the materials they collected, sometimes throwing together diverse documents, rather than rewriting the biographies in a consistent style.

Huihong also criticized the organization of the *Biographies*. As we have seen, although in the *Song Biographies* the section originally devoted to "practitioners of meditation" (*chan*) was increasingly reserved for members of the Chan school whether or not they were known for meditation, overall the interests of the compilers of the *Biographies* remained ecumenical: the *Biographies* cut across such divisions, attempting instead to highlight eminent monks regardless of their sectarian affiliation. It is precisely this refusal to presage the Chan school that Huihong objected to. In his *Linjian lu*, Huihong singled out Zanning's *Song Biographies* for criticism. "When Zanning compiled the *Song Biographies of Eminent Monks*, dividing the monks into ten categories, he put exegetes[52] at the head of the collection. This in itself is ridiculous enough, but what is more, he classified Chan Master Yantou Huo as an ascetic (*kuxing*) and Chan Master Xingzhi Jueshou as a benefactor. Grand Master Yunmen—a king among monks and a contemporary [of Zanning]—he did not record at all!"[53]

There is some justification for both Huihong's criticism of the style of the *Biographies* and his criticism of their system of classification. The compilers of the *Eminent Monks* series seldom composed the biographies themselves. Rather, they drew heavily on earlier sources, whether these sources were biographies composed soon after a monk's death and inscribed on a stele, or references to monks in collections of Buddhist tales, or from autobiographical references in the prefaces to a monk's works. Some of the accounts in the *Biographies* are awkward patchworks of these materials pieced together in a haphazard fashion, occasionally making for passages that are difficult if not impossible to understand.

Nevertheless, the modern historian is thankful for what we would now consider rampant plagiarism. Although the compilers of the *Biographies* seldom cite their sources, because they follow their original sources so closely it is often possible to determine the nature of the original source, whether it be a stele inscription, a miracle tale, or an oral story. Further, the heterogeneous nature of the *Biographies* means that the collections do not represent the opinions of the compilers alone, but also of the hundreds of different authors who composed the material on which the biographies were based; more than the work of three prominent scholar-monks, the *Biographies* can hence be used to reconstruct more general mentalities of the time.

Huihong's second criticism, his sectarian bickering about the organization of the *Eminent Monks*, presents us with a different problem— namely, how representative was the organization of the *Biographies* of mental categories of medieval Chinese? Did people think of monks as belonging to one of the ten categories established by Huijiao, or were these merely a formal principle of organization of a particular biographical genre without real social resonance? I lean toward this second interpretation. The ten categories of the *Biographies* are not found in any other biographical collections.

Even within the *Biographies* the division seems an arbitrary one, often masking themes that tie one figure to another. The biography of Daoxuan in the *Song Biographies*, for example, is placed in the category reserved for Vinaya scholars. This is understandable as Daoxuan composed a number of extremely influential works on the Vinaya. At the same time, Daoxuan's biography provides valuable information on his role in the "defense of the Buddha Law" and his views of thaumaturgy; and no survey of Buddhist thaumaturgy or monastic involvement in court politics during the Tang would be complete without some reference to Daoxuan.

Hence, while a careful analysis of the way these categories changed from one collection to another and the extent to which they influenced other writers may yet prove fruitful, I have chosen instead to cut across the ten categories in order to follow three prominent themes through the biographies. In the pages that follow I divide my discussion of monks into the three areas of asceticism, thaumaturgy, and scholarship. These should not be taken as absolute or distinct categories; most monks were seen by themselves and others as possessing some combination of characteristics from all three areas.

Monastic ideals of asceticism, thaumaturgy, and scholarship permeate Buddhist literature of all sorts and appear in various guises. Even when we focus our attention on hagiography, the expression of these ideals is not entirely consistent. Nevertheless, when we draw together the hundreds of examples of stories involving these three areas of monastic life, patterns begin to emerge, and it becomes possible to trace the emergence and development of these ideals in one particularly influential body of writings. The components of these ideals are many, and each raises its own set of questions. What forms did asceticism take in China, and how was it received by those outside the clergy?

If many monks were thought to be wonder-workers, where was their power thought to reside: in techniques or in inherent properties? In monastic debate, were monks expected to treat their opponents with tolerance and deference or to fiercely attack them in defense of correct Buddhist views? Let us begin with the most pervasive and visible characteristic of the medieval monk: the habits, clothing, and practices that marked the monk as an ascetic.

CHAPTER 1
Asceticism

The Monastic Distinction

When Yijing, a seventh-century Chinese pilgrim to India, composed a lengthy letter to his Buddhist brothers in China, he did not write about the universality of the Buddha nature or the latest Yogācāra tracts, or any other of a number of doctrinal issues with which Chinese exegetes of the late seventh century were engaged. Rather, he wrote about what at first seem the most mundane of matters: hygiene (monks should wash their hands after using the privy), decorum (one should not greet the host of one's destination immediately upon arrival, but should rest and wash first), and clothing (monks must learn to fold their robes properly). For Yijing these were not mundane matters at all, but among the most vital issues Chinese Buddhism faced, for it was through such matters that Yijing sought to define the Buddhist monk. The problem of definition was not one of discovery, but of implementation: the ideal monastic community was, for Yijing, already in place in India. While certain minor adjustments had to be made to fit the Indian model to a country with different climate and customs, the basic foundation of monasticism was sound.

But the problem of definition was never as straightforward as Yijing thought, for just as the full range of meaning of a given word differs from one language to another, or even within one language from one time to another, so too did the symbols of renunciation differ from India to China, from the second century to the tenth, from the monk to the layman. To the extent that the monastic community was essentially a "nonconformist subgroup,"[1] or "counterculture," its values were meaningful largely in relation to the dominant culture. Indeed, any set of values in which renunciation plays a central role is of necessity in a constant dialectic with mainstream values—values, it is important to note, that are themselves in a perpetual state of flux.

When applied to Chinese monastic ideals, all of this may seem to trivialize Buddhist ethics, to suggest that men in China became monks *simply* to be different. This is certainly not the case. Many monks were undoubtedly motivated by a genuine revulsion for the decadence of secular society, for facile materialism, and for violence. Many no doubt carefully considered the principles by which they hoped to live. But at the same time we must recognize that no one is capable of formulating a life-style that is ethically consistent in every respect. When pressed, even the most sophisticated theologian would be hard put to justify all of his or her actions according to theological tenets. To even contemplate such a project is mind-boggling. One would have to carefully consider the origin and nature of every sort of food one bought at the market or ordered at a restaurant, every article of clothing, every sentence uttered in every circumstance. What we need then are general parameters of behavior.

One of the appeals of monastic Buddhism was precisely that it represented a circumscribed set of rules centered on general notions of the proper way to live that were appealing to those who joined the Order. Taken together, monastic regulations and the stories of the lives of eminent monks provided models for a detailed system of practice, including instructions on how to act, eat, dress, and even sleep. In large measure the monastic life-style was based on carefully thought-out doctrines relating to the meaning of life, Buddhist cosmology, Buddhist ethics, and so on. But the evolution of Buddhist monastic ideals was more complex than this. The ever-changing social and material context in which monks found themselves also contributed to the standard of what was practicable and what was desirable at a given time and place, so much so that when we look closely we discover not one definition of what it was to be a monk, but many. The official, the peasant, the erudite monk, and the novice each had markedly different ideas of what a monk should be, ideas that constantly clashed, adapted, and developed in accordance with the social interactions of everyday life. Nevertheless, the vast majority of these various ideals of monkhood are in some way related to notions of asceticism loosely defined. Below I focus on several areas in which we can see in hagiography and other sources the meeting of divergent attitudes toward asceticism, as well as the role the *Biographies* played in these encounters.

Sex

One of the earliest references we have to a Buddhist monk in China occurs quite by chance in the "Western Metropolis Rhapsody," a long piece by the Han poet Zhang Heng depicting the glories of the flourishing capital of Chang'an in the second century A.D. At one point in the poem, Zhang describes the incomparably beautiful dancing girls of the capital skipping lightly "between plates and goblets" dressed in "vermilion slippers" and "gossamer silks." Zhang ends his flowing description by noting that one glimpse of these whirling girls with their "arched backs" and "darting glances," and "even Zhan Ji or a śramaṇa could not help but fall under their spell."[2]

In addition to helping us trace the rise of Buddhism in the capital, this short, chance reference reveals at least two important aspects of the image of the monk in early Chinese Buddhism. First of all, even at this early stage, the monk was a symbol of continence, the control of sexual desire; the fact that Zhang Heng could drop a reference to a śramaṇa, confident that his readers would grasp the allusion, indicates that the image of the sober Buddhist monk had already earned a place in the mental landscape of the capital's literati. Second, while the appearance of dark-skinned religious professionals[3] dedicated to a life of abstinence must have struck Han Chinese as novel, the reference in the poem to Zhan Ji reminds us that ascetic ideas were not entirely new to China. Zhan Ji, a figure from the seventh century B.C., was known for his spotless reputation, especially as exemplified by the story that he once allowed a scantily clad, unattached woman to sit on his lap in order to protect her from the freezing cold, without arousing suspicions as to his character.[4]

Nevertheless, while other early Chinese sources advocate restraint in sexual conduct and exhibit a suspicion of sensuality in general, the promotion of complete abstinence even for men who had as yet no offspring must have seemed peculiar, if not repugnant, to early Chinese.[5] In addition to the longstanding concern with the propagation of one's lineage through male offspring, medieval Chinese medical manuals warned that refraining from sex entirely was quite dangerous to a man's health.[6]

At the beginning of the sixth century when the *Liang Biographies* was compiled, many laymen apparently still found the notion of a continent clergy more puzzling than admirable. Take for example the biography of Kumārajīva, one of the most prominent monks of his day, in which the breaking of the monastic prohibition against sex is a recurring theme. According to the biography, Kumārajīva himself was the son of a monk who had been forced to marry a Kuchean princess against his will.[7] After the boy had come of age, a subsequent Kuchean king attempted to force the young Kumārajīva to marry yet another princess, a proposition the young monk steadfastly refused. Undaunted, the king then forced Kumārajīva to become drunk one night and locked him in a "secret chamber" with the girl, after which time, we are told, Kumārajīva "surrendered his integrity."[8] After Kumārajīva arrived in China, the northern ruler Yao Xing, impressed by the monk's intelligence, forced him to cohabit with no fewer then ten courtesans, arguing that otherwise his "seeds of the [Buddha]-Law would bear no offspring!"

"From this point on," the biography continues, "Kumārajīva no longer lived in the monks' quarters."[9] The repetition of the theme may lead us to question the historical accuracy of the account: the biography may be an amalgamation of three distorted versions of an original legend. At one point Huijiao himself laments the difficulty of obtaining reliable details concerning "Kumārajīva's transgression."[10] But setting aside the historicity of the story, it is significant that the author is at pains to explain Kumārajīva's helplessness in the matter: clearly, for the author and presumably his readers, monks, and especially eminent monks, were supposed to remain chaste. The reams of Indian scriptures translated into Chinese in the medieval period left little room for argument on this point. Vinaya texts are suffused with warnings and examples of the dangers of sex. In these texts, for a monk to engage in sexual relations, "even with an animal," is an offense entailing expulsion from the Order.[11] When "filled with desire, to approach a woman with improper intentions and speak to her in a vulgar manner" is a serious offense, warranting probation from the *saṅgha*.[12] And if Christian theologians projected their views of sexuality back in time to the days of Adam and Eve,[13] Buddhist thinkers projected their ideals of sexual relations upward toward the heavens where it was said that male and female gods no longer so much as touch, for they are able to have sex (*cheng yinyang*) simply by thinking about each other.[14]

Medieval Chinese did not all share this monkish enthusiasm for abstinence. The story of the king's treatment of Kumārajīva is indicative of a general disregard among non-Buddhists for the ideal of continence propounded by members of the Buddhist clergy, often coupled with a suspicion of the claims made for the sexual purity of monks and nuns. Aspersions on the sexual mores of monks, and especially nuns, were standard fare in anti-Buddhist polemic. The sixth-century official Zhangqiu Zituo, for instance, described the perverse conduct of monks in the palace, lamenting that "in the morning, [imperial] consorts enter the monks' quarters, while at night young men sleep in the nuns' rooms."[15] In 446, the first widespread persecution of Buddhism in China, that of Tai Wu Di, was justified by the reported discovery of a weapons cache on monastic property. Also found on monastery grounds were underground rooms where monks were said to have carried on clandestine relations with "fallen women of good families."[16]

Such dubious claims were reinforced by periodic court scandals, such as the notorious incident involving the prominent scholar-monk Bianji and the Gaoyang Princess, daughter of Tang Taizong. Only when a gift from the princess was found in Bianji's quarters during a routine inspection was it discovered that the monk and the princess had been carrying on a secret affair for some nine years! For his role in the affair, Bianji was summarily executed, severed at the waist.[17]

In later vernacular fiction, this suspicion of the sexual habits of monks and nuns found expression in the stock figures of the depraved monk and the fallen nun.[18] Already in the Tang, pornographic litera-ture depicting sex in the monastery circulated widely. For example, among the texts found at Dunhuang was a lengthy erotic prose-poem attributed to Bai Xingjian, younger brother of the famed poet Bai Juyi. Included in the poem is this brief description of the supposed sexual life of monks and nuns:

> There are famous worthy [śramaṇas] in the monasteries, and young nuns in the hermitages. Tired of living alone, they long to be together. Though they do not speak of it, in their hearts they silently surrender. [The monks may have been] profligate officials, or famous scholars of prominent families who 'in search of purity' entered the clergy. [They may be] closely shaven foreign men who speak Chinese despite their barbarian appearance, tall torsos, and thick pricks. Their thoughts are not of the Buddha Law, and [the nuns] finger more than rosaries.[19]

In short, sexual license rather than, say, the mystique of continence surrounding great ascetic figures in Indian literature, makes for the most memorable images of monks in Chinese letters.[20]

This sorry state of affairs must have been immensely frustrating to monks who had made considerable personal sacrifice in the face of enormous social pressures, only to be doubted and ridiculed. The *Eminent Monks* series was perhaps of some use in combating this image problem; for, not surprisingly, the monks of the *Biographies* are in this regard above suspicion.[21] Fachong, for example, refused to allow women to set foot in his monastery, saying that to do so would "at the highest level, harm efforts to spread Buddhism, and at a lower level give rise to vulgar rumors."[22] Similarly, the monk Lingyu only allowed women to enter his monastery when sermons were being delivered and insisted that they be the first to leave when the sermons were completed.[23] The seventh-century monk Daolin, citing women as the "source of all defilement," refused to look upon women, deliver sermons to them, accept food from them, or set foot in their homes. In the end, even when Daolin was on his deathbed and a female devotee wished to see him to bid farewell, he firmly refused her entrance to his chamber.[24]

The *Biographies* are particularly adamant in emphasizing the sharp lines of division between eminent monks and their female counterparts in the clergy. If monks were viewed with some suspicion for refusing to accept a clearly defined role in the Chinese family, full-grown women without husbands or sons were even more suspect. The *Biographies* do their utmost to put such doubts to rest. Though nuns often came to pay their respects to the monk Faxiang, he "never once spoke with them; he maintained the precepts with great purity."[25] Conversely, the monk Lingyu mentioned above exuded such an air of solemnity, that even the nuns who came to hear him speak dared not look him in the face.[26] Some monks are said to have simply refused to set foot in nunneries or to allow nuns into their monasteries.[27] Daoji refused to ordain nuns on the grounds that, in addition to giving rise to base rumors and "tainting one's reputation," the admittance of women into the Order had, as attested by the Buddha himself, "damaged the True Law."

The *Biographies of Nuns*, a sixth-century compilation, is even more acutely concerned with the chastity of its subjects.[28] A number of the stories in this collection recount attempted rape or forced marriage, which the nun in question heroically resists, maintaining her chastity.[29] Again, the relationship between nuns and monks is especially emphasized, as in the biography of the nun Jingxiu in which she is troubled when she finds herself the only one in attendance at a monk's lecture.[30] Interpreting these biographies of nuns is even more complicated than interpreting biographies of monks in that, while the biographies of monks were compiled by monks about monks, the biographies of nuns were written about nuns by monks. Hence, we cannot be sure that the concern for chastity expressed in the biographies of nuns was a concern of nuns themselves, and not just that of their male biographers. Nonetheless, from the later experience of nuns in China up to the present day, it seems safe to say that the chastity of young nuns was always the subject of much salacious gossip, gossip that biographies of upright nuns were intended to temper.

Rumors about the sexual lives of monks and nuns were surely not limited to court circles and literati, though these make up the bulk of the accounts left us; one can imagine the sort of suspicions and loose talk the wandering unattached monk must have aroused among gossiping villagers, or in town markets just outside monastery gates. Perhaps it is because of this environment of suspicion that one searches the *Biographies* in vain for stories of temptation—the sort of genuine inner-turmoil expressed in the *Lives of the Desert Fathers* where we read of a Christian monk who, to drive away mounting passionate thoughts of a woman in the adjoining cell, slowly burned his fingers in a lamp, one by one.[31] Monks in the *Biographies* have no such moments of doubt. When the charming young daughter of a donor attempted to seduce the Korean pilgrim Ŭisang, his "heart was like a rock and could not be moved."[32] When an attractive daughter of yet another layman attempted to seduce the young Guangyi, he locked himself in a room and severed his penis, not in order to subdue his own passions, but simply to render himself unappealing to the seductress.[33]

Stories such as these, in addition to other Buddhist attempts to spread an ideal of abstinence, were not entirely in vain. Some accounts suggest that Buddhist ideals of chastity gradually spread even beyond the clergy. We read of Layman Bao, for instance, who refused to take a wife, preferring instead to spend his spare time engaged in meditation.[34] Similarly, according to a secular source, layman Zhou Xuzhi, after studying on Lu Shan with the eminent exegete Huiyuan, "refused to take a wife for as long as he lived, wore garments of coarse cloth, and maintained a vegetarian diet."[35]

The notion of a continent clergy seems never to have been challenged in Buddhist circles in medieval China; the long, hard-fought struggle of leading clerics to wrest control of the monk's image from their detractors made a commitment to chastity an integral part of what it meant to be a monk. Recall that the *śramaṇa* of Zhang Heng's poem has no name; it was enough to mention his profession to know his life-style, part of which was that he should remain unmoved by the women of the capital.

Food

In China, as elsewhere, all sex was not equal. Medieval sex manuals reveal a highly developed aesthetic of sexuality that divided peasant from literati, official from emperor. But the "arts of the bedroom" were for the most part an intensely private concern, providing a relatively narrow range of possibilities for expression. Food, on the other hand, was a different matter. Food distinguished North from South, rich man from poor, connoisseur from plebeian. But if the monk could reject entirely social categories associated with sex, he could not renounce all food, at least not for an extended period of time. Nevertheless, the Buddhist renunciation of certain key types of food came to be one of the most important distinguishing features of the Chinese monk; for one of the most noticeable ways in which the monk differed from others was in his eating habits, particularly his refusal to eat meat.

Although meat seems to have played only a minor role in the everyday diet of early and medieval Chinese,[36] it was of great *symbolic* importance, particularly during rituals and feasts.[37] Meat, as a symbol of wealth, demonstrated the generosity of the host, or the sincerity of the sacrificer. Han funerary paintings of kitchen scenes and literary descriptions of feasts vividly document the preparation and consumption of huge amounts of all manner of flesh, prepared in a variety of ways.[38] In light of the status associated with the consumption of meat, inability to put meat on the table was considered a sign of pitiable poverty. Righteous officials would memorialize the throne, complaining that the "common people eat nothing but vegetables and wear their garments ragged. . . . If Your Highness does not save them, to whom will they turn?"[39]

For an official to give up the opportunity to eat meat for the sake of others was hence considered a great sacrifice worthy of praise and even official recognition. The Han official Cui Yuan, for example, was said ordinarily to have lived on a diet of vegetables and vegetarian stew in order to supply his frequent guests with fine and plentiful meats at hearty banquets.[40] Before usurping the throne, the Han official Wang Mang limited himself to a vegetarian diet whenever there was a drought, an act of conspicuous abstention that evoked a sympathetic response from the empress who pleaded with him to "eat meat regularly, and care for your health as you do for your country."[41] Other accounts tell us of how upright officials adopted vegetarian diets in order to set an example for the decadent people under their administration, or, even more commonly, as a demonstration of devotion to a recently deceased parent.[42] In short, meat was well established as a marker of prestige before the entrance of Buddhism to China, and never ceased to be so. Hence, aside from the ethical considerations at the heart of Chinese Buddhist vegetarianism, for a monk to abstain from meat altogether was an act of renunciation that must have carried considerable force in society at large.[43]

We may assume that some form of the monastic diet came to China with the first monks,[44] but the clearest written expositions of the ideal monastic diet are found in the various versions of the monastic regulations translated into Chinese over the course of centuries. By the sixth century when the *Liang Biographies* was compiled, most of the versions of the Vinaya that were to affect Chinese monks had already been translated, but the instructions these gave concerning the consumption of meat were hardly uniform. The *Si fen lü* (Skt. *Dharmaguptakavinaya*), for instance, states that in general monks should eat whatever is given them, meat included, with the exception of human, dog, serpent, elephant, and horse flesh. Monks are not to accept any meat, however, if they have seen, heard, or suspect that the animal has been killed especially for them.[45] The *Mohe sengqi lü* (Skt. *Mahāsāṃghikavinaya*) gives similar instructions, adding pork, monkey meat, and fowl to the list of taboo meats.[46]

While all versions of the Vinaya allow monks to eat certain kinds of meat under certain circumstances, other texts just as prominent in China, such as the *Mahāparinirvāṇasūtra*, forbid monks to eat any form of meat at all.[47] The biography of the fifth-century nun Jingxiu specifically states that she gave up eating fish and flesh after hearing a lecture on the sūtra.[48] Partly because the *Mahāparinirvāṇasūtra* was considered the final word of the Buddha and partly because of the association of meat with decadence, eventually Chinese monks came to consider the consumption of any form of meat under any circumstances as wrong. In addition to meat, the Buddhist diet also excluded the five "strong flavors"—usually given as garlic, onions, ginger, Chinese chives (*jiu*), and leeks (*xie*)—which were thought to stimulate the passions.

It is difficult to determine just when this more stringent definition of vegetarianism took shape in China; it is even more difficult to determine the extent to which it was implemented. Michihata Ryōshū argues that it was during the Sui-Tang period that the monastic leadership successfully championed strict vegetarianism for all of the clergy, a position that Chinese monks maintain to this day.[49] But already in the sixth-century *Liang Biographies*, we find examples of monks promoting vegetarianism.[50] In his sermons, for example, the sixth-century monk Huimi called for his listeners to give up the consumption of flesh. He himself was said to be a lifelong vegetarian.[51] That the adoption of the vegetarian diet was considered a difficult act of great renunciation is underlined by a sentiment attributed to the sixth-century official Guo Zushen: one way for the state to limit the size of the Buddhist clergy was to insist that it maintain a strict vegetarian diet.[52]

The severity of the Chinese Buddhist dietary ideal is vividly illustrated in stories like those of the monk Fakan who, after taking ill, went to his death refusing a doctor's prescription of pork,[53] or of Anlin who refused a doctor's prescription for chives to cure a gouty leg.[54] Before becoming a nun, the *Lives of Nuns* records, Huimu took care of her aged mother. Because her mother had no teeth, Huimu would chew meat for her. Although Huimu did not herself eat the meat, she considered her mouth impure and hence refused to receive the complete precepts of a full-fledged nun.[55] Here we move beyond a renunciation of decadent feasts and even, I think, beyond Buddhist concerns for merit and fault, to an overriding thirst for consistency, that is, a refusal to compromise, that was central to the identity of monks and nuns.

As vegetarianism was such a conspicuous act of renunciation, one may well ask to what extent it was inextricably tied to the monastic life-style. Did the monastic ideal of vegetarianism expressed in the

Biographies spread to the laity? Were laypeople who were not pre-pared to shave their heads, leave their families, and enter monasteries willing to renounce the standard Chinese diet?

Unlike the prohibition on sex, which was chiefly a monastic con-cern, Buddhist abhorrence of meat-eating applied to the laity as well. The biography of the monk Sengyai tells the story of a layman from Chengdu named Wang Senggui who, after witnessing Sengyai's self-immolation, swore off meat for both himself and his family.[56] Such examples are important indicators that, much more than in the case of monastic views about sex, monastic views concerning the con-sumption of meat and wine extended beyond the *saṅgha*. All three versions of the *Biographies* abound in stories of monks who, in addi-tion to maintaining strict vegetarian diets themselves, attempted to alter the eating habits of the laity as well, calling on people "through-out the land to give up the consumption of wine and meat, to release the hawks and hunting dogs, and renounce the practices of fishing and butchery."[57] After hearing the sermons of the monk Zhiwen, it is said that "the owners of wine shops smashed their goblets, while fish-ermen burned their nets."[58] When the Sui monk Huixiang spoke, "butchers gave up their profession, so that meat shops were no longer seen in the market."[59] As these examples come from Buddhist sources, we may question their accuracy, but the efforts they represent are undeniable.

From very early on, such proselytizing efforts extended beyond local butchers, fishermen, and pious laymen to the highest levels of the empire, and even to the emperor himself. In an audience with Wen Di of the Liu-Song Dynasty, Guṇavarman is said to have advised the emperor to take up a vegetarian diet and swear off killing of any living creatures.[60] We may be suspicious of such detailed transcriptions of conversations between monks and emperors, but in the case of at least one emperor, Liang Wu Di, such a conversation must indeed have taken place, for Wu Di eventually promulgated edicts calling on his subjects to adopt a vegetarian diet.[61]

The case of Liang Wu Di suggests that the accounts of successful proselytizing in the *Biographies of Eminent Monks* represent more than wishful thinking, that the monastic ideal of vegetarianism expressed in the *Biographies* was shared by at least some members of lay society. The Liu-Song official Shen Daoqian, for example, came from a family that had supported Buddhism for generations. When Shen was an old man, though he never became a monk, he did give up meat and live his remaining years on a vegetarian diet.[62] After his father's death at the hands of bandits, the Tang layman Li Yuan "abstained from wine and meat. He did not marry, or take on servants.

He often stayed at the Huilin Monastery, sleeping in a room there and eating vegetarian food with the monks."[63] Further, there are dozens of accounts in the Tang and pre-Tang dynastic histories of filial sons who adopted a vegetarian diet on the death of a parent, sometimes only for a brief mourning period, sometimes for the remainder of their days.

It is difficult to assess to what extent this practice is simply a continuation of an old pre-Buddhist Chinese tradition of abstaining from meat during the mourning period, and to what extent it may have been supported by the circulation of Buddhist ideas and the efforts of Buddhist monks.[64] The Chen official Wang Gu, for example, was known both for his filial acts following the death of his parents and for his devotion to Buddhism. When his mother died, Wang began to live on a vegetarian diet, a commitment he was to maintain for the rest of his life.[65] In part because of historical accident and in part because of the efforts of the clergy, a vegetarianism with Buddhist connotations became for many people an important vehicle for what was perhaps the most public moment of religious expression in a person's life in medieval China: the period following the death of a parent.

Yet even the dynastic histories, which tend to downplay the role of Buddhism in Chinese history, leave some accounts of lifelong Buddhist vegetarians who adopted a vegetarian diet more as a part of a regimen of personal cultivation than as an expression of sorrow at a parent's death. The well-known Tang Buddhist layman and high official Pei Xiu, for instance, was the only member of his family who did not eat meat. When his brothers prepared a dish of venison, Pei Xiu politely declined, saying that he had been a vegetarian all his life and could not justify making an exception for a single meal, even one prepared by his own brothers.[66]

Nevertheless, strict vegetarianism remained for the most part the responsibility of monks and not of the laity. While a monk was expected, through his diet, to set himself off from the laity as one following a completely different way of life, less demanding options were available to the Buddhist layman. The biography of the fifth-century figure Zhou Yong, for instance, indicates that the definition of vegetarianism among many laymen was more flexible than that of the stricter monks of the *Biographies*. Himself a devout Buddhist, Zhou was friends with one He Yin, also a Buddhist, who "kept neither wife nor concubine." When asked which of the two was the most vigorous (*jingjin*) in his practice, Zhou responded that they both continued to "carry certain burdens." When asked to explain just what these burdens were, Zhou replied: "For me it is my wife; for He Yin, meat."[67] Perhaps on Zhou Yong's urging, He Yin is said to have later given up "meat." Nevertheless, he still saw nothing wrong with eating fish and certain other types of seafood. Even Zhou himself, when asked what his favorite vegetable was, said that he was fond of eating leeks in early spring, a violation of the Chinese Buddhist proscription on the "five strong flavors."

In other words, though a monk was expected to keep to his rules, the same behavior in a layman might be seen as excessive. Outside of religious professionals, lifelong vegetarianism was never common in Chinese history. While the setting aside of periodic days for vegetarianism was seen as an acceptable if eccentric habit, certain occasions definitely called for meat. The *Song Biographies* relates the story of the Capital Director Gao Pian who had maintained a vegetarian diet for some twenty years. When Gao's granddaughter was to be married, "custom called for the butchering of animals [for the wedding feast]. At first Sire Gao did not want to go along with the idea, but his relatives said, 'You may keep a strict diet, but [if the same strictures are put on the feast,] how will we entertain the guests?' While Gao hesitated, unable to make up his mind, many animals were butchered."[68] Shortly thereafter, Gao contracted a mysterious illness and fell into a delirium during which he descended to the netherworld where he was reprimanded for this moral lapse. Gao's fate in this Buddhist source notwithstanding, the lay Buddhist had considerably more leeway in the question of meat than the monk. The definition of what it meant to be a Buddhist laymen was always quite flexible despite attempts to propagate standard sets of lay precepts. Monks, on the other hand, were under pressure from all levels of society—within the *saṅgha* and without—to keep to their rules.

It is as much because of social pressures from non-Buddhists as from monks or laypeople that diet became such an important part of the Chinese monk's identity. The importance of diet comes to the fore in stories of conflicts between monks and their enemies. When those hostile to Buddhism wished to humiliate a member of the clergy, they often attempted to trick or force the monk to eat meat. The *Liang Biographies* relates the story of Regional Inspector Xie Hui who, angered by the erection of a stupa in a monastery in his jurisdiction, ordered the images in the monastery destroyed. To complement this physical devastation, Xie also performed the symbolic act of granting a generous supply of wine and meat to the monks there.[69] In the same vein, during an interview with the fifth-century monk Fayuan, Emperor Wen Di of the Liu-Song Dynasty lost patience with the monk and his "insidious vegetarianism," and ordered his attendants to force the monk to eat meat. Even after a struggle that left his two front teeth broken, we are told, Fayuan refused to eat the meat, whereupon the emperor ordered the monk defrocked and returned to lay status.[70] Clearly, for Xie and Wen Di, a meat-eating monk was no monk at all; and for a monk to eat meat was an act of submission to an authority higher than any "barbarian teaching."

Monastic prohibitions against alcohol provide a parallel case to those against eating meat.[71] Despite the fact that, outside of the monastic community, the drinking of wine was equally if not more important socially than eating meat, Chinese Buddhists always maintained the ideal of abstention from wine. Perhaps the chief difference between the case of meat-eating and that of wine-drinking is that, if the Vinaya was ambivalent in regard to meat, it was quite clear in its prohibition of wine. The hagiographical literature suggests that these stories of the Buddha's admonitions to his disciples, brought to China by intrepid pilgrims and meticulously translated into Chinese, did indeed have an impact on the way monks lived, and even, in the case of one monk, on the way they dreamed.[72]

The *Further Biographies* relates the story of the monk Yancong who dreamt one night of an enormous yellow giant who gave him a beautiful bowl filled with wine. Yancong knelt down reverently before the being, saying, "I humbly accept the gift of this precious vessel, and am overwhelmed by the burden of gratitude it entails. But as the Regulations (i.e., the Vinaya) prohibit the consumption of wine, I dare not drink it." Later, Yancong realized the identity of the benefactor when he recognized the bowl in a painting of Guanyin.[73] On his deathbed in 416, the famous exegete Huiyuan is said to have refused the medicinal wine offered him by his disciples. When they offered him "rice soup" —presumably a euphemism for rice wine—he refused once again. Finally, when offered a mixture of honey and water, Huiyuan ordered an expert in the Vinaya to search through the Regulations and determine if this would be acceptable. But before the Vinaya Master had found the answer, the story concludes, Huiyuan died.[74]

The *Biographies* are replete with references to the sobriety of the *saṅgha*, of monks whose "feet never touched the ground of shop or wine house,"[75] and conversely, of negative examples, such as the story of the drunk monk who, after dying sends back a dream to his colleagues telling them that he has been reborn in an inferior realm.[76] The numerous references to the prohibition against wine in the *Biographies* may suggest that there was a need for repeating such admonitions, that the drinking of wine was widespread among the clergy. This is a subject to which we will return. For now, suffice it to say that in the *Biographies* the ideal Chinese monk was as strict in his refusal of alcohol as he was in his abstinence from sex and meat.

Clothing

Abstinence from sex, the vegetarian diet, and the prohibition against alcohol were all key components to the monk's identity, an identity that centered, on the one hand, on renunciation of social norms and, on the other, on embracing the ascetic alternative. However much particular laymen might admire or imitate the monk's life-style, one who left his family to dedicate himself to following the monastic ideal clearly belonged to a different category of person. Perhaps the most visible sign of this monastic distinction was the monk's clothing. Indeed, a common term for monks in medieval texts is the "black-robed ones" (ziyi). And when referring to monks and laymen, Buddhist texts commonly use the expression, "the black and the white" (zibai). Following this line of inquiry it would be possible to write a detailed study of the relationship between Indian styles of monastic clothing and indigenous Chinese fashion. But more than in the cases of sex or food, clothing provides us a glimpse into the ways in which monks distinguished *among themselves*, quickly dispelling the picture of a uniform clergy that is painted in secular sources. This is the aspect of the monastic uniform that I focus on below.[77]

As the term "black-robed ones" indicates, Chinese monks often wore black robes, but other colors were also worn. In his *Brief History of the Clergy*, Zanning includes a section on monastic garb in which he relates that during the Han-Wei period, most monks in China wore red robes. An expert in the Vinaya, Zanning further notes that the color of a monk's robes depended in India on the school to which he belonged. Pitch black (zao) for members of the Sarvāstivādins, deep red (jiang) for the Dharmaguptakas, blue (qing) for the Mahāsāmghikas, and so forth. After citing examples from the *Biographies* of Chinese monks who wore robes of various colors, Zanning goes on to describe the variety found in his day, that is, the late tenth century. At that time, a given color of robe was associated with a particular region: deep-black (hei) or red in the Jiangnan region, brown (he) in the area around the capital at Kaifeng, and so forth. Though some difference between the Chinese monk's robe and its Indian counterpart was tolerated, there were limits to the degree of innovation allowed. Zanning is critical of the practice of wearing deep-black robes, and even more so of monks who had in his day taken to wearing white robes. The wearing of either color, he insists, is forbidden in the Vinaya.[78]

Zanning was not the only leading Chinese Buddhist to express a concern for the diversity of attire within the *sangha*. When Yijing discussed the areas in which the Indian monastic ideal had been corrupted in its transmission to China, innovation in clothing, no less than in the performance of ceremony or the interpretation of scripture, comes in for criticism. Yijing writes: "If we come to India in Chinese garments, they all laugh at us; we get much ashamed in our hearts, and we tear our garments to be used for miscellaneous purposes, for they are all unlawful."[79] As Yijing is quick to point out, ideally, monks should limit themselves to three robes, each to be worn for a particular type of occasion: the *saṃghāṭī*, a heavier outer garment to be worn on special occasions; the *uttarāsaṅga*, a lighter garment to be worn during regular Buddhist ceremonies; and the *antarvāsaka*, another lighter garment to be worn for day-to-day activities.[80] But even Yijing admits that in India many monks kept more than just these three robes. And in the *Biographies*, monks who kept only the three robes are singled out for special praise.[81]

One sees in comments by Yijing and Zanning a tension between the ideal of a plain, subdued monastic uniform, setting the monk off from contemporary secular fashions, and a basic human need for distinction. Even within the confines of generally accepted norms for Buddhist clothing, there were opportunities to set oneself off from other monks. In the *Song Biographies*, in an addenda to the biography of the seventh-century monk Yuankang, for example, Zanning discusses the practice of wearing the *nabo*, a garment that had been described by Yijing some three hundred years earlier as a legitimate means of attire for monks living in colder climates. Zanning writes:

Question:
What was this *nabo* that Yuankang dragged behind him?

Response:
In Sanskrit it is called *"libo;*[82] in Chinese it is called a "garment for wrapping around the belly" [*guofu yi*]—it is also called the "belly wrap" [*baofu*]. It is shaped like a shoulder sash [*biantan*], with one end just reaching to the hand. Narrow at the shoulders, the garment is worn over the left side with the right side left open. The material is filled mostly with cotton floss.

This garment is used to keep out the cold, but in countries of hot climates it is used to demonstrate one's spiritual attainments. After the garment came east, monks began to make it of colored silk and to drape it over both left and right shoulders with the sleeves left hanging. The garment is worn to demonstrate that the wearer has mastered the scriptures and treatises. When one has mastered one book, one wears one of them; if one has mastered more books, one wears more. I do not know who started this custom. Today the term has been abbreviated to *bo*, leaving out the character *li*.

It has nothing to do with keeping out the cold and has become a sign of arrogance. Having lost its original meaning, it is manufactured with reckless abandon. The holy teaching is thus passed down to later sages in an altered form. From now on, let us not practice peculiar customs that upset the Grand Order. The *Book of Poetry* says: "He who has no right to his dress brings misfortune upon himself."[83]

This example is particularly interesting in that the *nabo* was not *inherently* extravagant and was in Yijing's time merely a useful garment for staving off the cold in northern climes. Such shifting attitudes and practices created a delicate problem for monastic leaders charged with dictating tastes to their fellow monks: when faced with such newfangled threats to the integrity of the monastic community, they had recourse to neither scripture nor consensus.

We see a similar dynamic at work in the more widespread and ultimately more threatening problem of positions and honors conferred by the state, an organization with much more power and experience in such matters than the *sangha* could ever muster. One of the most important of these markers of prestige issuing from the court was the purple robe (*ziyi*) bestowed on eminent monks by imperial edict.[84] This practice began in 690 when Empress Wu Zetian conferred the robe on a number of monks as a part of her project to legitimate her rise to the throne.[85] Such bestowals eventually became institutionalized, requiring a recommendation from a local administrator that was then submitted for review by court authorities before the robe was conferred. These regulations were marred by instances of bribery and corruption, and at one point the state simply sold the robes to monks or their supporters.[86] Nevertheless, in the mid and high Tang periods, before the overabundance of purple robes began to deflate their value, the conferral of such a robe was a great honor, warranting the respect of monks and laymen alike.

But it is precisely at such points that the ascetic imperative asserts itself; like the imperially conferred name or personal invitations to the palace, the purple robe became the focus of much ascetic angst, a symbol of the trivial trappings of the world. According to the *Song Biographies*, when emperor Zhaozong bestowed the purple robe on the monk Qingguan at the end of the ninth century, the monk "became gloomy and downhearted."[87] When, in 911, the first emperor of the short-lived Later-Liang Dynasty bestowed the purple robe on Hong-chu, he flatly refused to wear it, inspiring the poet Zheng Yue to write:

The purple robe is on the shelf, unused and unworn.
He sits instead staring at the golden characters etched in his mind.[88]

Finally, when the monk Hengchao received the purple robe on the recommendation of a local governor in approximately 949, he is said to have suddenly become depressed, and soon thereafter took ill and died.[89]

Similarly, there are numerous accounts in the *Biographies* of monks who, feeling the pull of the ascetic alternative, refused to wear robes made of silk, primarily because silkworms are killed in the silk-making process, but also because of the connotations of decadence associated with the fabric.[90] After recounting the life story of a monk named Daoxiu who "kept the three robes, and did not wear silk because it entailed the taking of life," Daoxuan notes that he had personally questioned monks from the western region regarding this matter, and that none of them had heard of the practice of monks wearing silk outside of China, even in Kucha and other Central Asian kingdoms to which sericulture had long since spread.[91] Writing roughly forty years later, however, Yijing notes that the use of silk in monastic garments was common in India, and complains of self-righteous Chinese monks who ostentatiously refused to wear it. After all, he continues, the manufacture of cloth also entails the death of earthworms.[92]

In this backlash against ascetic extremes, we catch a glimpse of what sociologist Pierre Bourdieu refers to as a "game of refusal and counter-refusal" in which those in a position to dictate tastes are in a constant state of interaction with their audience as they attempt to stay a step ahead of the game.[93] This is not to trivialize the sort of genuine intellectual struggle that a monk like Yijing engaged in when considering such issues, but simply to suggest that the need to take up such issues was driven in large measure by the irrepressible attraction of aesthetic and ascetic innovation.

Because of the nature of our sources, it is very difficult to determine just how much effect the campaigns of leading monks had on lesser members of the clergy. At least in the case of silk, Yijing's comments seem to have fallen on deaf ears. For well into the Tang, individual monks of an ascetic bent continued to reject silk, wearing instead rags or robes made of hemp.[94] Other monks went even further. Chujin "did not wear silk, only putting on a patched thatch robe when the weather turned cold."[95] Others wore "hair-shirts,"[96] ragged patched robes, nettle-hemp robes, robes made of tree bark, and so forth.[97] The *Biographies* are replete with stories of monks who kept the same robe for years, not changing their garments no matter how hot the summer or how cold the winter. Huikai refused to wash his robe until it reached the point that "those around him could stand it no longer, and took the robe from him in order to wash it."[98] Zhiyuan refused to remove his robe, even to sleep.[99] But here we begin to move beyond the basic forms of asceticism common to all monks to a more exceptional, rigorous way of life—that of the monk who even from within the monastic community was considered an ascetic.

Ascetics among Ascetics

As depicted in the *Biographies*, the practices discussed to this point—abstention from sex, the vegetarian diet, the prohibition on wine, restrictions on clothing—were considered basic requirements of any monk, though, as we have seen, there was some room for individual expression in all of these areas. Although medieval Chinese laymen would have found such practices extraordinary, and might well have labeled them as "ascetic"(*kuxing*), they would for the most part not have been seen to be so by monks. In other words, the standards for distinction between monk and layman differed from the categories of behavior that distinguished one monk from another, or for that matter monks of a previous, more rigorous age from the degenerate age of one's own day.

One should always be suspicious when reading the lamentations of monastic leaders on the sorry state of the *sangha*. The fact that such monks inevitably measure the contemporary clergy against an ancient Indian ideal that surely never existed makes such bleak assessments inevitable. Throughout Chinese history, leading monks complain that their brethren do not maintain the precepts with the vigor of days gone by. But regardless of the accuracy of such depictions of the state of the *sangha* in relation to the past, such accounts are important for what they tell us about how monks perceived themselves. One area of particular sensitivity was the fundamental issue of the sources of monastic income. In his *Brief History of the Clergy*, Zanning laments the fact that monastic leaders of his day received salaries from the state, an indication for Zanning of the gulf separating the monks of his time from the monks of the Buddha's time when, he believed, monks lived on alms alone.[100]

In addition to funds derived directly from the state, the growing body of secondary literature on the medieval monastic economy amply demonstrates the variety of ways in which monasteries, and especially large monastic estates, supported themselves through the rental of land to tenant farmers, the maintenance of orchards and mills, the performance of ceremonies for the dead, and so on. Begging seems to have played a relatively minor role as a source of monastic income.[101] Yet as Zanning's comments illustrate, the ideal of the mendicant monk was an important one to Chinese clerics, many of whom were undoubtedly uncomfortable with more lucrative sources of income. In other words, even though a relatively small proportion of monks were able to sustain themselves entirely on alms, the ideal of an independent, mendicant life continued to plague the thoughtful monk as he sat down to a hearty meal in the monastic refectory.

Those few who vowed to live on alms for long periods of time are singled out for special attention in the *Biographies,* according to which they were treated with a reverence reserved for the severest of ascetics. Daozhe, for example, "retreated to a small chamber, only eating once a day of food obtained from begging. He did not accept any of the benefits of the clergy, and the assembly held him in the highest esteem."[102] The monk Fazong "always sustained himself through begging, which he did once a day. He bore the rigors of this vegetarian diet throughout his days in order thereby to repent for his faults."[103] Other monks, like Zhu Tanyou, practiced begging while living the life of an ascetic mendicant, wandering the countryside in between long bouts of meditation.[104] Similarly, the rule that monks were only to eat before noon was well known among Chinese monks, though only the most dedicated carried it out for more than a short period of time.[105]

When we look closely at accounts of these distinctive monks in the hagiographical literature, patterns begin to emerge. Far from random anecdotes, we find in these stories nested systems of practice, life-styles within life-styles. This is to say, monks who vowed to eat only what was placed in their begging bowls, or to eat only before noon were not acting according to individual, eccentric impulses; they were following a carefully defined set of practices, specifically a regimen known as *dhūtāṅga* formulated for monks who wished to adopt a more demanding life-style.[106] These practices, described in a wide variety of Buddhist texts, are common in the *Biographies.* Zanning notes as the source for one of his biographies a monk he met "practicing *dhūtāṅga*" high atop Mount Kuaiji.[107] Mountains such as Kuaiji were sites for some of the most famous monasteries in China. But as presented in the *Biographies*, even when in these mountains, practitioners of *dhūtāṅga* retreated far away from the nearest monastery to the mountain wilds, ravaged by storms and populated by fierce animals and demons. The most rigorous of these ascetics were said to have lived in the open country, although there are also occasional references to "forest huts."[108] Shenxuan lived in a cave, "not building a hut, but practicing the 'open-air *dhūtāṅga*.' He did not even have a bed."[109] Like their counterparts on the mountains or in the forests, cave-dwelling monks are attacked by snakes and other dangerous animals during their long bouts of meditation.[110] Some, like Faren, are said to have "eaten from the trees,"[111] an expression found already in the *Zhuangzi* meaning to scavenge for berries, nuts, pine needles, and fruit.

In the discussion of *dhūtāṅga* in his *Notes on the Regulations in Four Divisions,*[112] Daoxuan quotes various Buddhist texts that recommend that monks should contemplate impermanence while in the graveyard, or, while sitting beneath a tree, think "as the Buddha thought" when he sat under the *bodhi* tree. But beyond an occasional reference to meditation, the *Biographies* are in general quite vague on just what monks were supposed to do while "practicing *dhūtāṅga*." Huizan "in body practiced the *araṇya* method [i.e., living in the forest], and in mind thought thoughts of wisdom."[113] Faxiang, while practicing *dhūtāṅga* spent his time "contemplating the Western Land [of Amitābha] and chanting *namo* Amitābha."[114]

In part because of the demands of narrative, the focus in the biographies of such monks is not on the content of meditative practices but on their context, on the eerie solitude of the ascetic monk, cut off from monastic as well as lay society. Huixiang "silently practiced meditation and chanted to himself, *for he was different from the others*."[115] Chan Master Na "practiced *dhūtāṅga* and therefore did not visit village settlements."[116] Huiming "wandered aimlessly, practicing the Way. None knew where he lived."[117] Huishi lived for more than fifty years "cut off from the world of men."[118] Elusive and strangely frightening, such figures appear in the *Biographies* as ascetics among ascetics, marginals among marginals.

Some of the ascetic practices described in the *Biographies*, particularly abstention from the "five cereals," derive from indigenous Chinese beliefs and medical theories.[119] Others fall neatly under the rubric of "reduction of desire." But what are we to make of a figure like Faqing, known to his contemporaries as "the human worm" because of his habit of eating dirt,[120] or Huizhu who lived on pine needles,[121] or Sengshan who eventually died after complications caused from eating small stones during a period of ascetic practice?[122] There are numerous stories of monks who, in accordance with one of the *dhūtāṅgas*, refuse themselves sleep for long stretches of time, or refuse to lie down for as many as thirty years! The *Biographies* are punctuated with haunting stories of monks who violently ravage their own bodies for reasons that, at least to this modern reader, are not readily apparent. These are the figures, the ascetic virtuosi, to which we now turn.

Self-Mutilation and Ritual Suicide

On the eighth day of the fourth month of the fourteenth year of the Xiantong era (873), the Buddha's birthday, Emperor Yizong of the Tang ignored the remonstrances of his officials and sent down an edict proclaiming that a segment of the Buddha's bone kept in the nearby Famen Monastery was to be brought into the capital.[123] The emperor hoped thereby, not only to accrue merit for himself, but also to usher in an era of peace and prosperity for the empire as a whole.

Su E (fl. 890), a Tang writer of the fabulous and the bizarre, left us an account of the event. Su describes the festivities in detail. The bone was escorted through the capital streets in a spectacular procession of thousands of chanting monks. The inhabitants of the city, from noblemen to commoners, came out to watch as the relic was brought within the walls of the capital. When the procession came to a halt, the emperor left the palace and personally went to the bone where he knelt down, wept, and formally welcomed the holy relic into the capital. Local inhabitants also became caught up in the devotional spirit of the moment, donating their jewels and clothing to the sacred bone. In the midst of the festivities, the following event took place. As described by Su E:

> A soldier cut off his left arm in front of the Buddha's relic, and while holding it with his hand, reverenced the relic each time he took a step, his blood sprinkling the ground all the while. Innumerable people walked on their elbows and knees, biting off their fingers or cutting off their hair. There was also a monk who covered his head with artemisia, a practice known as "disciplining the head." When the pile of artemisia was ignited, the pain caused the monk to shake his head and to cry out, but young men in the marketplace held him tight so that he could not move. When the pain became unbearable, he cried out and fell prostrate on the ground. With his head scorched and his deportment in disarray, he was the object of the laughter of all the spectators.[124]

Fifty-four years earlier, in 819, court scribes under Emperor Xianzong recorded a similar incident. Here again, the emperor ordered that the segment of the finger bone be brought into the capital so that "harvests would be abundant and the people tranquil." In the frenzy that followed,

> commoners abandoned their occupations and exhausted their fortunes, burning their heads and scorching their arms, saying that this was their offering. There were some hooligans from the shops who could endure the pain of burning and branding, deceptively saying that they were making offerings. They burned holes in their skin and bragged that the bones of the Buddha were within. There was much criminal activity. When caught they would all burn themselves. Peasants abandoned their plows and rushed to the capital city.[125]

The Famen Monastery was known chiefly as the home to this relic of the Buddha, for it was the only monastery in or around Chang'an said to house a relic of the Buddha himself. In 980, some 150 years after the event described above, what was purported to be an ancient stupa of Aśoka was discovered and found to contain yet another relic of the

Buddha. Once again, the discovery was accompanied by self-mutilation. "Monk and layman alike made burns on their heads and incinerated their fingers. Others burnt incense and candles. [Imperial] rewards were granted in various amounts."[126]

Each of the events cited above took place as part of a large communal activity—a spontaneous, ecstatic experience involving laymen as well as monks. But there was another type of raw, physical self-sacrifice in medieval China that on the surface at least seems to be of quite a different nature. The *Biographies* recount many stories of monks for whom corporal sacrifice, self-mutilation, and even suicide was a rational, premeditated ritual of offering. In other words, these self-inflicted monastic assaults on the body were an established form of ascetic practice.

Forms of Self-Sacrifice in the Biographies

More than an attempt to reduce desire, the forms of self-sacrifice lauded in the *Biographies* (chiefly, but not exclusively in chapters devoted to such figures) addressed the physical agent of desire, the human body. To give the reader a sense of the differences between self-sacrifice in the *Biographies* and the sort of collective self-mutilation described above, I begin with the biography of the Tang monk Wuran, an example of self-immolation in its most extreme form: suicide by fire. In the biography, Wuran, a monk of unknown background, goes on a long pilgrimage in search of the bodhisattva Mañjuśrī. Finally, in a remote section of Mount Wutai, he comes across a spectacular monastery populated by several hundred Indian monks. The abbot of the monastery turns out to be none other than Mañjuśrī who assures Wuran that he will be rewarded if he but perseveres in his practice. Wuran promises to do so. As he walks away from the monastery, it disappears into thin air.

> Wuran then followed Mañjuśrī's advice, doing all he could to support the clergy. Every time he had served one million monks, he would incinerate one of his fingers as a record. Little by little, the number of monks served reached five million. Monks came to him from near and far like sea water flowing into a bay. When he had finished supplying ten million monks, all ten of his fingers had been incinerated.
>
> During the Kaicheng era [836–840], Wuran announced to the assembly, "I have something of a karmic affinity with this mountain. I have traveled to all of the sacred sites seventy-two times, even going to places men have never before been, and have moreover never left this mountain. My deepest wish has been fulfilled; no one is more fortunate than I. Nevertheless, I am old—today seventy-four

years old, fifty-five as a monk. While I still have breath in me I wish to go to the pinnacle of the Central Terrace to burn one stick of incense[127] and say farewell to the Thus-Come-Ones of the ten directions and the ten thousand bodhisattvas. In resting me in death,[128] who could take my place? All of you are disciples of bodhisattvas, relatives of dragon kings implanted with the seeds of excellence. Living on this mountain, you are truly diligent night and day, reining in the three sources of karma.[129] We will meet again on the day of the three assemblies of the dragon-flower.[130] Now I will leave the mountain. Please do not try to keep me." Wuran then pressed his palms together and saying, "Preserve and protect yourselves," departed. At first the assembly, not understanding him, told him to come back soon.

Wuran took only his alms bowl and ring-staff. Burning a stick of fine incense, he ordered the devotee[131] Zhao Hua to bring two bolts of waxed cloth, a bundle of rough hemp, and a vial of fragrant oil. On the pinnacle of the Central Terrace, Wuran made obeisance and burnt incense from dawn to dusk, not resting even to eat or drink. He chanted the Buddha's name sincerely so that the sound of his chanting was unbroken. Late that night, Zhao became curious as to what Wuran was doing. Climbing up on a rocky peak, he saw that the monk had not moved, but was engaged in even more intense concentration. Wuran looked over at Zhao and said, "I have a secret wish. Help me fulfill my destiny and do not hinder me. Take the waxed cloth, the hemp, and the oil, and wrap up my body. In the middle of the night, at midnight, I want you to incinerate my body in offering to all of the Buddhas. If I attain the Way, I will deliver you as well." [At first] Zhao objected, advising against it. [But in the end he] took up the cloth and wrapped it around Wuran's body. Covering him with the hemp, Zhao doused the monk in oil [preparing to] burn him from the head down when Wuran said, "Take my bones and ashes and scatter them; don't make a fuss over them."

Zhao followed Wuran's orders, without the slightest alteration, burning him from the head down. Only when the flames reached his feet did Wuran's body fall over. Zhao exclaimed, "Of old, I hear, the Medicine King[132] incinerated his body. Today, I have seen a superior man. How marvelous! What pain!" Later, disciples collected Wuran's remains and erected a stupa south of Mount Fanxian that stands to this day.[133]

In the first three versions of the *Biographies*, there are numerous examples of monks who commit "self-cremation." It is a practice that in the twentieth century has evolved into a form of political protest, often bereft of religious connotations. Both in its medieval and modern manifestations, the practice has long attracted the attention of Western scholars.[134] But self-cremation is only one of many techniques of self-sacrifice extolled in the *Biographies*. Before returning to the practice of suicide by fire, let us first put the practice in context by looking at samples from a range of practices depicted in the *Biographies* that reveal much about Buddhist soteriology as well as medieval attitudes toward the body.

Stories of the many lives the Buddha passed through as a bodhisattva before finally becoming a Buddha in his life as Śākyamuni were translated into Chinese very early on and enjoyed widespread popularity. Many of these stories center on the Bodhisattva's willingness to sacrifice himself for others. In a former life as a merchant, the Buddha threw himself into the sea to feed the fish; once as an ascetic, he lay down before a ravenous tigress and her cubs; and so on.[135] Such stories of the Bodhisattva compassionately sacrificing himself for the benefit of others inspired many Chinese monks to imitation.

In the *Biographies*, one of the most common forms of self-sacrifice was for a monk to surrender his body to mosquitoes, leeches, and other bloodsucking insects. The Sillan monk Do-yuk, for example, "always wore a thick coarse robe, the weight of which was difficult to bear. At the beginning of summer and end of autumn, he would leave his chest, back, and legs uncovered in the afternoon, saying that he was giving the mosquitoes, gnats, gadflies, and leeches something to nibble. It reached the point where blood from the insect bites would flow to the ground."[136] During the hottest part of summer, Sengzang "would take off his clothes and enter into the midst of the thicket in order to allow the mosquitoes, gnats, and leeches to nibble and bite him. Clots of blood poured forth from his skin, yet he endured in silence, bathed in sweat. Throughout, he chanted the name of the Buddha Amitābha."[137] When the unexpected death of his parents left the impoverished monk Dinglan unable to provide for their funerals, he "stripped naked and entered Mount Qingcheng where he allowed the mosquitoes, gnats, gadflies, and flies to bite and nibble at his skin, all the while saying, 'I surrender my "inner wealth" to repay the grief and care of my parents.' "[138]

Other monks are lauded for the even greater sacrifice of giving themselves up to ravenous beasts. The *Song Biographies* relates the story of Wenshuang who, while practicing *dhūtāṅga* in the wilds, was threatened by a wolf. Taking pity on the hungry animal, Wenshuang announced, "I do not covet this filthy bag of meat. I give it over to you that I may quickly acquire a body of more enduring strength. This donation will thus benefit us both."[139] Similarly, Shouxian announced to his disciples, "I have a debt, and my mind will not be at rest until it is repaid." The next day Shouxian's disciples found only the master's legs, still inside his trousers, the rest of him having been devoured by tigers.[140]

All of these incidents were motivated by a compassion for pitiable, inferior beings. But often the self-sacrificing monk gives up his life for other people. In the *Liang Biographies* in a chapter devoted to monks who "sacrificed their bodies" (*wangshen*), we read of the monk Fajin, who offered himself as food to starving villagers during a famine. When they refused to kill him for his flesh, he proceeded to slice strips of meat from his own body until he eventually passed out and died.[141] The same chapter relates the story of Tancheng who saved a village from a hungry tiger by lying down in front of the animal. After eating the monk, the tiger left the village in peace.[142] Sengfu saved the child of a local villager when he discovered that the boy had been kidnaped by men intent on sacrificing the child's heart and liver to a deity. When Sengfu's offer to take the child's place is refused—evidently reflecting a belief that the spirits preferred child offerings—the monk shouted out, "Aren't the five viscera of an adult good enough for you?" and then took a knife and sliced himself open on the spot, thereby frightening the bandits away and saving the child.[143] Other monks died as martyrs proper. For example, when Hongxiu's monastery was about to be overrun by bandits, he walked out the front gates and said, "I hereby vow not to sully the pure grounds [of the monastery] with my blood," before slitting his own throat.[144]

The monks of these accounts are driven to sacrifice themselves for reasons that are fairly explicit: to save a starving tiger, or a village, or a boy; even those who surrender themselves to blood-sucking leeches and mosquitoes do so in order to "nourish sentient beings." But other, equally common practices are motivated by more abstract notions of worship and sanctification. Take, for example, the widespread practice of blood-writing in which monks copied out scriptures in their own blood, thereby joining personal corporal sacrifice with the vigorous Buddhist tradition that extols the virtues of copying scriptures. Dinglan, the monk mentioned above who offered his body to insects after the death of his parents, later "punctured himself in order to copy out scriptures in his own blood, made burns on his arms, and eventually went so far as to cut off his ears and gouge out his eyes in order to feed them to wild birds and beasts. After this if he did not have someone to support and lead him when he walked he would bump into things and fall."[145] Wen'gang is said to have copied some six hundred fascicles of scriptures in his blood, thereby "sowing seeds in the field of non-arising."[146] Others, like Zhenbian and Daozhou, painted images of Buddhist deities entirely in their own blood.[147]

It is not only the act of writing holy images and scriptures in one's own blood that was celebrated in the *Biographies*; the books and paintings themselves were venerated as precious holy objects. The *Song Biographies* notes that a copy of the *Lotus Sūtra* in the blood of the monk Hongchu "is kept to this day in Yongjia. The people say that even among the treasures of the clergy, this is an extraordinary treasure."[148] The two hundred eighty three fascicles of Buddhist scriptures copied out in the blood of the monk Zengren were kept by his disciples and eventually submitted to the throne, a gift that resulted in the monk receiving the purple robe posthumously.[149] Even today such books can be found on display in prominent Chinese monasteries.

Just as enduring among Chinese monks is the practice of cutting or burning off one or more fingers, a practice that has continued into the twentieth century and been vividly documented in interviews and photographs by Western scholars.[150] The motivations for such acts in the numerous references to monks severing or incinerating their fingers in the *Biographies* are diverse. At times the slicing off of a finger is a dramatic sign of commitment. Such is the case in the biography of Daibing in the *Song Biographies*. When his father died, the seven-year-old Daibing asked his mother to allow him to become a monk, but she refused him permission. He then chopped off one of his fingers and asked again. This time, the astonished mother gave in.[151] Similarly, the famous Chan monk Huiji convinced his parents to permit him to become a monk by kneeling before them and presenting them with a severed thumb in order to "repay them for the toil of rearing him."[152] Stories such as these provide a backdrop for the most famous incident of self-mutilation in Chinese Buddhist history, that of the "second Chan patriarch," Huike. The most well-known incident in Huike's life is the legend that he cut off his own left arm in order to demonstrate his sincerity before Bodhidharma, who had at first refused to take him on as a disciple.[153]

More often, the incineration of a finger is associated with "offering" (*gongyang*). When Xichen, who had previously incinerated a number of his fingers, learned that a segment of the Buddha's finger bone was kept at the Famen Monastery, he went there to pay reverence to it. "On seeing this rare and marvelous sight, he burned off yet another of his fingers, leaving him with only two fingers on both of his hands."[154] When relics were escorted to a local monastery as a part of Sui Wen Di's campaign to distribute relics to prominent monasteries throughout the empire, the śramaṇa Tanyi, a "renown monk of lofty practice," traveled to see the relics, and then proceeded to burn off his fingers as "candles of offering" during an all-night vigil.[155] When Changyu arrived at the Huayan Monastery, the first stop on his pilgrimage to Wutai Shan, home of Mañjuśrī, his first act of devotion was to bow down before the image there of Mañjuśrī, coat the middle finger of his right hand in oil, and set it ablaze, whereupon "the countenance of the Holy One seemed pleased."[156]

Other monks variously cut off ears, gouge out eyes, make burns on their arms, and pierce their foreheads, all in the name of "offering." A similar language is used to justify the dozens of accounts of monks in the *Biographies* who, like Wuran, burned themselves to death in what was often a drawn-out, elaborate ritual. But surely there is a significant distinction between offering, say, fruit to a deity, and offering a finger or an arm. As we will see, the language used to describe offerings of the body differ markedly from that used to describe offerings of other sorts of objects. Similarly, the desire to nourish insects or to demonstrate one's sincerity only partly explain these practices. More than any one element, it was a nexus of ideological, psychological, and social factors that together provided the motivation for monks to hurt themselves, to voluntarily embark on a graded path of self-destruction ranging from mosquito bites to suicide.

Motivation

In these stories of self-sacrifice, we see an example of the formation and propagation of what anthropologist Victor Turner would call a "root-paradigm," by which he means a set pattern of special behavior with particular symbolic associations. Turner, for instance, interprets the actions of Thomas Beckett in his conflict with King Henry II as an example of the playing out of the root-paradigm of Christian martyrdom. Beckett's actions have struck many political and institutional historians as irrational and self-destructive, but when we read Beckett's behavior as the actions of a man who saw himself as a martyr, his decisions seem perfectly reasonable and in keeping with well-established symbolic and literary conventions.[157] The self-mutilation described in the *Biographies* is not simply a Buddhist version of Christian martyrdom, though it does share much in common with the self-mutilation of Christian ascetics. Let us look more closely at the ideology behind self-mutilation.

All of the practices discussed so far have canonical correlates that marked them as distinctly Buddhist forms of asceticism. In addition to the Jataka tales relating stories of self-sacrifice and a number of other, lesser texts,[158] the most important source for self-mutilation and suicide was in what may be the most influential book in all of premodern Asia, the *Lotus Sūtra*. In the "Medicine King" chapter of the *Lotus*, Śākyamuni describes how in time past, "beyond *kalpas* as numerous as the sands of innumerable Ganges rivers," a bodhisattva decided to offer his body to the Buddha of that distant age. After drinking fragrant, flammable oils for two hundred years, he lit himself on fire. One thousand two hundred years later, his body was finally consumed, and the bodhisattva was reborn in a paradise. Later, when the Buddha he had worshiped passed into Nirvana, the bodhisattva made an offering to the Buddha's stupa by burning his forearm. Having told this story, Śākyamuni says, "If there is one who, opening up his thought, wishes to attain *anuttarasamyaksaṃbodhi* [supreme enlightenment], if he can burn a finger or even a toe as an offering to a Buddha stupa, he shall exceed one who uses realm or walled city, wife or children, or even all the lands, mountains, forests, rivers, ponds, and sundry precious objects in the thousand-millionfold world as offerings."[159]

Clearly, monks like Wuran were following the example of the bodhisattva and reading the *Lotus* story as a set of guidelines for practice—a handbook for the ascetic virtuoso who hoped to acquire great merit through such arduous acts. Indeed, monks described in the chapter devoted to those who "surrendered their bodies" in the *Liang Biographies*, the earliest accounts of Chinese monks to commit self-immolation, go to their fiery deaths chanting the "Medicine King" chapter.[160]

Nevertheless, while Chinese monks drew inspiration from the scriptures, they were as innovative in methods of ascetic practice as they were in matters of doctrine or ceremony. One of the most pervasive of these innovations was the belief, held by laymen and monk alike, that by making an offering of their own flesh, they would be reborn directly in a "pure land." The most famous illustration of this belief is contained in the biography of the Pure-Land patriarch Shandao. In the biography, after Shandao explained to a congregation of laymen that they could be reborn in the Pure Land of Amitābha simply by reciting the Buddha's name, one of the layman promptly climbed to the top of a tall tree, chanted the name of Amitābha, and leapt to his death.[161] And just as classical scriptures like the *Lotus* provided monks with a set of ascetic guidelines, so too did hagiography. The Tang monk Xingming, for instance, makes reference both to the *Lotus Sūtra* and to the monk Sengyai—one of the most famous of the Chinese self-immolators, eulogized in the *Further Biographies*—before throwing himself before ravenous tigers.[162]

Another factor involved in these practices, though much less explicit than the famous story from the *Lotus Sūtra* or the Jataka tales, or even the association between pious suicide and the Pure Land, was nonetheless every bit as pervasive and revealing for what it tells us about the give-and-take logic of self-sacrifice. The principle behind this mentality is apparent at the juncture at which the examples of monks who mutilate themselves and of laymen who mutilate themselves meet. This is at the site of the remains of the greatest of all self-sacrificers: the Buddha. In all of the examples of lay self-mutilation cited above, the soldiers, peasants, and townsfolk who burned and cut themselves did so when in the presence of the Buddha's relics. We find similar occurrences in the biographies of eminent monks. Recall that on hearing of the famous finger bone of the Buddha housed in the Famen Monastery outside of the capital, the monk Xichen, who had risen all the way to a position in the Palace Sanctum based on his reputation for burning off his fingers, rushed to the site, paid obeisance before the reliquary, and burnt off one more of his three remaining fingers on the spot.[163] Yuanhui, another Tang monk, made burns on his arm when in the presence of a relic of the Buddha's tooth.[164] One of the most prominent of finger-burners was Fazang, the great Tang exegete and architect of Huayan thought, who at the tender age of sixteen went before an Aśoka reliquary and incinerated one of his fingers.[165]

These monks were, of course, following the instructions of the *Lotus* to burn their fingers before a Buddha stupa, but there is also a more complex dynamic at work in this particular form of self-sacrifice. As the language of the accounts reveals, in these incidents the monk or layman through self-mutilation drew on the power of the relic in an attempt to transfer or internalize the sanctity of the sacred object. Remember the passage from the incident of 819: "There were some hooligans from the shops who could endure the pain of burning and branding, deceptively saying that they were making offerings. They burned holes in their skin *and bragged that the bones of the Buddha were within.*" Self-mutilation before relics of the Buddha was not only a sacrifice; it was an appropriation. By burning himself, the adept drew on the power of the Buddha's body, purifying his own body and transforming himself into a holy, living relic. Hence, while negative Buddhist attitudes toward the body as a source of defilement certainly encouraged the destruction and mutilation of the body, there was at the same time a more positive interpretation of the act.[166]

In other words, as in the case of cremation, self-mutilation and suicide were not merely attempts to destroy an impure body, but also to create a new and better one. As Zanning puts it, ritual suicide "is what is known as 'true returning.' Through it, they gain a body as firm as adamantine, and leave behind kernels of *dhātu* [i.e., relics] as a sign of their attainments."[167] It is to "cast aside this body, in order to obtain a body of self-mastery. When one has obtained a dharma-body of self-mastery, one can roam through all realms of existence."[168] They give over one body in order to "quickly acquire a body of more enduring strength."[169] The reader may well doubt that a notion as abstract and erudite as this would compel people to expose themselves to extreme physical pain, but a connection between self-sacrifice and relics is undeniable. From the earliest accounts to the *Song Biographies*, monks, nuns, and laypeople burn and cut their bodies before not only relics of the Buddha, but relics of eminent monks as well.[170]

The relic connection does not stop here. The importance of relics in medieval Chinese Buddhism has been amply documented in a number of recent studies,[171] and as Zanning's comments indicate, monks who had purified their bodies through self-mutilation and suicide were prime sources for these numinous pieces of bone. Recall the final instructions of Wuran to his disciple Zhao ("Take my bones and ashes and scatter them. Don't make a fuss over them.") and the discreet, matter-of-fact statement easily overlooked at the very end of the biography: "Later, disciples collected Wuran's remains and erected a stupa south of Mount Fanxian that stands to this day."

The touching story of the monk known only as Master Bundlegrass (Sucaoshi) vividly illustrates the allure of the prestige associated with self-immolation, as well as the value placed on the remains of monks who had immolated themselves. An odd, ugly monk of uncertain origins, Master Bundlegrass lived for several years beside a monastery, refusing to enter the sleeping quarters, preferring to sleep instead on a bundle of grass under the eaves of the monastery buildings. When the monastic administrator reprimanded the ragged monk because of the ridicule he attracted, Bundlegrass replied, "Do you detest me so? The world holds no affection for me. How can I remain here any longer?" That night the monk burned himself with the same bundle of grass. After this, we are told, "the faithful of the capital city made an image of the monk from his ashes and placed it next to the Buddha Hall. The people called him Master Bundlegrass, and prayers to his image were often rewarded."[172] Years later, in the middle of the ninth century, the famous Tang writer, bibliophile, and Buddhist aficionado Duan Chengshi related the same events, describing the image of Bundlegrass in his account of the important religious centers of the capital.[173]

By burning himself to death, the lowly Master Bundlegrass elevated himself to a position warranting enduring reverence. Stories such as these lend credence to a disturbing reference in Yijing's work to the pressures put on monks to make such sacrifices: "Two or three intimate friends combine and make an agreement among themselves to instigate the young students to destroy their lives."[174] Scattered hints such as these remind us that while ideological motivations stressed in the hagiographical literature were certainly important, monks were also influenced by the pervasive though vaguely defined mentalities and social pressures of the time.

The Reception of These Practices

One of the most jarring references to relics in the *Biographies* comes at the end of the biography of the sixth-century monk Puyuan who bled to death after cutting off his own hands in an act of self-sacrifice. After this, "inhabitants from the various villages were all grieved at this ascetic act and competed for the right to bury the corpse. Unable to resolve the dispute, they divided the body into several pieces so that each village could erect its own stupa."[175] Here we begin to get a sense for the complexity of public reaction to Buddhist self-mutilation. The villagers in this story seem to be acting more in their own self-interest than out of reverence for the monk himself; they would have their relics, even if it meant tearing apart the sacred corpse to get them. While it could be argued that the passion for relics reflected in this story does in fact stem from a profound reverence for the deceased, it is clearly a different form of respect than that shown, for example, to a deceased parent. I know of no stories in Chinese literature of, for instance, feuding sons dividing the body of a deceased parent. And if there were such a story, the sons would certainly be condemned for their actions.

In addition to attaching importance to the relics of monks who sacrificed themselves, many were impressed by such awful acts in and of themselves. At the same time, others found these displays of self-destruction repugnant. In fact, the responses to Buddhist self-sacrifice were remarkably diverse. Buddhist sources are replete with references to pious lay people, weeping mournfully and sighing in admiration at the death of a self-immolating monk. As we saw in the examples cited at the beginning of this section, others found the practices variously morally offensive, socially disruptive, or ludicrously funny. Several prominent figures from both within and without the *sangha* left more detailed, thoughtful accounts of their reactions to these practices.

For instance, some leading Buddhists singled out for criticism the practice of blood writing. In an inscription dedicating a new set of scriptures carved in stone, the prominent poet and Buddhist layman Bai Juyi noted that scriptures written in blood deteriorate just as quickly as those in ink.[176] More pointedly, the eighth-century monk and poet Jiaoran once noted that it is wrong to copy scriptures in one's blood because "the body is a putrid, vile thing, inappropriate for pure books."[177]

Huijiao, who had himself set aside a chapter of the *Liang Biographies* for those who "surrendered their bodies," discussed some of the objections raised from within the clergy to self-sacrifice at the end of his chapter. The most curious of these objections is that "according to the Buddha himself," each individual's body houses some eighty-thousand minuscule worms that perish only when one dies. The fear then was that when burning himself to death the monk would unwittingly murder a myriad of innocent creatures. Huijiao also gives voice to the more persistent concern that suicide was expressly prohibited in the Vinaya.[178] From the monk's point of view, this was the most serious charge raised against self-immolation.[179]

The most prominent spokesman for the criticism that self-sacrifice was counter to the Regulations was Yijing, a monk well-versed in the Vinaya, who takes a characteristically consistent stand on the issue. According to Yijing, while the Vinaya clearly prohibits suicide,[180] lay people are not required to follow the monastic regulations. Therefore, it is suitable for a layman to "offer food by roasting his own arm," for "it is right for them to offer, not only any treasure in their possession, but even their own life, when needed." But for a monk, "These actions are entirely out of harmony with the Vinaya Canon. Even those who consider such practices to be wrong are afraid of [committing faults] if they prevent such actions. But if one destroys life in such a way, the great object of one's existence is lost. That is why the Buddha prohibited it. The superior [monks] and wise teachers never acted in any such harmful way."[181]

Yijing was certainly a respected and influential monk as testified by his biography, the very first in the *Song Biographies of Eminent Monks*. Nonetheless, when compiling the *Song Biographies* Zanning continued to reserve a chapter for monks who sacrificed their bodies, including self-mutilation and suicide by fire. In his discussion at the end of the chapter, Zanning first relates the corporal self-sacrifices of the Buddha in his many lives before attaining Buddhahood. He then discusses other precedents for self-sacrifice in the scriptures. Finally, he turns to Yijing's critique.

> Question:
> In his correspondence and in his translations, Yijing repeated again and again that men should not incinerate their fingers. He personally went to the Western Regions. He was thoroughly familiar with what is appropriate, and he was well-versed in all of the teachings. Yet he did not permit self-mutilation. What are we to make of this?

> Response:
> This perspective is restricted to the teachings of the Āgamas.[182] How could such concerns restrict the Mahāyāna Law? If someone gives up inner wealth he will certainly attain the "perfection of giving."[183] Therefore, the *Solemnity Treatise*[184] states: "He who gives of his own life is rare. Such a one can attain a bodhisattva's perfection of giving."

In other words, no matter how well documented Yijing's claims were in the Vinaya, all such views could ultimately be relegated to the "lesser vehicle." It is important to note, however, that Zanning, like Daoxuan before him, was known for his expertise in the Vinaya. Zanning even had the nickname "Tiger of the Regulations." Apparently, such fields of expertise were less restricting than one might think; Zanning was able to choose when and where to play the "tiger." This is largely because of the enormous body of resources on which a learned monk like Zanning was able to draw. The *Solemnity Treatise* is only one of a number of well-respected Buddhist scriptures to which Zanning could have turned to make his case for the legitimacy of self-sacrifice. By his time, that is by the early Song Dynasty, Chinese monks had access to an immense body of "orthodox" Buddhist literature riddled with contradictory claims, thus providing a creative thinker like Zanning with a considerable amount of flexibility when formulating a stance on a pressing issue like self-sacrifice. Indeed, in cases like this one, it is contemporary practice which inspires and shapes the formulation of doctrinal stances, and not the other way around.[185]

Of course non-Buddhist officials needed have no qualms about reconciling conflicting passages in the scriptures, and many such figures no doubt found the practice of self-mutilation as dangerous as it was offensive. The most famous articulation of official opposition to Buddhist self-immolation is found in the writings of the scholar-official Han Yu. After the spectacle of 819 when the bone of the Buddha was brought into the capital, Han Yu submitted a memorial to the throne that has been held up ever since as a model of concise, forceful prose —one of the greatest pieces of invective in all of Chinese literature.

Most of the memorial is taken up with traditional Confucian complaints against Buddhism. Buddhism is foreign. The Chinese sages of antiquity did not practice Buddhism. The reigns of Chinese emperors have grown increasingly short since the introduction of Buddhism, and so forth. Finally, the memorial refers to the practice of self-mutilation with rank disgust.

> The people are stupid and ignorant; they are easily deceived and with difficulty enlightened. . . . Burning heads and searing fingers by the tens and hundreds, throwing away their clothes and scattering their money, from morning to night emulating one another and fearing only to be last, old and young rush about, abandoning their work and place; and if restrictions are not immediately imposed, they will increasingly make the rounds of temples and some will inevitably cut off their arms and slice their flesh in the way of offerings.[186]

With his carefully chosen reference to "burning heads and searing fingers," Han Yu paints a picture of mass chaos. Unrestrained violence, even when self-inflicted, can only make the thoughtful official nervous.[187] Han Yu was not alone in this concern. Various attempts were made to regulate the practice of self-mutilation among both monks and laymen. The *Biographies* contain several references to monks who submitted memorials, requesting official permission to burn themselves to death.[188] And while Han Yu was banished for his presumptuous memorial, other emperors were more receptive to such concerns, issuing edicts forbidding the populace from mutilating themselves.[189]

In an article entitled "The Indianization of China," Hu Shih remarked that "the Chinese in their moments of calmer judgment could not but regard [self-mutilation] as revolting and inhuman."[190] The main reason for this reaction, Hu argued, is the Chinese view of the body as a sacred inheritance, as embodied in the passage from the *Book of Filial Piety*: "The human body, even every hair and every skin of it, is inherited from the parents and must not be annihilated or degraded."

The polemical literature seems to bear out Hu's claim. Even Zanning, in the discussion following his chapter on self-sacrificers, finds it necessary to quote the passage from the *Book of Filial Piety* and dismiss it as a veiled form of selfishness. One would think along with Hu Shih that the pervasive importance attached to the notion of filial devotion would have been a major impediment to the spread of the practice of self-mutilation. But surprisingly, when we look more closely at the reception of these practices by Chinese society as a whole, we find precisely the opposite: for many Chinese, self-mutilation was one of the most venerated, sincere forms of filial devotion imaginable.

When Chen Shuling, a sixth-century noble, wished to demonstrate his filial devotion at the death of his mother, he claimed to have copied out the *Nirvāṇa Sūtra* in his own blood. Shortly thereafter, Shuling shamelessly broke the period of mourning by eating fine foods and having sex, actions for which he was soundly punished on imperial orders.[191] But the interest of this story for our purposes is that already at this time the relationship between filial devotion and what began as a distinctly Buddhist form of mutilation, blood-writing, were taken for granted. The *Tang Histories* also make occasional reference to the practice of copying out blood scriptures as a demonstration of filial devotion.[192] The Tang figure Wan Jingru, for instance, earned official recognition for his filial behavior at the death of his parents, behavior that included copying out Buddhist texts in his blood and chopping off two of his fingers.[193]

When the mother of a certain Zhang Quanyi died, he cut off one of his fingers as a sign of respect for her, an act that earned him a reputation for filial devotion. Earlier, when his mother had taken ill, Zhang cut off a piece of his thigh and fed it to her as medicine.[194] The *Song Biographies* record a similar story of a boy cutting off a piece of his thigh to feed it to his sick father; because of this action, the boy became famous for his filial devotion.[195] This gruesome practice, which seems to be rooted in Buddhist Jataka tales, apparently became quite widespread, provoking the famed Tang poet and essayist Pi Rixiu to condemn the practice of feeding one's flesh to an ailing parent in an essay on filial piety.[196] When the mother of Zhu Shouchang, an eleventh-century figure, was missing, Zhu "burned his back and scorched the top of his head *according to the Buddhist method*, also puncturing himself and copying out Buddhist scriptures with his blood."[197]

Indeed, virtually every example of Buddhist forms of self-mutilation recorded in the dynastic histories is in some way related to the concept of filial piety. Thus it is clear that from quite early on what were originally considered Buddhist forms of self-mutilation—copying scriptures in blood, chopping off fingers, burning one's arm—were considered appropriate means for expressing filial piety. More than simply a marginal Buddhist practice for monks and madmen, self-mutilation had become a distinctly Chinese form of self-expression.

Clearly, the subject of corporal self-sacrifice was a controversial one, evoking a variety of passionate responses, pro and con. Critiques of these practices were not limited to righteous officials like Han Yu, but included members of the *sangha* as well. Further, the practice itself quickly spread from the clergy to peasants, soldiers, and even high-level literati and members of the court. Against the backdrop of this wide variety of heated opinions on these practices, the *Eminent Monks* series consistently affirmed the validity of self-mutilation.

It is important to recall that the *Eminent Monks* collections are just that, *collections* of already extant biographies composed by hundreds of different authors and read by thousands in various forms, from the stele inscription at a local monastery, to tales of the marvelous in the library of the literatus. In other words, the mere existence of biographies of monks who sacrificed their bodies attests to the widespread respect for the practice. At the same time, once these stories were collected in the *Eminent Monks*, they were imbued with an even greater air of legitimacy and were hence even more influential. While it may be argued that the self-mutilators represent only a small minority of monks, they are important because of the role they played in pushing the limits of ascetic possibility to a more violent extreme. Not only did they encourage the most radical monks to cross the line dividing the guarding of the senses from an attack on the body, they were also the models against which more timid or circumspect monks judged themselves.

Most scholars would agree that the *Eminent Monks* series was a powerful voice for the virtues of Buddhist asceticism. Nonetheless, interspersed with stories of monks who swore off bodily comfort and at times went out of their way to cause themselves discomfort are stories of monks who did precisely the opposite, that is, ate meat, drank wine, and generally ignored the monastic regulations. These monks, the anti-ascetics, are the subject of the following section.

The Meat-Eating Wine-Drinking Monks

The sixth-century work *Chu sanzang jiji*—one of our earliest sources for biographical information on Chinese monks—contains a curious account of the eccentric layman Zhu Shulan. Born in China to descendants of Indian nobility, Zhu was raised a Buddhist. After quickly mastering several languages at an early age, the boy demonstrated an aptitude for Buddhist scriptures. But despite his promising credentials as an exegete, Shulan had a wild streak: he hunted voraciously and, ignoring the protestations of his pious mother, refused to become a vegetarian, eating meat and drinking wine with reckless abandon. One day, after a particularly wanton drinking bout, he collapsed drunk by the side of the road and was subsequently sent to the prefectural jail. The story continues:

> The Governor of Henan, Yue Guang,[198] had been drinking with some guests and was already drunk. He said to Shulan, "You're an immigrant [*qiaoke*]. How is it that you drink like us?" Shulan said, "Du Kang [the inventor of wine] fermented wine for all the world to drink. Why make distinctions between immigrants and natives?" Yue Guang then said, "It's all right to drink, but why [drink to the point of] being wild and out of control?"
>
> "I am wild but far from out of control," Zhu replied, " just as your honor is drunk but not wild."

Yue Guang then laughed and let him go.[199]

Here, the Buddhist layman Zhu Shulan is clearly a part of an established triangle of associations—wine, wit, and literati—prominent in the secular literature of the day.[200] But for a Buddhist author to draw on this secular tradition was problematic. If literati-poets distinguished themselves from their dull-witted but politically powerful contemporaries through excessive drinking, the Buddhist defined himself, as we have seen, through precisely the opposite means, namely, strictures on the diet. Sengyou, compiler of the *Chu sanzang jiji*, resolves this tension in the end of the biography when Zhu Shulan dies, descends to hell, and realizes the error of his ways. In the end, Zhu is given a reprieve and allowed to return to the world of the living where he devotes himself to good deeds and the translation of scriptures.

In the *Liang Biographies*, composed soon after the *Chu sanzang jiji*, Zhu Shulan's reckless behavior is toned down; the biographer concentrates instead on his activities after his "conversion."[201] But in other biographies in the collection the same motif emerges again: this time having to do with monks, and this time without a repentant ending. The monk Beidu, for example, was given his name, meaning "cup-crosser," when he pilfered a golden Buddhist statue from a layman at night. As Beidu was sneaking away with the statue, its owner awoke and gave chase. Coming to a river, Beidu tossed a small cup onto the water and wondrously floated across on it, thereby effecting his escape.

Later, Beidu is described as one who did not "strictly keep the dietary regulations, but drank wine and ate meat."[202] Here we are given no conversion experience and no doctrinal justification; Beidu is an eminent monk just like any of the others described in the collection except that he steals, cheats, lies, eats meat, and drinks wine. Two other similar monks also appear in the *Liang Biographies*, both in the *Shenyi*, or "Divine Marvels," chapter of the book. Shaoshuo, a remarkably ugly monk whom "children were fond of chasing after and teasing," would "enter into the wine shops and drink with the others there."[203] Huitong would "travel through the hamlets and villages eating and drinking no differently from anyone else."[204]

In the *Further Biographies*, a dozen more meat-eating, wine-drinking monks appear. In addition to violating the dietary restrictions mentioned above, they defecate and urinate in public, eat entire hogs, and vomit profusely after obscene bouts of drinking and gluttony.[205] By the next installment of the *Biographies*, the *Song Biographies of Eminent Monks*, there is a veritable avalanche of accounts of these unpredictable monks, not only in the chapter devoted to "wonder-workers" (*Gantong*), but also in the "Chanters and Reciters" (*Dusong pian*) chapter. Again, they violate the monastic code by gambling, fighting, and butchering helpless animals.[206] Who are these monks, and what are they doing in collections of what are supposed to be accounts of *exemplars*—paragons of Buddhist virtue?[207]

The meat-eating, wine-drinking monks of Buddhist hagiography fit into the broad category of a nebulous archetype known as "the trickster," common to the religious literatures of many, if not most, cultures. First examined by scholars such as Paul Radin, MacLinscott Ricketts, and Robert Pelton in their studies of the mythology of North American and East African tribes, tricksters, such as Coyote and Hare in North America or Spider and Hyena in East Africa, are characterized by their exaggerated body parts, scatological episodes, and above all, insatiable libidos, often directed at daughters, grandmothers, and sisters-in-law.[208] In the Chinese Buddhist biographies, there is only an occasional, oblique reference to sexual deviance, such as the following story of Nantuo (Nanda):

> When Nantuo first entered Shu, he traveled with three young nuns. He would either get roaring drunk and sing like a madman, or gather a crowd and preach on the Law. [A certain] General Zhang found all of this reprehensible and ordered the monk's arrest. When Nantuo was captured and taken to General Zhang, the monk said, "I

am merely a member of the clergy and have no knowledge of the medicinal arts."

Then he pointed to the three nuns and said, "But they are all excellent singers and dancers." The general then valued him and kept them there. Calling for wine and meat, Zhang held an evening banquet in order to drink and dance with his guests. Zhang loaned the nuns jackets, trousers, washcloths, and combs. The three nuns each wore powder and lipstick. They sat in a row casting furtive glances and giggling—lascivious beyond compare. When they were all half drunk with wine, Nantuo said to the nuns, "Perhaps you could do a skip-dance for the officer." The nuns then rose slowly and began to dance, twirling the white damask of their garments like swirling snow. They kicked their legs in rapid succession with unparalleled skill.

After some time the music stopped but the nuns kept on dancing. Nantuo flew into a fury, shouting at the nuns, "Are you girls mad?" Then he suddenly drew the general's sword. Thinking him drunk, everyone quickly backed away in terror. Nantuo then cut off the heads of the three nuns who fell dead to the ground, their blood spreading for several yards. The astonished general called for his attendants to apprehend the monk, whereupon Nantuo laughed and said, "Don't act so rashly." Then he picked up the bodies of the three nuns one by one. As he did this their bodies became bamboo staffs; their blood turned out to be the wine that they had been drinking.[209]

This is a far cry from the rape scenes of the Coyote and Raven stories, or the incestuous battles of Susanō-no-mikoto and Amaterasu-no-Ōmikami in the *Kojiki*; here sex is replaced by dancing and make-up, and the "lascivious nuns" are not, as it turns out, real at all. In the *Eminent Monks* series, the focus of the transgression is not on sex, and there are only occasional references to excrement; the focus in these biographies is rather on food, clothing, and manners.

Master Tante "although he had received the tonsure, was wild and unrestrained, drinking wine, eating meat, and mumbling strangely."[210] The monk Shijian "lived in no set place, but would often go to visit his relatives, saying his belly was hungry and asking for some chicken. He would also obtain fine wine, drinking a few cups and then leaving, without ever even saying thank you."[211] The monk Fazhao who "drifted about randomly" wandered into a tavern one rainy day, "suddenly shaking himself so that mud splattered everywhere. Since noon had already passed, he could not obtain food by begging (recall that stricter monks were expected to refrain from eating after noon), so he shouted at a boy to buy him some venison, boil it, and sandwich it inside of a biscuit. Fazhao gobbled it down in an instant, without the least sign of remorse, as if there was no one else about."[212] The monk Weigong associated with "drinkers and gamblers, acting wildly, without the least sign of remorse."[213] Hanshan would walk slowly through the corridors, "sometimes raising a ruckus and insulting others, and sometimes shouting curses off into space. When the monks of the monastery could no longer stomach him and chased him away with their staffs, he would turn around, clap his hands together, and slowly walk away laughing. His clothing was always in tatters, his face old and battered."[214] Shide, as a child apprentice charged with care of the Buddha Hall, was demoted to dishwasher after ridiculing an image of the holy man Kauṇḍinya.[215]

The "Grand Master of Guangling" demonstrates all three characteristics—improper diet, clothing, and manners—in the first few lines of his biography, which reads:

> The Grand Master of Guangling was ugly in appearance and of a perverse nature. Possessing a straightforward disposition like a butcher or a wine merchant, he was only distinguished from them by the accoutrements of the śramaṇa. He was fond of wine and meat and would go about in a coarse hemp cloak, the weight and thickness of which can be imagined. Yet even in the midst of summer he did not take it off for a moment, so that fleas and ticks gathered on him in clusters.
>
>   The Grand Master stayed at the Xiaogan Monastery where he kept a room to himself, closing the door every night to sleep in a seemingly normal fashion. But at times the crazed aspect of his character would assert itself, and he would slaughter a dog or a pig. During the day he would gather some of the local toughs together for a fist fight. Other times he would get drunk and sleep by the side of the road. For all of these reasons, the people of Yangzhou despised him.[216]

Thus we are confronted in these biographies with a "type," a frequently appearing figure defined by behavior that is not as unpredictable as it first appeared; a trickster, but one who transgresses only certain taboos in certain situations. Nevertheless, the question remains: what is such a figure doing in collections of accounts of *eminent monks*?

As we have seen, the *Biographies of Eminent Monks* were written for two distinct audiences. On the one hand they were to present politically powerful figures with examples of the worthiness of the *saṅgha*;[217] on the other hand, they were to provide monks with *exemplars*, or ideals worthy of emulation. Temporarily putting aside the reception of such stories at court, how are these meat-eating, wine-drinking monks worthy of emulation? What is the doctrinal justification for their actions, the moral these stories were intended to convey?

The most obvious, orthodox precedent for their actions lay readily at hand in one of the most popular scriptures in all of Chinese Buddhism: the *Vimalakīrtinirdeśasūtra*. Not only is Vimalakīrti a layman with wife and children, but like the "hedonistic" monks described above, he frequents brothels and wine shops. Vimalakīrti is not, however, a trickster—for his trips to the brothels and wine shops are for a most sedate purpose: to preach the holy *Dharma*. But the sūtra is vague on just what Vimalakīrti does when he goes to the wine shops and brothels. Does he actually drink with the drunkards and sleep with the prostitutes, or is he exceptional because he resists their temptations? The symbolic language of the *Vimalakīrti* is tantalizingly vague: like Shaoshuo, Vimalakīrti "may follow the ways of the weak, the ugly, and the wretched, yet he is beautiful to look upon." Like Nantuo, "He may show himself engaged in dancing with harem girls, yet he cleaves to solitude, having crossed the swamp of desire." Like Tante, "He follows the ways of the dumb and the incoherent, yet, having acquired the power of incantations, he is adorned with a varied eloquence." In short, "He follows the ways of the heterodox without ever becoming heterodox."[218]

Like Vimalakīrti, some of the monks depicted in the *Biographies* enter the "sea of passions"[219] with strictly didactic intentions. Ācārya Xiang, for example, promotes vegetarianism through his meat-eating. Among the people of Yi Prefecture[220] the story goes, there was a custom of climbing the nearby Qingcheng Mountain each year on the third day of the third month for a lavish picnic of meat and wine. Ācārya Xiang repeatedly urged the people to stop this practice, but they ignored him. One year the monk went along with the people, eating and drinking with the rest of them. In the midst of the saturnalia, he stood up, saying, "I'm really drunk, and stuffed too! Somebody help me over to a ditch so I can throw up." When he opened his mouth to vomit, "the chicken meat that emerged cried out and flew off. The mutton that came out galloped away. Wine and food came out chaotically until it just about filled the ditch to the top with fish and ducks swimming about in profusion. All of the people sighed and vowed to abandon their practice of killing animals."[221] But this kind of easily recognizable didactic message is rare in these stories.

In the *Song Biographies*, when the accounts of carnivorous monks make their way into the "Chanters and Reciters" chapter, they are put to a new, more subtle use: glorification of the power of scripture. Here the 'bad monks' are a foil for sutra recitation as if to say, if even these lowly monks can derive benefit from the scriptures, the books must be powerful indeed. Take, for example, the biography of Shi Xiongjun.

Shi Xiongjun, whose secular surname was Zhou, was from Cheng-du. He was a skilled orator, but did not keep the precepts, using donations from laymen unlawfully and, immersed in his own deception, caring only for wanton lawlessness. What is more, he once betrayed his [holy] garments and entered the military. Only in order to avoid some difficulties did he return to the clergy. During the Dali era [766–779], he suddenly passed away and entered the netherworld.

When the king [of the netherworld] had finished scolding and reprimanding him, Xiongjun was led into hell. The monk protested, shouting out, "If I enter hell then the sayings of all the Buddhas of past, present, and future are a pack of lies. I once read in the *Contemplation Scripture*[222] that if he recites [the name of the Buddha] ten times when on the verge of death, even one of the lowest class of the lowest types of sentient beings who has committed the five abominations[223] will still be born beyond [in the pure-land]. Although I have my faults, I haven't committed the five abominations, and if you speak of reciting the Buddha's name, I don't know how many times I've done it! If the sayings of the Buddhas can be believed, since I've died a sudden death, I ought to return."

[Soon thereafter] Xiongjun said to someone who was with him, "If you see monks or laymen from the city, tell them I've already been reborn in the West." When he had finished speaking, he mounted a jeweled dais and went directly to the Western [Paradise].[224]

Xiongjun's characterization of the *Guan wuliang shou jing* (the *Contemplation Scripture*), one of the most popular texts in all of Chinese Buddhism, is in fact accurate. In the sutra, the "lowest type of sentient being" is used as a foil for the sutra itself, as if to say, if even the most despicable, immoral scoundrel can be delivered by the scripture, how much more efficacious it must be for the average reader. The *Contemplation* is not the only scripture so treated in the *Biographies*. Weigong "associated with gamblers and drunkards, telling lies and speaking wildly without a trace of shame." But because he chanted the *Diamond Sūtra*, he was reborn in the Western Paradise along with the most pious of monks.[225] Other monks appear to be coarse but demonstrate their hidden virtue through scripture recitation. Again and again we read accounts of monks, usually through the eyes of a third party, who wander into taverns to eat meat and drink wine, spitting out foul language at all who would question them. But at night, when passing by the door of the scoundrel's room, the narrator peeks through a crack in the door and sees the monk sitting upright, chanting scriptures and emitting a radiant glow from his mouth—a telltale sign of high attainments.[226]

The behavior of these monks could also be justified by the antinomian strain in Buddhist thought, particularly as it emerged in late Tang Chan.[227] But all of this puts the elite, orthodox compilers of the *Biographies of Eminent Monks* series in an awkward position. If all monks followed the examples of these exemplars, there would be little need for monasteries, much less carefully designed monastic regulations. As we have seen, many leading monks championed a complete prohibition on both meat and wine for monks.

Curiously, one of the most prominent figures to advocate a strict prohibition of meat and wine was none other than Daoxuan, compiler of the *Further Biographies of Eminent Monks*.[228] Judging by the vast majority of the biographies in the *Eminent Monks* series, Huijiao and Zanning seem to have taken a similar stance on the question of diet. In a commentary to the biography of the mysterious "Abbot" (Shangzuo), Zanning attempts to reconcile the contradictory messages he sends his readers. First, the biography:

The background of Shi Wangming is not known. He lived several tens of *li* west of Baocheng[229] in a place called Mount Zhongliang. He grew up there against a backdrop of rows of winding peaks where the verdure of vegetation hangs as if frozen in the air. The Abbot was most peculiar in his behavior, and his way of speaking was unusual as well. Though those who were accustomed to him did not find him startling, those who saw him for the first time thought him most strange. He would often satiate himself with wine and meat and act crudely in public. Yet he concerned himself with the affairs of the monastic assembly, often mediating in their disputes. The other monks feared and respected him, giving him the nickname "Abbot."

At that time, there was a group of monks who modeled themselves on the Abbot. They were the only ones who did not fear him. When the Abbot learned of this he sighed and said, "Not yet abiding at the stage of pure mind,[230] how dare you carry out unorthodox practice? Unorthodox practice is not for all men. It is said that gold is tested by fire. Wait for the day when I will test you with fire!"

One day, during the Kaicheng era [836–840], the Abbot made a large biscuit. Calling the other members of the assembly together he said, "Let's go to the *śītavana* [i.e., graveyard]." On the outskirts of the city there were many graves. People abandoned corpses there, and that is why it was called the *śītavana*. The Abbot squatted on the ground, opened up the biscuit, and filled it with pieces of flesh from a rotting corpse. Then, putting it in his mouth, he swallowed it with an expression of pleasure while the monks who had come out with him covered their noses and vomited on the ground as they ran away. The Abbot shouted after them in a loud voice saying, "Only when you can digest this meat can you eat other meat."

This incident shocked the monks into enlightenment. They changed their ways, becoming serious and devoted. People from near and far took refuge in the master.

In an addendum to this biography, Zanning gives a sophisticated doctrinal explanation for the distinction between the Abbot and his epigones: the meat-eating wine-drinking monks, he tells us, are exceptions.

ADDENDA:

At first the Abbot demonstrated the teachings he himself followed. Later, others emulated him. Let it be known that those who have achieved the "verification of fruition"[231] may make use of unorthodox means in the service of Buddhism. In the end, the unenlightened are aroused and then return to the truth. According to the *Treatise on the Law*,[232] great bodhisattvas of awe and virtue are sustained through the manifestation of their powers.[233] If someone falsely claiming to have attained fruition were to follow their example, would it not be like a squirrel trying to imitate the roar of a lion?[234]

In this way, these monks are easily explained away: because of their high spiritual attainments, they recognize the fundamental nonduality of the phenomenal world, transcending the distinctions between pure and impure, life and death.[235]

If this explanation seems perfunctory and forced, it is for good reason. In this passage, Zanning is attempting to explain a baffling contradiction that confronts him, a tension between an admiration for those who rigorously keep the rules and those who openly transgress them. The story is not told to illustrate the doctrine; rather, the doctrine is invoked to explain away the story. In other words, the stories of trickster monks reveal a deeper ambivalent logic of religious values in which, under the right circumstances, there is no contradiction between the maintenance of monastic regulations and their violation, between stricture and excess.

In the previous two sections, I made the case that to a large extent it was asceticism that defined the monk, for it was asceticism even in its most formal aspects that set the monk apart, that pushed him into the outer boundaries of society—repositories of prestige, respect, and power. Ironically, the trickster derives *his* power from precisely the same source, though in his case it is not separation from secular society that distinguishes him, but rather, his separation from the monastic community, from the ascetic. If the ascetic violates the rules of ordinary life by maintaining a strict diet and refusing to eat or sleep, the trickster violates monastic taboos, eating meat, drinking wine, sleeping all day long, and cursing when he awakes.

This implicit juxtaposition of ascetic and trickster is made explicit in the story of an encounter between Daoxuan and the famous Tantric master Śubhakarasiṃha recorded in the *Taiping guangji*.[236] According to the biography, Śubhakarasiṃha shared a room with Daoxuan at the Ximing Monastery in Chang'an. It soon became apparent that the two roommates were incompatible.

> Tripiṭaka Śubhakarasiṃha drank wine and ate meat; in word and deed he was crude and uncouth, always getting drunk, raising a ruckus, and vomiting on the mat. Master of the Regulations Dao-xuan could not tolerate him in the least. Once, in the middle of the night, Daoxuan caught a flea and was about to toss it to the ground when Śubhakarasiṃha, half-drunk, repeatedly called out, "You've killed a child of the Buddha!" Only then did Daoxuan realize that Śubhakarasiṃha was an exceptional man."[237]

In the *Song Biographies* version of the story, Daoxuan realizes that Śubhakarasiṃha is not only "exceptional," but is no less than a bodhi-sattva!

In fact, as I pointed out in the Introduction, such an encounter between these two men could not have taken place, as Daoxuan died a half century before Śubhakarasiṃha arrived in China. The existence of carefully dated biographies of both of these figures made this dating problem quite apparent to the scholar-historian Zanning. Hence, the *Song Biographies* version of the story included in Śubhakara-siṃha's biography explains the discrepancy by marveling at Śub-hakarasiṃha's ability to transcend the confines of space and time. When the story appears once again in Daoxuan's biography, Zanning suggests in a note that there must have been another monk by the name Śubhakarasiṃha alive during Daoxuan's day. Evidently, despite evidence clearly separating the two figures, there was a need to bring them together. Similar juxtapositions occur between the staid exegete Chengguan and a madman,[238] and between the famous translator Xuanzang and the profligate young genius Kuiji, known for his taste for wine and women.[239]

One of the factors bringing such figures together may well have been a literary one. One character was needed to act as a foil, to high-light the characteristics of the other. The more clever and playful the jester, the more foolish and humorless Lear appears; the more dull and straitlaced Tang Seng, the more outrageous his companion, Monkey.

Like the ascetic, the trickster's attainments are revealed through supernormal means. Their wild, nonsensical mutterings are later revealed to have been predictions.[240] They invoke spirits and demons at will.[241] The story is told of one trickster-monk who drank poison to save his fellow monks from an evil minister, and when he relieved himself, split open solid rocks with his urine.[242] And again, like the ascetic, their bodies are transformed into numinous relics upon their demise.[243] The easy coexistence of ascetic and anti-ascetic in the hagiographic literature points to the underlying structure of the values system of its compilers and, potentially, its audience. If we imagine a spectrum running from ascetic to trickster, the key to prestige and power is not which end of the spectrum a figure belongs to, but rather that he be at one or the other extreme: if the ascetic is a marginal figure, the trickster is a marginal among marginals.[244]

If we can now understand how these seemingly contradictory messages—that of the trickster and that of the ascetic—illustrate a common principle that governs a particular mentality, the question arises as to just whose mentality this principle belongs. In the preface to the *Song Biographies*, Zanning explains the methods used to assemble the five hundred some accounts of his collection. Zanning writes:

> We based some of the biographies on stele inscriptions. For others we sought out written accounts and records. For some we questioned official envoys, while for others we interviewed local elders. We did research to match this information against treatises and scriptures, did editing work to compare this information with historical documents, and compiled it all into three cases in order to assist the palace. We have narrated these wondrous accounts of the clergy that [the reader] may know of the wealth and value of the house of Buddha.[245]

As we have seen, both Huijiao and Daoxuan make similar comments in the prefaces of their works. Unfortunately, my attempts to trace the original sources for the stories of meat-eating, wine-drinking monks have yielded mixed results. In most cases, it is impossible to recover the original sources on which the compilers of the *Biographies* relied. It is tempting to assume then that these stories came from popular, oral traditions, but the evidence is inconclusive.

The final sentence of the quotation above is equally significant: "We have narrated these wondrous accounts of the clergy that you may know of the wealth and value of the house of Buddha." In other words, if it is difficult to determine the original authorship of these stories, we are on much firmer ground when attempting to determine intended audience. The *Biographies of Eminent Monks* were compiled in part for a specific polemical purpose: they were meant not simply to describe the ideals of the Buddhist community, but to present a picture of the Buddhist monk palatable to the emperor and his court.

Did the emperor and other court officials share a values system that respected and admired the marginal? I think not. In fact, the imperial ideal was precisely the opposite: a citizenry without marginals, a populace neatly compartmentalized into manageable units. The massive construction of Chang'an, the capital city of the Tang, is a testimony to this obsession with compartmentalization. The city was divided into symmetrical geographic units, each surrounded by a wall and connected by gates that were closed at dusk.[246] The clergy, likewise, was divided into administrative units: in the capital, one official was in charge of the monasteries to the left of the main street; another official of the monasteries to the right. Each prefecture was allowed only a certain number of large, officially sponsored monasteries to which other, smaller monasteries and shrines were, at least in theory, subservient. Within these larger monasteries, monks were administered by state-appointed representatives—namely, the Abbot (*shangzuo*), the Head Monk (*sizhu*), and the Deacon (*duweina*).[247] The image of the wandering trickster, responsible to no one and contemptuous of all, is clearly a threat to this regimented, orderly system. Even more striking is that Huijiao compiled his work precisely during, or perhaps slightly after, Liang Wu Di's famous campaign to promote vegetarianism.[248] In this context, the glorification of meat-eating monks would seem to border on sedition.

Authors of anti-Buddhist polemical literature—of which there is a great deal—recognized the dangerous marginal element in the clergy and attempted to bring it to the attention of the throne. Most of the memorials to the emperor calling for the restriction or persecution of Buddhism rely chiefly on arguments concerning the economic dangers of the foreign religion: monks do not pay taxes; they do not produce anything (including offspring); ordination provides a means for the populace to avoid conscription; and so on.

But tucked away in these documents is another more subtle attack, an attack against the *moral* character of the *saṅgha*. The regulations of the Vinaya, critics contended, were seldom upheld; they were in fact a smokescreen used to cover the illicit activities of depraved minds. Take, for example, a memorial to the throne by the Tang official Peng Yan who writes, "The monks of today are all ignoramuses of the lowest sort. Even if they kept their regulations strictly they would be useless to a ruler. How much more [despicable] that they avoid corveé labor and commit crimes of murder, robbery, and perversion."[249] Fu Yi —next to Han Yu, the most famous early critic of Buddhism—charged that the clergy was made up of "soldiers who, to avoid service, shave their heads and hide in [the clergy's] midst, not serving their parents, but only practicing the ten abominations. Every coin they distribute hides a plot to reap ten thousand in return; every day of their fasting disguises a plot to garner a hundred days worth of food."[250] Similarly, other critics charged that monks "practice the three poisons and spread harm to all directions."[251] Recall that the persecution of 446 was justified by the reported discovery of a weapons cache on monastic property. Also found on monastery grounds, the report claimed, was a large storage room *filled with wine* and underground rooms where the monks carried on clandestine relations with fallen women of good families.[252]

Apparently, the memorials had the desired effect, for the edicts they provoked mirror their sentiments; to nervous emperors, the dissolute nature of the *saṅgha* was shockingly apparent. Emperor Xuanzong, for example, promulgated an edict entitled "Edict Forbidding the Transgression of the Rules and Regulations by Monks and Priests," that specifically called for the prosecution of monks who "drink wine, eat meat, wander and sleep in inappropriate places, who loiter about among city shops, doing nothing to ward off suspicion, and show disrespect for their own teaching."[253] The response to this realization was not to disband the clergy as a whole; rather it was to "weed out" (*sha-tai*) undesirable elements, to push unorthodox monks back into their neatly defined social / political roles—as Tang Gaozu proclaimed "to separate the jade from the rubble."[254] In a vitriolic memorial, the Liang official Guo Zushen demanded that all monks maintain a strict *vegetarian* diet and that eleven clerics who did not keep the precepts be immediately defrocked.[255] An edict of 842 proclaimed that all monks *"who do not observe the Buddhist rules*, should be forced to return to lay life."[256] And, following the persecution of 845, an edict rejoiced over the discipline enforced on those "lazy and idle fellows."[257]

Throughout these memorials and edicts there is an attempt to create an image of the monk as a lazy, greedy scoundrel who takes advantage of his special status to eat and drink as he pleases without working or paying taxes to support himself. Like his female counterpart, the nun, he is a lascivious rogue who abandons spouse and family not for spiritual reasons, but so that he can engage in perverse, illicit sex. The thrust of the *Biographies of Eminent Monks* can be better understood in the context of this polemical dialogue. If the image of the monk in the anti-Buddhist literature was a gross exaggeration, a transparent exercise in propaganda, the same can be said of its Buddhist counterpart.

At first glance, the appearance of trickster monks in the *Biographies* seems incongruous. A monk like Nantuo, described above, seems to mirror the debased monk of anti-Buddhist polemic. He does not keep the Vinaya, but eats and drinks excessively. He is disrespectful to his superiors and even associates with the notoriously promiscuous nuns. But the key to the biography of Nantuo comes with the ingenious twist at the end when the bodies of the nuns become bamboo staffs; their blood, wine. As the biography of the Abbot points out, these trickster figures are not like ordinary monks, much less ordinary laymen. They run "counter to the common principles" and, "when they appear within the world, we can observe them, but they are difficult to fathom."[258] In other words, Zanning seems to say, for all of their rhetorical flourish, the anti-Buddhist polemicists had missed the point: for Zanning there was no such thing as a bad monk; there were only "misunderstood" monks.

From Huijiao's *Biographies of Eminent Monks* to Zanning's version, this "misunderstood" monk came to play a more and more prominent role. Although Zanning wrote and compiled several important works in the course of his career, the monumental *Song Biographies*—his final work—was his tour de force. On his deathbed, Zanning could claim to have tamed the trickster. No longer a dangerous subversive figure of the popular imagination, viciously manipulated by enemies of the faith, the meat-eating, wine-drinking monk was now thoroughly entrenched in his position as spokesman for the Buddhist establishment, an emblem of the spiritual elite whose activities and esoteric cultivation were not only to be permitted by the authorities, but to be sponsored by them.

Or so it would seem; for in the years that followed, the meat-eating, wine-drinking monk was to go through one more transformation—the trickster had one more trick up his sleeve. Hagiography is, of course, bound by the constraints of economics, politics, and ideology. But happily, at certain points in time, this dreary, inevitable progression of rationalization and institutionalization is broken by startling shifts, disruptions, and reversals that subvert the very purposes for which the rhetoric was constructed. Perhaps it is not surprising that a figure as slippery as the trickster provoked just such a shift. For while the transcendent, unfathomable monk continued to play a prominent role in the dominant narrative forms of the southern Song, of the Ming and Qing, and even into the kungfu novels of today, he also produced an even more popular figure known as the "phony monk" (*jia heshang*), the "filthy monk" (*lai heshang*), "Reverend Tramp" (*hua heshang*), or "meat-eating, wine-drinking monk" (*jiurou seng*)[259] who for many readers confirmed their suspicions that, for all of his claims to spiritual attainments, the average monk was nothing more than a deceptive showman, a false ascetic no different from anyone else—a mere trickster.

Conclusion

At this point the reader may well want to set aside *exempla* and rhetoric and ask the more down-to-earth question of whether or not
monks in fact ate meat and drank wine. The picture of the dissolute
monk presented in anti-Buddhist polemic is certainly not a reliable
measure of the state of the *saṅgha*. And material like the erotic prose-
poem by Bai Xingjian cited earlier, though not expressly hostile to
Buddhism, is more representative of collective fantasies than it is an
accurate depiction of the sexual lives of monks and nuns. As we have
seen in the last section of this chapter, even the accounts of meat eating and wine drinking in the *Biographies of Eminent Monks* were
included in the collection for rhetorical, polemical purposes and have
only limited value when we attempt to reconstruct actual practice.

There is some evidence from later periods that, far from restricting
their monks from drinking wine, some monasteries even produced it
for sale.[260] Archaeology may some day shed light on the pervasiveness
of wine drinking among medieval monks. In the meantime, we come
closer, perhaps, to actual practice when we look at the more personal
writings of leading monks. The eminent Tang monk Huaisu, for example, known both for a commentary on the Vinaya and for his fine
calligraphy and connections with talented literati, composed a short
essay on eating fish.[261] In the essay Huaisu remarks, "When I lived in
Changsha I ate fish, but since coming to the city of Chang'an I have
had my fill of meat. Yet I have often been ridiculed by the common,
which has made matters most inconvenient, and it is for this reason
that I have taken ill." Elsewhere, in a poem, Huaisu exclaims, "Everyone brings me wine; I never have to buy a drop!"[262] In fact, numerous
references to wine-drinking can be found in the essentially secular
poetry of Tang monks.

Nevertheless, it must be granted that these references are no more
free of the restraints of genre than the biographies of eminent monks
—the wine-drinking persona was virtually a requirement of Tang
poetry. Conversely, while Huaisu the poet may drink wine and eat
meat, it comes as no surprise that the Huaisu portrayed in the *Biographies of Eminent Monks* does neither. It may well be that practice
followed even these contradictory ideals, that there were "genres of
practice" just as there were genres of textual presentation. In other
words, while a monk in the somber setting of a mountain monastery
would frown upon meat and wine, a monk matching couplets with
literati friends in the capital would feel no compunction in sharing the
standard diet with his friends.

Even at the more abstract level of ideals, when all segments of the *saṅgha* are taken into consideration, monastic ideals are seen to be quite fluid. Many Chinese monastic leaders considered the consumption of meat and wine acceptable if these were necessary as medicine for a sick monk. And some stretched the definition of "sickness" to include melancholy or fatigue, justifying wine and meat for all manner of circumstance.[263] Nonetheless, with all of these qualifications, we can still assert that in general, in the eyes of monks and lay people alike, monks were expected to lead lives of restraint and abstention; with the exception of the peculiar antinomian tricksters introduced for specific polemical purposes, the vast majority of monks in the *Biographies* conform to an ascetic ideal.

As we have seen, this ascetic ideal extended from choices in sexual habits, diet, and clothing, to the extreme cases of self-mutilation and even suicide. Why then was the ascetic ideal so appealing? To voluntarily inflict physical discomfort on oneself seems, on the surface, counter-intuitive. To the modern scholar, the extremes of the ascetic life-style seem sheer madness. Many would sympathize with eighteenth-century historian Edward Gibbon who described medieval Christian ascetics as "a swarm of fanatics, incapable of fear, or reason, or humanity."[264] Similarly, Hu Shih saw Chinese Buddhist ascetics as pathological: "China seems to have gone completely mad in one of her strange periods of religious fanaticism."[265] But to dismiss ascetics as madmen is to miss an opportunity to understand them. Fortunately, there is another strain of scholarship, beginning with Nietzsche, that has taken a more empathic approach to asceticism in an attempt to understand the enduring appeal of ascetic practice. In *On the Genealogy of Morals*, Nietzsche argued that asceticism was a means of coping with that most difficult of all brands of suffering—meaningless suffering. Through ascetic practice, Nietzsche claimed, the adept invests suffering with meaning and regulates where and when he will suffer, thereby achieving a qualified victory over suffering—a grim victory, but a victory nevertheless.[266] Similarly, William James referred to asceticism as "the fruit of highly optimistic religious feeling" rather than simple self-destruction.[267] Joseph Swain spoke of asceticism as a form of purification,[268] while Peter Brown describes how stories of ascetics of the past spoke to Christians of "the eventual transformation of their own bodies on the day of the Resurrection."[269] In sum, through efforts to see asceticism from the ascetic's point of view, Western asceticism has become considerably easier to understand.

The biographies of self-sacrificing monks discussed in the second section of this chapter betray sensibilities similar to those of their Western counterparts. The *exempla* in these biographies sacrificed themselves for merit, or in order to be reborn in a pure-land, or as a part of a more esoteric longing for sanctification. They attacked their senses not because they wanted to destroy themselves, but because they wanted to be better. Once one appreciates the intellectual environment in which they lived, it is easier to understand even self-mutilation and suicide as rational choices, sacrifices toward well-defined ends.

At the same time, we miss much if we focus exclusively on the individual psychological aspects of asceticism. Asceticism was an inherently social practice that was meaningful largely in relation to societal norms. It is for this reason that asceticism was central to the image of the monk and to the monk's identity. The basic forms of asceticism required of all monks separated them from the rest of society, marking them as a fundamentally different category of person. Finally, even within this select group, the range of ascetic practices available to the monk allowed him to distinguish himself from fellow members of the *saṅgha*.

CHAPTER 2
Thaumaturgy

LET US RETURN once more to the story of Wuran, the monk who ended his life by burning himself to death atop Wutai Shan. According to the story, Wuran set upon the severe life of austerities and self-mutilation that characterized his final days when he unexpectedly came across a holy monastery on Wutai inhabited by hundreds of divine Indian monks and governed by the bodhisattva Mañjuśrī. After receiving instructions from the bodhisattva and walking out of the monastery gates, Wuran turned around for one last look only to discover that the monastery had vanished from sight.

Whether or not this manifestation of Mañjuśrī was in fact a vision experienced by a historical figure named Wuran is of course impossible to determine, though one could compare Wuran's description with those of other visionaries of China and elsewhere in an attempt to come to a better understanding of what a monk like Wuran *might* have experienced under such circumstances.[1] But the historian of mentalities quickly brushes aside such ethereal questions and insists that we treat the monks in these fabulous stories as *exempla*, as models of behavior. Certainly the case can be made that stories like the biography of Wuran inspired monks, nuns, and lay people to make the pilgrimage to Wutai in search of visions of Mañjuśrī. Indeed, Wuran himself was said to have made the trip to Wutai after hearing a tale of a similar experience by the famous pilgrim Buddhapāli. Nonetheless, most of the readers of the story never made the trip to Wutai and probably had no intention of doing so. And even if they did hope one day to make the pilgrimage, few would have endeavored to follow the gruesome example Wuran set, after his vision, of mortification and suicide.

The tough-minded historian of institutional history may contend that we come closer to grasping the significance of the story if, instead of looking exclusively at content or audience, we scrutinize the ideological structure that produced the story. That is, by emphasizing the glory of the bodhisattva Mañjuśrī, the story validates a complex of beliefs, practices, and social organizations attached to the deity, most notably, the monastic institution that produced and propagated the story in the first place. Indeed, the hagiographers admit as much when discussing stories of the divine. The first line of Huijiao's treatise on "divine marvels" (*shenyi*) reads, "The purpose of these divine acts is 'proselytism,'" that is, the propagation of Buddhism.[2] "Without this [thaumaturgy]," Daoxuan tells us in the treatise to his chapter on wonder-workers, "it would be difficult to spread [Buddhism]."[3] The same lofty motivation, the spread of the Teaching, lay behind the labors of the hagiographer who scoured the empire in search of wondrous demonstrations of the power of Buddhism.

But if such an explanation goes a long way toward explaining the hagiographer's motives, it tells us less about why the stories were read. Surely brute attempts at sanctimonious proselytizing held as little appeal for the medieval Chinese audience as they do for us today. And even from the hagiographer's perspective, we occasionally come across stories in the *Biographies* that have little to say about Buddhism and its propagation. What, for instance, are we to make of the biography of the fifth-century monk Zhiyi who was famous for rearing a white monkey? After Zhiyi's death, "Whenever the monks finished eating, they would have the leftover food sent to an area where monkeys gathered. They would have a mountain boy call out several times, whereupon all of the monkeys would race to the spot. During the persecution of the Teaching under Wuzong of the Tang [ca. 845] when this monastery was reduced to rubble, the practice of feeding the monkeys ceased."[4]

We are here confronted with a side of these stories that is at once more elusive and more personal than the institutional or doctrinal aspects of the *Biographies*. Both the majestic accounts of the wondrous manifestations of Mañjuśrī and more trivial stories of unusual plants, animals, and prodigious occurrences issue, I think, from the same font: a fascination with the marvelous shared by monk and layman alike.[5] While one might argue that the story of the monkeys was intended to demonstrate Buddhist compassion for sentient beings, it is more likely that it was out of a more visceral thirst for the exotic that readers were attracted to the curious image of monkeys gathering daily for their dinner.

We see this same sense of wonder in a more intense form in the comments of Wuran's faithful assistant Zhao at the end of Wuran's biography. After witnessing the master's fiery death, Zhao can only exclaim: "How marvelous! What pain!" (*qi zai, tong zai*). Even in literature as formalistic and stereotyped as hagiography, the reaction "How marvelous" discloses a profoundly ambivalent sensation, perched precariously between delight and horror, belief and incredulity.[6] It was in search of this sensation, in Buddhist parlance, the "inconceivable" (*bu ke siyi*), that many leafed through the pages of the *Biographies of Eminent Monks* over the centuries, looking for wondrous stories of events occurring just beyond the horizon of tedious everyday experience.

The *Liang Biographies* relates that once when Emperor Ming Di (r. 465–473) took ill, he called for acupuncture and moxibustion to cure what ailed him. But to treat his spirit the emperor needed something more. "Aching and listless, he summoned Zhou Yong, Yin Hong, and others to tell him stories of ghosts and spirits and other such things to relieve his troubled mind. Zhou then read from the scriptures the *Words of the Law* and the *Wise and the Foolish*,"[7] two collections of Buddhist tales.[8] In other words, Buddhist stories of the marvelous were not only read because they were informative; they were read because to do so was pleasurable. This may seem an obvious point, but it is easily forgotten in our tendency to focus on the doctrinal and social aspects of hagiography.

The medieval reader in search of accounts of the marvelous did not need to limit himself to Buddhist literature. For many, the *Eminent Monks* series was probably seen as a subset of a larger body of secular literature that eventually became known as *zhiguai*, or "records of the strange." Also growing up alongside the *Biographies* was the genre usually referred to in the West as "miracle tales," that is, stories of the intervention of Buddhist deities in the world of ordinary mortals.[9] The chief difference between these writings and the stories of the marvelous in the *Biographies* is a formal one: true to its title, the stories in the *Biographies of Eminent Monks* center on monks.

The monks of these stories can be divided into two general categories. The first consists of monk protagonists who are not particularly remarkable in themselves. There are a number of stories, for example, of ordinary monks who, while wandering through the mountains, come across spectacular monasteries "not of this world" staffed by divine monks. In these cases the monk serves not only as a reliable source for the story, but also as a conduit through which the reader is permitted to experience the marvelous for himself, vicariously. Even with the distance of time and culture, we as modern readers cannot help but place ourselves in the shoes of Wuran as he peers through the mountain mists at a shimmering monastery in the distance.

The second category consists of monks who are themselves the focus of attention. They are thaumaturges with wondrous properties and powers all their own. In the discussion that follows I focus chiefly on these monks. As an unattached figure, versed in vaguely perceived foreign teachings and taken to long bouts of wandering through mountains and other sparsely populated areas, the monk was well suited for the role of bridge to the marvelous. The success of Buddhist narrative in China can to a certain extent be attributed to the effectiveness of the monk in precisely this role. In other words, just as monastic estates succeeded in large measure because they were able to fill a niche in the Chinese economy, monks came to find a niche in what might be termed "the economy of the imagination."

Forms of Thaumaturgy in the *Biographies*

Properties

There is a long and rich Buddhist exegetical tradition of categorizing and evaluating the thaumaturgical powers that accrue to monks of superior attainment. Much of this project is devoted to mapping out the ascending path of the enlightened, for whom supernormal powers are incidental manifestations of spiritual progress. In other words, the powers come naturally to the adept in the course of his practice; and he is usually expected to discount them as of relatively minor significance. The most common exposition of supernormal powers (*shentong*) in Buddhist texts divides them into six basic types: magical powers (*ruyi*), supernormal hearing (*tianer*), the ability to read minds (*taxintong*), knowledge of one's previous existences (*suzhutong*), ability to discern the previous lives of others (*tianyan*), and finally, the state of having "no outflows" (*wuloutong*), a state in which one is no longer plagued by any form of defilement.[10]

Although these categories are common throughout the canonical literature, they had surprisingly little impact on Chinese Buddhist narrative. The *Liang Biographies* refers to the supernormal powers only once, in the treatise to the "Chapter on the Practice of Chan" (*Xi chan pian*) in which Huijiao emphasizes that the six supernormal powers are the products of attainments in meditation.[11] Even the more extensive *Further Biographies* refers to the six powers on only two occasions. Hence, if the *Biographies* are any indication, up to the early Tang, familiarity with the six supernormal powers was for the most part limited to those versed in abstruse technical commentary on Buddhist doctrine.[12]

In the *Song Biographies* the situation changes somewhat, and we read occasionally of monks said to possess these powers. Master of the Regulations Quan, for example, was said to know "everything that happened near and far. The people said that he had the power to read minds."[13] The monk Zhengzhi worked in a layman's field during the day, and every night returned to his monastery some seven hundred *li* (200 miles) away. In abhidharma theory, the ability to travel great distances in an instant is attributed to "divine feet" (*shenzu*) a subcategory of "magical powers." But, tellingly, the biography makes no mention of the "divine feet," instead attributing the monk's ability to a knack for "shrinking the veins of the earth," a concept borrowed from Daoist literature.[14]

While we do find occasional references to the ability to "divide the body," that is, to appear in more than one place at the same time, most of the six supernormal powers were apparently more topics for sophisticated doctrinal discussions than they were the stuff of stories. This gap between the popular imagination and Buddhist technical literature is well illustrated by the curious case of Yongan, the "Master of No Outflows."

In Buddhist technical literature, the term "no outflows" (Skt. *anā-sravā*) is used to indicate the freedom from afflictions of liberated individuals for whom the mind's defilements (ignorance, sexual desire, desire for existence, and so on) do not "flow outward" and come into contact with external phenomena.[15] In the biography of Yongan, however, the monk was given the name "Master of No Outflows" when it was discovered that he had transcended the need to relieve himself. When word of the monk's abilities reached the local general Bai Minzhong, the general set a guard around the monk's quarters with orders to make sure that he ate and drank regularly, and to prohibit him from going to the privy. Yet throughout the ten days under observation, Yongan never relieved himself once.[16] In an addendum to the biography, Zanning is at pains to explain that a mistake has been made, and the term "no outflows" misapplied. "It was incorrect," he writes, "for the people of Shu to call Yongan 'Master of No Outflows.' Only when one has cut off all afflictions, does not again allow them to increase, has therefore cut oneself off from 'karmic seeds' and does not again [allow afflictions] to increase (*suizeng*, Skt. *anuśaya*), can one be said to be without outflows."[17] Nevertheless, one suspects that Zanning's comments, couched as they are in the abstruse, quasi-legal language of the abhidharma, had little effect on popular monk-centered folklore.

Prophesy, on the other hand, is one of the most common themes in all three versions of the *Biographies*. Leading Buddhist thinkers in India, Inner Asia, and East Asia maintained a persistent concern with ancient prophecies of the eventual decline and even demise of Buddhism. Chinese scholars pored over texts, some truly old and some only claiming to be old, in an attempt to flesh out these prophecies and calculate the years remaining before the moral collapse of the world.[18] Similarly, students of the Vinaya and of Church history were particularly interested in the ancient canonical prophesies of the division of the *sangha* into a set number of schools. As the supposed dating of the texts that made these "prophecies" was never questioned (most were in fact written after the events foretold had occurred), such prophesies not only renewed the scholar's faith in the ability of Buddhist adepts to make predictions, but also served as a useful historical tool for making sense of a more complex reality; for example, the numerous Indian schools must have at some point come from an earlier division of five in accordance with an even earlier prophecy.[19]

Although leading Chinese thinkers were undoubtedly concerned with the prophesies of ancient Indian texts, the *Biographies* seldom make mention of these sorts of grandiose long-term schemes. They tend instead to relate short-term prophesies on a smaller, more personal scale. In the *Song Biographies*, we read for example of a monk named Chiren ("fool"), known for his ability to predict the future in "wild songs" and "muddled speech," who accurately predicted the arrival at his monastery of the great Huayan exegete Chengguan and ordered the other monks to clean up in preparation for his visit.[20] Similarly, Chuji ordered preparations to be made for a "foreign visitor" the day before the Sillan monk Musang arrived at his monastery.[21]

More striking are stories like that of the monk Xuanjue who through a dream recognized the imminent death of the great translator-pilgrim Xuanzang,[22] or of the prominent Chan monk Puji who predicted the death of his disciple Yixing.[23] In a similar vein, the stories of monks who predict the precise time of their own deaths are so numerous as to make this ability a virtual requirement for the status of "eminent monk." These stories follow patterns that are clearly of Chinese rather than Indian origin; with minor emendations, many of the stories of prophetic monks in the *Biographies* could easily be mistaken for Han Dynasty accounts of the "scholars of the [esoteric] arts" (*fangshi*).[24]

Most of the stories involving prophecy serve chiefly to demonstrate an intangible quality of eminence, a natural by-product of the monk's spiritual attainments. The monks do not fall into a trance before making their predictions and do not necessarily resort to special techniques of divination, though, as we will see, such techniques were practiced. Further, only in the brief comments of Daoxuan in his treatise on wonder-workers is allusion made to the connection between meditation and supernormal powers. Rather, their abilities issue from an inherent supernormal quality that is never analyzed in detail. It is this mysterious, unearthly property that allows the thaumaturge to see the causes of future events invisible to mundane eyes. Take for example Xingzun's sighting of the cause of a future fire.

> Someone from the Li family ordered a vegetarian feast [for the monks]. As they were eating, Xingzun suddenly stood up and ran out the gate shouting, as if someone had done something wrong. [He then returned and] said to Mr Li, "There will be a fire tonight. It will travel from the southeast to the northwestern streets. You should order the residents of the area to make the necessary preparations." That night, sure enough, there was a fire that reduced everything to ashes. When the other monks asked Xingzun what had happened, he said, "Yesterday I saw a woman in red pass by carrying a torch. Unfortunately, I couldn't catch up to her."[25]

Xingzun needed no special technique or divine assistance to predict the coming fire; he simply saw it. Curiously, the Mr. Li of the story seems to have ignored Xingzun's warnings, for in the end, everything was "reduced to ashes."

Yet, if in fact beliefs in the abilities of extraordinary monks to predict the future were widespread—and I believe they were—one can imagine the use to which such monks would be put by political and military figures. The biography of Fotucheng (var. Fotudeng), one of the most famous Buddhist thaumaturges in China, is filled with references to services rendered to the military leadership of the day. In the biography, Fotucheng repeatedly predicts the outcomes of battles waged by the northern ruler Shi Le and his generals. Shi Le outwits raiding brigands and enemy assaults all on the basis of Fotucheng's ability to see into the future.[26] In the *Song Biographies*, the monk Hongyin takes Qian Liu (soon to become the first ruler of the Wuyue Kingdom) by the hand and correctly predicts that he will one day rise to a position of great prominence.[27]

The biography of the famous Tang thaumaturge Wanhui suggests that even low-level officials may have had recourse to the services of extraordinary monks. Wanhui's biography relates the story of the Tang official Cui Xuanwei who served during a time when the court was rife with dangerous political machinations. In the story, Cui's wise mother invites Wanhui to their house to tell her son's fortune, offering the monk a pair of gold chopsticks as a reward. But Wanhui merely mumbles a few words and throws the chopsticks up on their roof as he leaves. The disappointed family only realizes the import of his actions when they fetch the chopsticks from the roof and find there documents planted by "treacherous officials" in an attempt to frame Cui. Cui quickly destroys the documents, just before the arrival of official inspectors who search his house in vain for evidence of sedition.[28]

If the medieval Buddhist reader might be expected to take such stories at face value, the modern reader is more circumspect. In addition to rejecting outright the possibility of seeing into the future, we may also question the historical context of events described in the *Biographies*. The secular biographies of Cui Xuanwei in the *Tang Histories*, for example, while referring to an incident in which Cui was falsely accused at court, and relating a story of Cui's wise mother, make no reference to Wanhui, prophecy, or Buddhism.[29] Similarly, we can note that the biography of Fotucheng was compiled some one hundred and fifty years after the monk's death, and clearly contains as much fabulous as factual material. Hence any attempt to understand the role of prophesy in the lives of the historical figures alluded to in the *Biographies* seems a lost cause. To return to the discussion at the beginning of this chapter, we may be on firmer ground when we look for the appeal of these stories to the Buddhists who told them and to their audience.

In the biography of Fotucheng, when Shi Le first meets the monk, he asks him, "What numinous efficacy does Buddhism have?" At this point, the biographer comments, "Knowing that Shi Le did not understand profound principles, Fotucheng determined to prove [the potency of Buddhism] through the use of magical arts [*daoshu*]."[30] Tellers of stories about monks and the compilers of the *Eminent Monks* series may well have shared this line of reasoning; that is, wondrous stories were an effective tool for spreading "the Teaching." This is not to question their belief in Buddhist thaumaturgy, which is beyond doubt, but simply to suggest that they emphasized these aspects of received biographical information when compiling the biographies of prominent monks in order to demonstrate the efficacy of Buddhism to men and women in positions of power. They seem to be saying that, with their ability to predict the outcome of battle and foresee assassination plots, figures like Fotucheng (and by association, all monks) are not to be taken lightly. This explanation—reading the stories as a form of proselytizing to officialdom—would go a long way toward explaining the prominence of political figures and events in stories of Buddhist prophecy in the *Biographies* were it not for the curious fact that, even in the stories, the prophecies of monks seldom do anyone any good, political figures included.

Take, for example, the case of the hapless Military Commissioner Qian Renfeng who on taking ill sent a messenger with a gift of incense to the renown monk Deshao to ask for the monk's blessing. Deshao sent the messenger back with a missive reading "eighty-one (*ba shi yi*) your honor." The Commissioner was delighted, saying to himself "I will live to the age of eighty-one." In fact, Qian had misinterpreted the prediction: he died on the eleventh day of the eighth month of that very year (*ba yue shiqi ri*).[31] When the prominent Tang official Wei Chuhou was awarded a new position, he was baffled by the pronouncement of an anonymous monk who remarked, "Marvelous indeed for the Minister to die in such a place." Later, when delivering a memorial, Wei collapsed dead on the steps leading to the throne. Only then was the monk's prediction understood.[32] Indeed, coding prophesy in cryptic language fraught with deep meaning was one of the distinguishing characteristics of the thaumaturge, shrouded as he was in unspeakable mystery. We are told that the well-known thaumaturge Wanhui "disliked the florid and decadent, and very seldom spoke. When he did speak it was always a prediction of future events, *the accuracy of which was only realized after the events had occurred.*"[33]

The prophesies are often so enigmatic that even after the events predicted occur considerable skill is necessary to decipher their meaning. In the 780s, the itinerant monk Puman left a poem on a monastery building that read: "This river runs to the waters of the Jing. With the two Zhu, the river fills with blood. When the green ox apprehends the red tiger, an era of great peace will arrive." Our hagiographer points out that "this (*ci*) river" stood for (Zhu) Ci, a late Tang rebel who instigated his rebellion at a place called Jing(zhou), alluded to as "the waters of Jing" in the poem. The "two Zhu" referred to Zhu Ci and his younger brother Zhu Tao. The "green ox" corresponds in Chinese cosmology to the cyclical date *yichou*, which fell on the first year of the Xingyuan era (784), the year of the outbreak of the rebellion. The rebellion was pacified in 786, represented in the calendar by *bingyin*, which corresponds to the element fire and the animal tiger.[34] Needless to say, even in the story, no one at the time of the prediction understood the events that it foretold.

If the compilers of the *Eminent Monks* hoped to assure powerful figures of the usefulness of monks, they surely could have exercised greater skill in selecting their stories. If we set aside such unlikely political motivations, it is tempting to read these stories as simply outgrowths of the same fascination with the bizarre alluded to above. That is, we marvel not only at the ability of the monk to predict the future, but also at the clever way in which he frames his predictions, much in the way we delight in mystery novels even when it is impossible to identify the killer until the clues are interpreted for us at the end of the novel. As Kenneth Dewoskin puts it, "An element of suspense is inherent in any divination event."[35]

But the stories may also have played a more general role in the collective consciousness of the time, and this role may help to explain why so many of the stories related to prophesy center on political and military events. When confronted with the same phenomenon—the preponderance of military and political themes in prophetic stories—in sixteenth-century England, Keith Thomas suggested that retroactive stories of prophesy provided a much-needed sense of stability in the face of radical change.[36] In other words, while purporting to provide a link between present and future, such stories were in fact providing a link between the present and the past.

We are familiar with the seamier side of this tendency in the crass attempts by rulers to resort to retroactive prophecy in campaigns intended to legitimate their reigns. Wu Zetian, as the only woman ever to claim the title of emperor in Chinese history, was of course in special need of legitimation, and her use of Buddhist prophecy to confirm her right to the throne has been well studied.[37] But here in the *Biographies* we see in the prophetic stories a less conscious longing for order, a search for a sense that even if the tempestuous, chaotic events of the day are not understood, one day they will be seen to have followed a logical and immutable pattern.

From this perspective then it is not so surprising that many of the prophecy stories emerge in the turbulent Five Dynasties period, or in the aftermath of the An Lushan rebellion. Similarly, stories relating prophesies of officials doomed to disgrace and execution provided some sense of order and meaning to byzantine court intrigue of infinite complexity. And the frequent stories of monks who foresaw the great Huichang persecution of Buddhism reminded the faithful that such events did not escape the calculations of the loftiest members of the clergy. At the same time, stories relating the accurate prophesies of monks of the past must surely have reinforced belief in prophesy, providing as they did evidence for the ability of monks to predict the future.

Techniques

The preceding discussion, with all of its talk of prophecy after the fact and the role of narrative in Buddhist thaumaturgy, may lead the reader to suspect that mantic monks were the stuff of stories, that the Buddhist thaumaturge never really existed outside of the religious imagination. In fact, as even a cursory knowledge of the role of monks in contemporary societies suggests, monks were seen by many as ritual specialists, and as such were all expected to have some facility with thaumaturgy. Unlike the random, natural manifestations of supernormal powers or spontaneous prophecy described above, many monks performed thaumaturgic functions through established techniques that could be studied and refined.

In the *Biographies*, the most striking examples of such techniques are the stories of monks who summoned rain. In the *Song Biographies* we read, for example, of the Tantric monk Vajrabodhi (Ch. Jin'gang-zhi) summoned to the court of Emperor Xuanzong to make rain after all of the efforts of court ritual specialists to bring rain through offerings to the five sacred mountains and the four sacred rivers had failed. In an elaborate ritual, Vajrabodhi made offerings to the deity Amoghāṅkuśa[38] and constructed a platform, at the same time painting an image of the Bodhisattva of Seven Koṭis.[39] Later, on a set date, the monk finished the image by painting in the eyes, a ritual known as "opening the vision" (*kaiguang*). At that moment,

> a wind whipped up in the northwest. Tiles flew off of roofs and trees were uprooted. Thundering clouds burst forth with rain, startling those near and far. And in the place of the altar, a hole broke through the room so that the sanctum was deluged. When dawn broke the next day, gentlefolk and commoners of the capital all said, "Vajrabodhi captured a dragon, which broke out of the room and flew away." Hundreds of thousands of people daily came to look at the place. Such is the divine efficacy of the "platform ritual."[40]

Śubhakarasiṃha—known along with Vajrabodhi and Amoghavajra as one of the three great Tantric monks of the Tang—performed a similar feat by chanting spells over a bowl of water.[41] While we may question the efficacy of such rituals, there is little reason to suspect that they were not in fact practiced at court, as they are perfectly consistent with an array of non-Buddhist court rituals intended to influence the weather. More generally, these monks fit into a very old Chinese tradition of ritual specialists at court that extends as far back as the state itself.[42]

But there is also a more local face to the monk's role in Chinese ritual life manifested in the *Biographies* in references to techniques of divination loosely defined.[43] Even to the present day, monasteries often serve as the spiritual centers of their communities. Just outside monastery gates, one is likely to find a number of tables set up by local fortune-tellers to serve visitors to the monastery. And occasionally one of the most visible activities in the monastery itself is the practice of divining one's fortune by shaking a single bamboo stick loose from a tube containing many such sticks. By reading the (often cryptic) characters written on the stick, one discovers one's fate.[44] Although our earliest descriptive accounts of this practice in the monastery seem to come from the thirteenth century, Michel Strickmann has shown that the practice goes back at least as far as the fifth century when a Buddhist manual for this type of divination was composed.[45] The manual, the tenth chapter of the *Consecration Scripture*,[46] though actually com-

posed in China, purports to be a translation from Sanskrit. In the
scripture, the god Brahmā complains to the Buddha that while the
various non-Buddhist schools provide their adherents with techniques
for resolving doubts about the future, Buddhism fails to supply its
followers with similar forms of divination. The Buddha then consents
to allow Brahmā to lay out a system of divination, which comprises
the rest of the chapter. As Strickmann pointed out, the conversation
between Brahmā and the Buddha discloses the distinct uneasiness
monks felt with regard to divination. This apprehension arises from
the explicit prohibitions on divination in the canonical literature.

The *Āgamas*, translated into Chinese early on, contain hundreds of
references to divination. The diviners, however, are not monks. And in
several well-known instances, the Buddha specifically forbids monks
from practicing palm-reading and other forms of divination for material gain.[47] Elsewhere, the prohibition is categorical: monks must not
tell fortunes.[48] These prohibitions carried over into the monastic regulations proper. In the *Mahīśāsakavinaya*, for instance, the Buddha
singles out divination for criticism and establishes it as a minor offense
(Skt. *duṣkṛta*).[49] In the *Dharmaguptakavinaya*, the Buddha specifies that
monks are not to tell the fortunes of women, nor are they to have their
fortunes told by others.[50] The most influential prohibition of all is that
of the *Fanwang jing*, mentioned above, which categorically prohibits
monks from practicing fortune-telling.[51]

Nevertheless, we detect no such ambivalence toward divination in
the *Biographies*. The fifth-century Indian traveler and exegete Guṇabhadra was said to have "studied the non-Buddhist [Indian] classics
and understood *yinyang* [divination]. More than once his predictions
of future events proved accurate."[52] The fifth-century monk Xuanchang forecast good fortune and bad with unfailing accuracy."[53] Perhaps it was because of the legitimation provided by works like the
Consecration Scripture that monks felt no compunction in practicing
divination. More likely, the creative scenario involving Brahmā and
the Buddha proposed by the *Consecration Scripture* was born of the
same sentiment that inclined monks to overlook scattered passages in
the Vinaya: in China monks considered the practice both valuable and
relatively harmless when in the hands of well-intentioned clerics. The
reaction to divination by those outside the monastic community was,
as we will see, somewhat different.

Monks do seem to have drawn the line, however, at receiving
payment for the performance of divination. It seems likely that some
monks probably performed divination for money, but the *Biographies* make no mention of such vulgar practices. The biography of the
tenth-century monk Huaijun comes tantalizingly close to describing a

shadowy economic side to divination. After Huaijun had gained a reputation for the mantic arts, "whenever anyone passed by, they would
always anchor their boats and go to pay a visit to the master. He told
fortunes to people along the gorges;[54] and passing merchants asked him
for prognostications on their business ventures. When a traveler would
ask him for a fortune, Huaijun would only write three or five lines.
They could never understand what he meant, yet the subtle mysteries
[contained in the lines] were later borne out."[55] In accounts like this
one, it is difficult to determine whether the hagiography avoids discussion of payments received because this was considered beneath an
upright monk, because monks did not in fact receive payment for
divination, or simply because such matters were considered too trivial
to be included in a good story. Suffice it to say, whatever their attitude
toward payment for divination, the *Biographies* show little concern
with the propriety of divination itself.

Through stories such as these we begin to get a sense of the general
thirst for knowledge of the future, for tips on how to avoid imminent
disaster, and for assurances that one's future and the future of one's
children would be prosperous. The social position of monks, spiritual
figures with the leisure to pursue such matters, made them eminently
fit to satisfy the need for oracles, whether or not the questions asked
or answers given related to distinctly Buddhist concerns. Even geomancy, a Chinese tradition with very old and respected roots, was an
area in which some monks gained expertise. A number of monks were
known for their skill in determining the proper location of the family
graveyard, a decision believed to influence the fortunes of the family
for generations to come.[56] The Tang monk Hongshi, for example, was
said to have advised a number of high-ranking officials on the correct
placement of their family graveyards and the proper positioning of
their homes.[57] We also know that, previous to this, Emperor Yuan Di
of the Liang possessed a manual on grave placement written by a
monk named Tanzhi of the Toutuo Monastery.[58]

Despite the easy coexistence of Buddhism and divination in the
Biographies, no mention is made of distinctly Buddhist forms of divination. Indeed, the *Biographies* suggest that the monks themselves did
not consider divination to be a particularly Buddhist activity. That is,
like medicine, divination was a separate discipline that monks mastered "on the side." The fifth-century monk Fayuan, for instance, "in
addition to understanding the [Buddhist] scriptures and treatises, also
learned the 'arts of calculation.' "[59] Similarly, at one point in the biography of the great monastic leader Daoan, the biography emphasizes
the monk's wide learning: "He ventured into a wide variety of fields,
looking through various books on non-Buddhist as well as Buddhist

matters. He came to master divination and calculations in addition to attaining a great facility with the marvelous doctrines of Buddhist scriptures."[60]

If there were any doubts about the propriety of a monk studying the arts of divination, the example set by a figure of Daoan's prominence quickly set them to rest. In the *Further Biographies*, the Tang monk Daobian specifically cites the example of Daoan's mastery of the "arts of calculation" as inspiration for his own interest in the field.[61] The "arts of calculation" (*shushu*) mentioned in these biographies is a technical term encompassing various forms of divination that was used to represent a considerable body of mantic literature already in the Han.[62] As the term implies, these forms of divination were not supernormal powers shrouded in mystery, but rather calculations following learned rules and executed in the matter-of-fact manner common to Chinese fortune-tellers of more recent times.[63]

As we have seen, Chinese monks drew on a rich tradition of mantic techniques developed long before the entrance of Buddhism to China. Nonetheless, it is interesting to note how many of the early monks known for divination were foreigners, reflecting not just tolerance but respect for the mantic lore of India. Foreign monks such as Buddhayaśas and Dharmakāla were both known for their ability to predict the future on the basis of the movement of the stars.[64] The interest in Indian astrology reached a peak in the Tang with the translation into Chinese of related texts by Amoghavajra and others.[65] Apparently the demand for such texts was greater than the supply, for Ōmura Seigai has suggested that several texts from this period claiming to be translations of Buddhist texts concerning Indian astronomy were in fact composed in China.[66]

Perhaps it was precisely because of the importance attached to divination in society at large that the *Biographies* deliberately downplay the importance of fortune-telling. That is to say, by at once affirming the ability of monks to see into the future, and at the same time dismissing this ability as insignificant, the *Biographies* underline the greater importance of the specifically Buddhist concerns that separated the monk from the local fortune-teller. Further, this rhetorical move, suggesting that divination was a small matter for eminent monks, suggests even greater, unspoken powers. We read, for instance, of the humble Ratnamati who, after receiving wide acclaim for his abilities to predict future events, exclaimed, "This is not difficult; it is simply a matter of the arts of calculation. Ignorant people have done me a disservice by labeling me a holy man."[67] In the same vein, it was said of the monk Yu Fakai that he "used the arts of calculation to spread the Teaching."[68] That is, prognostication was an expedient

device and not to be taken too seriously for its own merits. Nonetheless, divination was taken very seriously indeed, not just by the
benighted masses implied in the condescending tone of the hagiography, but also by many of the monks themselves. And one suspects that
few outside of the monastic community felt it necessary to distinguish
between the "tools of the Teaching" and the Teaching itself.

Not everyone in early China sought out masters of prognostication.
There were those who rejected divination outright as a bundle of
superstitions and went to great lengths to expose the absurd premises
on which it is based.[69] But such views were confined to an extremely
small minority of radical mavericks. For most, the question concerning divination was not one of belief or disbelief, but rather of which
methods were the most effective and to what purpose they were employed. If the *Biographies* are any reflection of reality, then ordinary
people often found references to future events more disturbing than
comforting. Yishi "at the beginning of the Zhenyuan era [785] traveled
in Wuyuan[70] to beg. He had many premonitions of events yet to come,
and for this reason *people held him in suspicion*."[71] The Sui monk Faxi
"was normally silent, but when he met someone he would always say
something, and his words always contained profound implications.
His predictions of good or bad fortune were [realized] as surely as a
shadow [following an object] or an echo [following a sound]. *People
did not like meeting with Faxi, for they feared his predictions of misfortune and disaster*."[72]

These apprehensions were intensified in the case of the state, for
which prophecy of national disaster was tantamount to sedition. The
Tang house itself claimed legitimacy on the basis of Daoist and Buddhist prophecies of the fall of the Sui and rise of a new order.[73] It is not
surprising then that officials saw fit to arrest prophetic monks like
Huaijun and to execute imitators of the prophetic monk Wanhui for
"deceiving the people."[74] Of course political prophecy was complicated
by the possibility that it disguised more tangible plots against the
throne. Earlier I cited the story of the monk Wanhui who saved an
innocent official from the machinations of enemies at court who had
planted incriminating material on his roof. The material in question
was a book of predictions (*chenwei*), presumably detailing the fall of
the dynasty.[75] As the compilers of the *Tang History* stated: "The sage
rulers [of antiquity] banned books concerning the stars and divination
with good reason."[76] The discovery of such material would no doubt
have been labeled sorcery and punished with death.

Nevertheless, to refer to thaumaturgy in general as "sorcery," even
when taking the state's perspective, would be misleading. For the
state, the distinction between "the arts of yin and yang" and "sorcery"

was more rhetorical than substantive and was based on the intention of the diviner rather than divination itself, which as we have seen was often at the very foundation of the state's claim to legitimacy. Chinese attitudes towards "magic" become clearer when we look at the case of what is perhaps the most common technique falling under the category of Buddhist thaumaturgy, the spell.

Spells

Long before the introduction of Buddhism to China, Chinese were intensely concerned with the far-ranging problem of how to deal with demons. Until the modern era, demonology and medicine were often closely tied; rather than the ubiquitous bacteria and viruses of modern popular medical conceptions, demons were a common source of illness, and possession was an everyday occurrence. Demonic malevolence was at the root of both physical and mental maladies, from warts and rashes to seizures and even nightmares. It is not surprising then that the Chinese early on developed techniques for combating the spooks and specters that harassed them. Entries in the bibliography included in the *Han shu* indicate that by the Han there was a thriving demonographic literature. Unfortunately, these texts are no longer extant, but manuscripts discovered in the 1970s at the Mawangdui and Shuihudi sites give us a fascinating glimpse of pre-Buddhist conceptions of the demonic and ways for protecting oneself from it.[77]

A demonography discovered at Shuihudi dating to the third century B.C. describes measures to be taken in the event of demonic mischief. It advises, for example, that "the dwelling places of the great spirits cannot be passed through. They like to injure people. Make pellets from dog excrement and carry them when passing through. Throw them at the spirit when it appears, and it will not injure people."[78] In addition to expelling demons with unpleasant substances, readers were also taught to drive them away with prophylactic postures. When in danger, the demonography advises, recline in a crouch or sit "like a winnowing basket" to ward off demonic attack.[79]

Among the various techniques for dealing with demons included in one Mawangdui manuscript were spells—incantatory formulas used to exorcise demons. Take, for example, this spell, recited to exorcise fox spirits:

> Spirit of Heaven send down the sickness-shield.
> Spirit Maids according to sequence hear the spirit pronouncement.
> A certain fox is poking into a place where it does not belong.
> Desist.
> Not desisting, let the ax cleave you.[80]

It seems likely that this preoccupation with protecting oneself from the demonic through incantatory formulas was not limited to the aristocratic figures in whose tombs the Mawangdui and Shuihudi manuscripts were found: surely spells were a part of the everyday life of people at all levels of Chinese society.

Meanwhile, an incantatory tradition had been developing for centuries in India and had been readily incorporated into Buddhist doctrine and folklore.[81] In the *Liang Biographies* we read that Guṇabhadra who "was originally of Brahman stock, as a child mastered the various discourses concerning the 'five sciences,'[82] as well as astronomy, mathematics, medicine, and the art of spells."[83] Similarly, Tanwuchan (Skt. Dharmakṣema) in addition to studying the "five sciences" and the "lesser vehicle," also learned to chant spells as a part of his childhood education.[84] It was monks like these, steeped in the Indian tradition, who bridged the gap between Indian and Chinese practices, introducing Indian spells to the Chinese incantatory repertoire.

In addition to foreign missionaries, Buddhist texts concerned with spells appear to have been translated into Chinese from an early date. While a number of Buddhist spell texts have been attributed to the earliest translators, the authenticity of these attributions is difficult to determine.[85] Nevertheless, it seems safe to say that certainly by the end of the third century, Chinese readers had been introduced to texts in which Buddhist spells play a central role.[86]

A glance at the *Chu sanzang jiji*, a catalog of Buddhist books compiled in the early sixth century, reveals that by that time the libraries of Buddhist aficionados were well stocked with a wide variety of Buddhist spell texts. Although most of the spell books listed in this catalog have been lost, their titles give us some idea of their contents. Most of the titles point to spells of a decidedly practical nature. Medical texts like *The Spell for an Aching Tooth*, *The Spell [to Treat] Poison*, and *The Spell for Sore Eyes* were all in the library of the sixth-century cataloger.[87] The catalog also records *The Scripture of the Water Spell*, *The Scripture of the Dragon King and the Bathing Spell*, and *Spells to Request Rain, Stop Rain and Extract Blood Humors*.[88] The titles of these long-lost texts point to two of the most common uses to which Buddhist spells were put in China: treating illness and controlling water. Considering the efforts of missionary monks and translators as well as the Chinese predisposition towards spells, it is not surprising that the Buddhist spell came to play a prominent role in the image of the Buddhist thaumaturge in China. By examining the evolution of the spell in Buddhist hagiography, it is possible to gain a purchase not only on the history of incantations in early Chinese Buddhism, but also on the development of the image of the Buddhist wonder-worker in China.

Spells in the Liang Biographies

Huijiao attributed the spread of Buddhist spells in China to the fourth-century monk Śrīmitra, credited with translating a version of the spell text known as the *Peacock King Scripture*,[89] and of introducing Buddhist spells to the eastern part of China.[90] Later scholars of Buddhist history, from Zanning in the tenth century to modern scholars, have followed suit, citing Śrīmitra as a key figure in the early spread of Buddhist spells. Nonetheless, the *Liang Biographies* also attribute a knowledge of spells to even earlier figures, like the third-century monk Heluojie who during an epidemic "treated the ill with spells, curing eight or nine out of every ten,"[91] or the fourth-century Zhu Fakuang who "traveled through the villages and hamlets, saving the gravely ill."[92] Thus, if the *Biographies* are any indication, monks were associated with the spell-casting arts almost from the beginnings of Buddhism in China.[93]

In the *Liang Biographies*, the content of the spells and the rituals into which they were incorporated remain for the most part obscure. For Śrīmitra we are told only that he chanted a spell in "several thousand [foreign] syllables." For others we are given only a few tantalizing details. On learning of an official named Teng Yongwen, bedridden with a crippling illness, the early fourth-century Indian monk Jīvaka went to him and asked, "Do you wish to be cured?" The monk "took up a bowl of clean water and a tooth-cleaning stick [*yangliu*]. He then stirred the water with the stick, pointed it in Yongwen's direction, and intoned a spell. After doing this three times, he stroked Yongwen's knees and ordered him to arise. The man then arose and walked as he had before his illness."[94] Fotucheng was said to have effected even more dramatic results, bringing a dead prince back to life with a tooth-cleaning stick and a spell.[95]

Here we see one of the major uses of spells in the *Liang* and subsequent versions of the *Eminent Monks*: the treatment of sickness. The stories cited above make no mention of demons and do not necessarily suggest that such cures were regarded as exorcisms. Other stories, however, point to just such a notion; that is, when stricken with an illness brought on by a demon, exorcism was the only sure cure; and the proper incantation administered by a specialist, the best medicine. According to the biography of the fifth-century monk Puming, when the wife of a local villager took ill, Puming was asked in to chant a spell. As soon as the monk did so, the woman's breathing returned to normal. Immediately thereafter, a "creature that looked like a fox scurried out of the dog gate. She thenceforth recovered."[96] The connection between spells and the spirit-world is further illustrated in the lines of the story that follow: "Puming once walked past a shrine by the side of a river. The shaman there said that when the spirits saw him they fled in fear." Similarly, the fourth-century monk Dharmakṣema in one story sensed that demons had entered a village and warned of an imminent epidemic. At the time one of the villagers doubted Dharmakṣema's abilities, whereupon the monk chanted spells for three consecutive days and announced, "The demons have gone." Just at that time someone reported that they had seen hundreds of plague demons fleeing the village.[97] If these stories are more than exotic fantasies, and reflect, however imperfectly, the way real monks behaved in society, then spell-casting, like fortune-telling, was an important point of contact between monks and ordinary people—one of a set of soundly practical services the monk offered to the community.

The belief in the value of spells for curing demonic illness reflected in the hagiography jibes with views expressed in more theoretical Buddhist writings. Speaking at the end of the sixth century, the great Tiantai exegete Zhiyi divided the causes of illness into six categories, including improper balance between the "four elements" (si da), improper diet, disorders brought on by improper meditative practices, and karmic conditions. Also included in his six categories were illness caused by ghosts and by demons. For these later two types of illness, Zhiyi prescribed spells of which he gave two examples.[98] As the passage from Zhiyi illustrates, sickness was not attributed exclusively to demonic influence; the spell was seen as one of a number of potential remedies for illness, only to be prescribed under the proper circumstances.[99] Nonetheless, when something as mysterious and terrifying as an epidemic struck a community, demons were the natural focus of attention. It is equally understandable that at such times people would turn for help to the spiritual figures in their communities, guardians of unspeakable secrets who in many cases were monks.

In addition to the belief that incantations were effective in exorcising malevolent spirits, it was also believed that spells could be used to manipulate nature and specifically to attain water. One story tells that Dharmakṣemsa, known as the "Great Master of Spells," once when accompanying a king into the mountains produced water for the thirsty sovereign by casting an "esoteric spell" on a boulder, which, like Moses' rock in the desert, bubbled forth with fresh spring water.[100] The prevalence of this kind of story in the Liang Biographies reflects a fascination with the dramatic thaumaturgic solution to drought—a fascination not surprising in an agricultural society justifiably preoccupied with the proper allocation of water. The biography of Guṇabhadra relates that in 462 China suffered from a great drought. After making supplications to the mountains and rivers for several months to no effect, the emperor summoned Guṇabhadra and commanded him to pray for rain, adding that if his efforts were unsuccessful his presence would not be requested again. Guṇabhadra from that moment refused all food and drink, lit incense, and began to "silently chant scriptures, secretly intoning esoteric spells at the same time." Needless to say, rain fell the following day.[101] It may well be that behind these stories lay the assumption that the availability of water in wells and in the form of rain was subject to the whims of the spirit-dragons who were believed to control water; again, the function of the spell was to manipulate the spirit-world.

The connection between spells, dragons, and rain is occasionally made explicit in the *Liang Biographies*, as in the case of Shegong who "could call down the spirit-dragons through the use of esoteric spells. Whenever there was a drought, [the ruler] Fu Jian would ask him to cast a spell, whereupon a dragon would appear in his alms bowl. The heavens would then break forth with torrential rains. Fu Jian and his officials would look into his bowl and sigh in astonishment at these marvels."[102]

With this last example we return to the more general appeal of the thaumaturge in hagiography as a source of wonder. Illustrative of this function of the hagiography is the fact that many of the stories relate the use of spells to achieve less practical results. When Fotucheng was faced with the challenge of demonstrating the merits of Buddhism to the martial ruler Shi Le, "realizing that Shi Le could not understand the profound doctrines [of Buddhism]," he resorted to a simple demonstration of the efficacy of Buddhist spells. "Taking up a vessel filled with water, he lit incense, and said a spell over it. Moments later, a green lotus flower sprouted up, dazzling to the eye. From this time on, Shi Le believed."[103] Whether we read this as a record of some sort of magic trick or as a later legend, its inclusion in the *Liang Biographies* discloses a fascination with the power of these esoteric foreign words apart from the pressing concerns of drought and disease.

Two characteristics of the *Liang Biographies* are particularly important for tracing the evolution of Buddhist spells in China. First, the reader may have noticed that virtually all of the spell-casting monks mentioned so far were foreigners. Second, the spells mentioned in the *Liang Biographies*, unlike spells in later biographies, are known only as generic "spells" (*zhou*), and do not reflect widespread knowledge of the technical spell literature that assigned specific names and attributes to various spells. No attempt is made to transcribe the spells or to distinguish the spells of one master from another. Apparently, up to this time (that is, the early sixth century), the Buddhist spell was seen as chiefly the domain of foreign, dimly understood figures versed in exotic arts deemed incomprehensible by native Chinese. The great translator and exegete Kumārajīva was enormously influential in China not only because of his own work, but also because of the brilliant Chinese disciples he trained. Nonetheless, according to the *Liang Biographies*, when Kumārajīva was on his deathbed, "he intoned three spirit-spells and ordered his *foreign* disciples to chant them in an attempt to save him."[104] For Kumārajīva, or perhaps only for the author of his biography, Chinese monks were deemed inappropriate students for the art of spell-chanting. At this time, it was perhaps this exoticism, this inaccessibility, that allowed Buddhist spells to compete with a rich indigenous incantatory literature.[105]

Specialization and Sinification in Later Biographies

While Indian Buddhist texts featuring specific spells came to China early on, it is not until the *Further Biographies* that the names of such spells begin to punctuate the hagiography. The monk Fayun chanted the Spell of Seven Buddhas in order to "save others," while Huiyu chanted spells from the larger version of the *Perfection of Wisdom*[106] in order to save several men dying from an attack by a prodigious poisonous snake.[107] Narendrayaśas repeatedly made use of the *Spirit Spell of Guanyin (Avalokiteśvara)*, as did Dharmagupta who used the *Guanyin Spell* in order to bring down rain.[108] In addition to the oral training in these spells that we must assume was taking place, many spells were elucidated in instructional manuals either translated into Chinese from Sanskrit or purporting to be translated from Sanskrit.[109] It was becoming increasingly possible for Chinese monks who had never made the trip to India, or even learned rudimentary Sanskrit, to dabble in incantatory arts that had in the past been reserved for foreigners.

Nevertheless, in the *Further Biographies*, the association between the foreign monk and thaumaturgy remains strong. Once, we are told, when Bodhiruci was sitting alone beside a well, he stirred the well water with a tooth-cleaning stick and cast a spell. In a moment the water came bubbling to the top of the well, whereupon Bodhiruci washed himself. A monk happened to see this thing and exclaimed that the Master was a great and holy man. Bodhiruci responded sharply, " 'You must not give praise lightly. This [spell-casting] is a practice that we all cultivate abroad. It is just because you here do not practice it that you call me holy.' Fearing that he would mislead those still caught in the web of worldly ways, Bodhiruci henceforth kept [his spells] secret and did not make them known to others."[110] Here we see the same sort of rhetorical device we saw in the case of supernormal powers: dismissing spells as insignificant only adds to the respect due the monk, or, as in the case of Fotucheng cited above, adds to the respect due the profundities of Buddhist doctrine.

Despite the continued fascination with the foreign thaumaturge, as we move into the seventh century we read more and more accounts of *Chinese* monks like Sengfan who at the age of twenty-three mastered the "art of Indian spells," or of Faan who wandered about treating the ill with "charmed water."[111] Ironically, this democratic spread of Buddhist spells to Chinese monks was accompanied by increasing specialization in the form of technical books and theories. Thus, although more and more monks claimed competence in the use of spells, Buddhist spell-casting was still confined to the specialist; there is no evidence to suggest that at this time many outside of the clergy learned Buddhist spells with their long strings of strange and meaningless syllables.

A part of this specialization was the increased use of technical terminology. The *Further Biographies* introduces to the series the specialized type of spell known as *dhāraṇī*. In many instances, *dhāraṇī* and spell (Skt. *mantra*) were used indiscriminately in China, but at this time (pre-Tang), the hagiography reflects an awareness of the more technical sense of *dhāraṇī* as a distinctively Buddhist mnemonic device used to help the adept memorize Buddhist writings.[112] The term *dhāraṇī*, sometimes given in its Chinese translation of "all-retaining" (*zongchi*)—which includes the ability to retain memories—appears only twice in the *Further Biographies*. In one case it is associated with the ability to master scriptures; in the other, it is linked to spells.[113] Hence, while the idea that *dhāraṇī* could be used like regular spells was in circulation at this time,[114] the restricted use of the word "*dhāraṇī*" in the *Further Biographies* suggests that these particular Buddhist spells may not yet have achieved widespread acceptance within the *saṅgha*.

In addition to documenting the use of *dhāraṇī* as a mnemonic device for studying scriptures, the *Further Biographies* also introduces the use of spells (*zhou*) for purposes more abstract than the treating of illness or prayers for rain. "During the Zhenguan era [627–650]," the biography of Huikuan relates, "there was a monk named Ce who cast spells with efficacy. He suddenly died in Luo District. When he saw King Yama [king of the netherworld], the King said: 'The faults of the people in hell are many. You should chant spells for them, and ask Master Huikuan to speak on the *Hell Scripture*.' "[115] The biography of Tanxuan also mentions the notion that spells can be used to eradicate one's faults.[116] Finally, it is said that the sixth-century monk Huiyuan chanted spells "in order to repay his four debts" (to parents, all sentient beings, teachers, and ruler).[117] The ideas represented by these stories lay behind the eventual incorporation of spells into Buddhist liturgy.

The translation of spell texts and the use of spells in liturgy prepared the way for the three great Tang ritual specialists Amoghavajra, Vajrabodhi, and Śubakarasiṃha, characterized in the hagiography by their use of *mudrās*, *maṇḍalas*, and spells, known in the technical literature as the "three mysteries" (*san mi*). For a sense of the sort of impressive ritual acts with which these three monks came to be associated, consider the story of Vajrabodhi and the twenty-fifth princess, daughter to Tang Xuanzong.[118] According to the *Song Biographies*, the twenty-fifth princess, Xuanzong's favorite daughter, took ill and was on the verge of death. At this point the emperor summoned Vajrabodhi to administer her last rites. But then something unusual happened.

> Vajrabodhi went to the princess, and, selecting two seven-year-old girls from the palace, wrapped their faces in red silken gauze and had them lie on the ground. Then, he ordered Niu Xiantong [a high-ranking official] to compose an edict and burn it elsewhere. Vajrabodhi then cast a spell with esoteric words. The two girls memorized and recited [the spell], not dropping a single word. The monk then entered *samādhi*, and with inconceivable power ordered the two girls to take the edict to King Yama. In the time it takes to eat a meal, Yama ordered the princess' deceased nurse, Dame Liu, to escort the princess' *hun* soul back with the two girls. The princess thereupon sat up, opened her eyes, and talked as usual. When the Emperor heard the news, he raced back to the Outer Rooms without waiting for his guard. The princess said to him, "The numbers [set] in the netherworld are difficult to change. King Yama has sent me back only that I might gaze on your sacred countenance once more." After about half a day, she passed away. From this time on, the Emperor took refuge in and worshiped [Buddhism].[119]

While we have no contemporary sources testifying to this particular incident, the close ties between the court and the three Tantric masters is beyond doubt. The credence the court placed in Buddhist ritual is illustrated by the vast corpus of ritual texts the three monks were ordered to translate or compose on imperial directive. The impact of the influx of this spell literature is apparent in the *Song Biographies*. In place of the generic spells common in the *Liang Biographies*, monks in the *Song Biographies* keep spells with such impressive sounding titles as *The Heart Spell of Great Compassion*, *The Scripture of the Eight-syllable Dhāraṇī*, or *The Spirit Spell of the Buddha's Uṣṇīṣa*.[120] This last spell was particularly influential as it became the chief spell inscribed on "*dhāraṇī* pillars" (*jingchuang*), hundreds of which were erected throughout the Tang empire.[121] For many monks it was no longer enough to chant a common spell; spell-casting now required expertise in a vast body of technical, esoteric lore.

At the same time, the influence of these technical manuals can be overemphasized, and it would be a mistake to think of the use of Buddhist spells as a direct, unadulterated appropriation of purely foreign practices. The monk Quanqing, for example, was said to have cured a woman of possession through the use of spells and a grass doll, a practice with origins in pre-Buddhist China.[122] Similarly, Buddhist spells became intertwined with the traditional topos of Chinese folklore. Zhixuan, for instance, employed "Indian spells" to save a young gentleman from a fox spirit disguised as a damsel in distress, a familiar motif to students of Chinese literature.[123]

Unfortunately, in the *Biographies* we can only dimly perceive the changes in the day-to-day ritual life of the monastic community brought on by this new influx of ritual texts. The *Song Biographies*, like the two collections that came before it, is for the most part concerned with the most dramatic uses to which spells were put: curing illness, invoking rain in villages and at court, and subjugating malevolent spirits in the mountain wilds. Ethnographic descriptions of ordinary rituals did not, for the medieval reader, make for a good read.

Scripture as Spell

The *Biographies of Eminent Monks* contain important material for the history of Buddhist reading, that is, how Buddhists understood their own scriptures.[124] It is of course necessary to balance the attitudes reflected in the *Biographies* with the more formal, sustained attempts to understand scripture found in the writings of the great Chinese Buddhist exegetes; hagiography is not conducive to the inner grappling of a Zhiyi or a Zongmi. On the other hand, perhaps more than commentaries or compendiums of scripture, hagiography reveals the connections that existed between scripture and practice, the circumstances under which sacred books were read, and the impact they had (or were supposed to have had) on their readers. One of the ways in which Buddhist scriptures were read was as spells.

The *Biographies* disclose an overriding concern with the power of the sutras themselves—with the physical object of the book, the characters on the page, and the sounds of the words when read aloud—apart from doctrinal or philosophical meaning of the texts. This will come as no surprise to readers familiar with the major Mahāyāna sutras. The *Lotus Sūtra*, for instance, contains so many self-referential passages insisting on the marvelousness of the scripture and the merit accruing to all who recite and copy it, that first-time readers are often baffled by just where the "message" of the scripture lies, if not in these very self-referential passages themselves. The *Perfection of Wisdom*, *Diamond*, and *Flower Adornment* all display similar characteristics, and were all key players in the growth of the cult of the book in Indian and subsequently Chinese Buddhism.

One of the uses to which these spiritually powerful books were put was, as in the case of spells, to protect oneself from demons and to manipulate the spirit-world.[125] When the Sui monk Xingjian travels to Mount Tai, known in China from ancient times as the destination of the dead, he is warned not to stay in a particular room in a mountain monastery because it is known to be haunted; "All who stay there inevitably meet with violent death," warns the monastery caretaker. Nonetheless, Xingjian fearlessly spends the night there, confidently chanting the scriptures to protect himself from whatever demons might appear.[126] In the biography of the eighth-century monk Qingxu the association between spells and scripture is made even more explicit. On retreating to the famous Shaolin Monastery for summer medita-tion, Qingxu learns of a room said to be inhabited by a fierce demon. He is further told that a monk who had mastered the *Fire-Head Vajra Spell* (*huotuo jin'gang zhou*) once attempted to spend the night there, but was hurled down the mountain by the demon. "For seven days he could not speak and was mentally disturbed." Undaunted, Qingxu goes to the room where he chants the *Eleven-Face Guanyin Spell*." When the statues in the room begin to shake, Qingxu realizes that the spell is ineffective, and so begins to chant the *Diamond Sūtra* instead. "From this time on," the story concludes, "those who lived there came to no harm and the spirit moved away."[127]

If these sorts of heroics seem far removed from the needs of the average reader, the biography of Hongzheng relates a story of a kind of protection that all would find useful: protection against the envoys of death. While a monk was sitting in meditation, we are told, he saw two envoys of death come to collect Hongzheng whose allotted life-span had expired. The monk then overheard a ghostly conversation between the two spirits who complained that they could not approach Hongzheng, for he was chanting the *Diamond Sūtra*. Eventually, in order to satisfy their superiors in the underworld, the frustrated spirits decided to take in Hongzheng's place another man in the capital who happened to share his name.[128]

There was of course a more pervasive, less dramatic notion drawn upon to combat the spirits of death: accumulation of merit. The scrip-tures themselves are the first to testify to the merit derived from their recitation. The hagiography is full of accounts of monks and laymen who temporarily descend to the netherworld where Yama praises them for chanting the scriptures and extends their life span, or chastises them for failing to chant scriptures and sends them back for another chance.

But this notion seems too removed and abstract for the ideas we associate with the word "spell," and may be closer to what we mean by "incantation," or even "prayer." It is likely, however, that such distinctions would have been quite alien to the medieval Chinese Buddhist. Reciting the *Lotus Sūtra* both accrued merit and protected one from demons in times of danger; scriptures could be read both for their philosophical insights and as apotropaic spells. The very multivalence of the act of reading Buddhist scriptures is part of what made them so appealing.

Much of our uneasiness with the term "spell"[129] stems from our own experience of the Reformation when "magic" was juxtaposed to "religion," and later, magic distinguished from religion and science—categories of belief and practice with which leading scholars of religion continue to grapple to this day.[130] I will return to these larger questions of the theory behind thaumaturgy in the next section. But first let us look at the reaction to spells and incantations within and without the *saṅgha* in medieval China.

Reception

The vast corpus of extant works by Li Bai includes a poem dedicated to an Indian monk. The poem begins,

> There is a monk whose Dharma name is Saṅgha.
> At times he discusses the three carts [of the *Lotus Sūtra*] with me.
> I asked him how many times he had chanted his spells.
> "Twice the number of the grains of sand in the Ganges," was his
>   reply.[131]

As this poem indicates, along with ascetic practice and the ability to discuss lofty, erudite doctrines, in the layman's eye the spell had become an integral part of the image of the monk. The diary of Ennin, the ninth-century Japanese pilgrim to China, illustrates that by this time the spell had become a part of a monk's everyday life. In addition to chanting spells on behalf of an ailing ship captain and for favorable winds on his journey to China, Ennin also chanted spells at the funeral of one of his disciples who died in China.[132] In 838, Ennin had the opportunity to observe an annual ritual in Yangzhou honoring the anniversary of the death of the former emperor Jingzong. Part of the ritual, attended by representatives of the state, included the recitation of spells intended to assist the spirit of the deceased ruler in the afterworld.[133] This final example raises the curious matter of the attitude of the state toward the use of Buddhist spells. The attitude of the state toward spells was more complicated than that of the average layman. If a layman could call on monks to chant spells only when ill or on the occasion of a funeral, and otherwise ignore them, the state felt the need to regulate such practices, to draw a line between beneficial incantations and sorcery.

Judging by legal documents, the state seems to have taken a dim view of the use of spells. In the Han code, sorcery, widely defined, was a punishable offense. The first-century *Xin lun* recounts the story of a certain Mr. Han who was arrested for chanting incantations against nightmare bogies in the morning in the privy.[134] This suspicion of spell-casting continued into the Tang legal code, which stipulated that monks apprehended casting spells were to be arrested and executed.[135] One of the first anti-Buddhist edicts of the famous Huichang persecution of 842 called for the laicization of monks who cast spells.[136]

But when we look more closely, we see that the position of the state concerning spells was hardly consistent. Take for example the official policy of Xuanzong. According to the *Tang History*, Xuanzong's mother was killed after being falsely accused of using spells for evil ends.[137] If indeed the accusations were false, the unfortunate event did not deter Xuanzong from carrying out his own furious purges of spell casters, for sorcery consistently played at least a minor role in the tense drama of intrigue and suspicion among court rivals. Xuanzong made his stance clear in an edict of 726 in which he states:

> We have been informed that among the clergy and the laity, there are those who falsely prognosticate, wildly deceiving gentlemen and commoners alike. Claiming [to foretell] disaster and good fortune, [drawing up] talismans, and [casting] spells, they practice sorcery [*zuodao*]. Previously, orders were issued that these practices were to cease. Yet it seems that the foolish are unwilling to change their ways. Let it be known that officials shall henceforth make known the [relevant] statutes and edicts and rigorously examine [those under their administrations].[138]

Another of Xuanzong's extant edicts, issued thirteen years later, singles out Buddhists for criticism:

> Sorcery is extremely damaging to the state. It is for this reason that the former kings established the principle that those who commit these crimes must be executed in order to extirpate destructive [elements]. Yet not all of [the sorcerers] have been seized. From this day on, the law cannot abide those who, in the name of the Buddha Law, want only to make magic, speaking wildly of good and bad fortune, and specializing in pernicious deception. It shall be commanded to all senior officials in office that all of this type are to be rigorously apprehended.[139]

While members of the royal family might dabble in sorcery, this edict indicates that it was the specialists in such arts who were most feared; and monks were counted among these specialists. Obviously Xuan-zong's efforts to curb the use of spells by the clergy during this time met with at most limited success, or the second edict would not have been necessary. Curiously, it was during precisely this period, the reign of Xuanzong, that the bulk of Buddhist spell texts were trans-lated. Further, the texts translated by monks like Amoghavajra, Vajra-bodhi, and Śubakarasiṃha almost always bear the heading *feng zhao* "[translated] on imperial edict." Xuanzong's case is representative of the state's attitude toward such matters in general. Spells were not conceived of as universally evil in the way that theologians during the Reformation denounced all such practices as the work of the devil. In China, spells were thought of as weapons: in the right hands they could be used to summon rain and cure the sick; but in the wrong hands they could be used for malevolent purposes. Hence it is under-standable that during the Huichang persecution—a time in which the clergy felt great animosity toward the imperial house—yet another imperial edict was issued banning monks from using spells.[140]

For their part, leading clerics sought to convince the laity that monks would only use powerful spells for righteous causes. This ten-dency is reflected in monastic reactions to an incident said to have taken place at the court of Taizong in 639. According to the *Zizhi tongjian*, a foreign monk appeared in the capital in 639 claiming to possess the ability to cast a spell that would kill a man in an instant. It was said that after killing a man, he would then use another spell to bring the victim back to life. Fu Yi, a staunch opponent of Buddhism, reported to the emperor: "This is a false art. I have heard it said that the false cannot overcome the true. I request that the monk be asked to cast his spell on me. It will certainly not work." When the monk attempted his spell, Fu Yi remained unharmed, while the monk him-self fell down dead.[141] In his *Longxing biannian tonglun*, the Song monk Zuxiu states that since the arrival of Śrīmitra in the Jin, "any number of charlatan *bhikṣus* have come from foreign countries, equipped with arts with which they startle the ignorant." The story of Fu Yi and the foreign monk, Zuxiu continues, is no doubt a fabrication, so absurd that "even a child would not believe it." Even if it were true, he contin-ues, then clearly the monk's spell was not a real spell and could indeed be termed a false art.[142] Of course Zuxiu's main point here is to refute the superiority of an enemy of Buddhism to one of its representatives. But in doing so he seems to be saying that it was the inefficacy of the spell that proved that the monk who cast it was not Buddhist. Zhipan, the Song Dynasty compiler of the *Fozu tongji*, makes a more powerful moral argument in his own commentary to the story in which he claims that Buddhist spells can only be used for compassionate ends, and that it was the foreign monk's failure to understand this basic tenet that led to his own death.[143] Both the original story and the reactions to it reflect an ambivalence toward spells, a sense that the mere uttering of certain esoteric syllables could wreak horrible consequences, especially if used by unscrupulous individuals.[144]

Although incantations evoked a certain uneasiness, spells continued to attract monks to their mysteries, often at the expense of less dramatic fields of Buddhist knowledge. In the biography of the sixth-century monk Zhixiang, a monk uses a spell to invoke a powerful spirit who lifts him several feet above the ground before Zhixiang expels the spirit through recitation of the precepts. Zhixiang then informs the monk that he has been practicing a false art that he should abandon forthwith.[145] As in the story cited earlier in which the recitation of scripture proved more powerful than a spell, this story was an attempt to emphasize the superiority of the more conservative, collective practice of reciting precepts over the pursuit of mastery of spell-casting. Similarly, in his commentary to a collection of Pure-Land stories, the prominent Ming monk Zhuhong complained that the monks of his day put little faith in the value of chanting the name of Amitābha. Instead, "in recent times men who keep spells read that the merit of *dhāraṇīs* can move mountains and seas, quell demons and spirits, and grant all manner of wishes. This they gleefully believe. But they also read that the merit of the pure-land can allow one to directly climb the sacred stairs and immediately transcend the three realms. This they quietly dismiss!"[146] While spells never supplanted scriptures, the Vinaya, or recitation of the name of Amitābha, they nevertheless held a consistent attraction for monks who perceived them to be as potent as they were mysterious, and the layman's apprehensions served only to bolster the appeal of the incantatory literature for monks.

The organization of my discussion of spells (beginning with indigenous Chinese spells, and then describing the entrance of Buddhist spells to the Chinese scene) may seem to argue that Buddhist spells *replaced* Chinese spells—another chapter in the Buddhist conquest of China. This is not at all the case, for while Buddhism certainly made inroads into Chinese demonology—texts used in modern Daoist ritual, for example, sometimes contain *dhāraṇī*—even mainstream Buddhist monks continued to use old-fashioned Chinese methods for warding off demons. Zanning, best known for his *Song Biographies of Eminent Monks* and his *Brief History of the Clergy*, also left us some of his more personal writings, including a lengthy treatise on bamboo and a book of techniques for warding off malevolent influences, the *Record of Res-*

onance by Category. This text includes methods for dealing with demons that are reminiscent of the techniques prescribed more than a thousand years earlier in the Shuihudi manuscripts. Zanning recommends, for example:

> When lying down to sleep at night, place a blade of grass sticking up from the ground by a little more than three *cun*, and the demons and bogies will not dare to bewitch you. If when out in the fields you see a roving glow[147] that [looks like] fire, it is Shining Demon Fire. It may become a wild fire when someone dies and their blood collects on the ground. Roving Glow is unpredictable. It may appear and then disappear. It comes to harass people and to snatch their breath and essence. Make a noise by slapping the sides of your saddle, and the fire will be extinguished.[148]

Here we see neither *dhāraṇīs*, *mudrās*, *mantras*, nor Buddhist deities. The definition of orthodoxy hinted at in the discussion over the story of the evil foreign monk and his death spell was not so narrow as to exclude non-Buddhist methods for dealing with the demonic. Buddhist spells, despite their pervasive influence and the extensive literature prescribing their use, were but one contribution to a vast repertoire of techniques available to those troubled by seen and unseen specters. This being said, in the *Eminent Monks* it is the spell and not these other techniques that lies at the center of stories of encounters between monks and the demonic.

Miracles

Étienne Lamotte, the eminent modern scholar of Buddhist history and doctrine, scrupulously avoided the word "supernatural" in his writings on Buddhism, preferring instead to refer to miraculous phenomena as "supernormal." Although he never made explicit the reasoning behind this decision, it is probable that Lamotte, himself a Jesuit priest, wished to dissociate Buddhist ideas of miracles from their Christian counterparts. Christian theologians have differed over the mechanism of miracles, but the dominant view has held that miracles are without exception acts of God and God alone. God created Nature, and only God can alter Nature through supernatural intervention. Therefore, according to these same theologians, even when prayers to a saint are answered with a miracle, it is not the saint who *makes* the miracle. The saint, who is close to God, can only *intercede* on behalf of the supplicant; in the final analysis, it is God who creates the miracle.[149] Neither of these assumptions—that wondrous occurrences involved the intercession of a force outside of Nature, or that all miracles could ultimately be traced to a single source—hold true for Buddhism.[150]

Lamotte focused most of his attention on Indian Buddhism. When discussing the Chinese world view distinct from Indian influences, Joseph Needham expressed a similar discomfort with the term "supernatural." "It should be noted," Needham states, "that for the characteristic and instinctive Chinese world view in all ages there could be nothing supernatural sensu stricto. Invisible principles, spirits, gods and demons, queer manifestations, were all just as much part of Nature as man himself, though rarely met with and hard to investigate."[151]

The conjunction of Chinese and Buddhist beliefs meant that for Chinese Buddhists, Buddhism fell within the purview of Nature. Although Buddhist cosmology and ideas of karma and reincarnation were invoked to explain the workings of Nature, the idea that one could overstep the boundaries of Nature was not entertained. Hence, in an addendum to a biography describing the persecution of Buddhism in the 840s, Zanning could comment that the teachings of Buddhism were themselves "conditioned elements" and consequently subject to the inevitable progression through the "four states" (*sixiang*) of birth, stasis, decay, and death.[152]

One doubts whether abstract theories of the nature of miracles held sway with the average Christian; in, say, medieval France, when a peasant prayed to a saint for a miracle, he or she doubtless believed that the saint himself had the power to effect it and that miracles could come from any number of sources. Nevertheless, the relevance of the theological position to the Church as a whole becomes important when we examine the use of the English word "magic." For many Christians, since God created the universe, any attempt to alter the universe by unnatural means was seen as wrong, as an abrogation of authority.[153] As we have seen, the Chinese definition of "magic," or "sorcery," was based more on the intention of the practitioner than on the act itself. This difference stems in part from a difference in interpretation of the relationship between miracles and Nature. Unlike the Judeo-Christian model of miracles based on the notion of the supernatural, the Chinese model for miracles was based instead on the idea of "resonance."

Resonance

The *Song Biographies* recount the story of the efforts of the eighth-century monk Sengjie to build a monastery that was to include a pavilion near water's edge.

When it was decided to build the pavilion by the water, Sengjie worried that living creatures would be harmed in the process and so he erected a sanctum and held rituals for three days, warning the many-legged and no-legged creatures to move clear so that the construction of the holy site would not result in disaster. Let it be known that *supreme sincerity evokes resonance*, for a sign was made manifest, demonstrating that his efforts had not been in vain: when [the workmen] dug into the ground and reached the spring, not a single insect was seen.[154]

The phrase "supreme sincerity evokes resonance," a paraphrase of a passage from the *Book of Documents*,[155] occurs with regularity in the *Biographies* to describe the responses of animals, plants, spirits, and people to the holy monks with whom they came into contact.

A similar expression, *ganying*, variously translated as "stimulus and response" or as "resonance," is also frequently invoked to describe miracles associated with eminent monks. We read, for example, of the miracles at the site of the corpse of the thaumaturge Housenghui. As the monk had once asked a villager for a pair of straw sandals, after his death, the local people would make offerings of straw sandals at his tomb. These offerings, we are told, evoked much "resonance," that is, miracles.[156]

There is nothing distinctly Buddhist in the idea of resonance, and by the end of the Han it had become a part of the general Chinese heritage rather than a proposition of a given school of thought.[157] Indeed, a number of the biographies relate stories of monks who evoke miracles through the "resonance of their filial devotion" (*xiaogan*)—returning sight to a blind mother, or miraculously finding a father's bones on an immense battlefield—rather than, say, through the use of a Buddhist spell, or the assistance of a Buddhist deity.[158] In post-Han China, the ability to "stimulate resonance" had become a requirement of any holy figure, Buddhist or otherwise.

One of the clearest expositions of resonance in this technical sense is in the *Huainanzi*, which illustrates the concept with the musical example of sympathetic resonance. "When the lute-tuner strikes the *gong* note [on one instrument], the *gong* note [on the other instrument] responds; when he plucks the *jiao* note [on one instrument], the *jiao* note [on the other instrument] vibrates. This results from having corresponding musical notes in mutual harmony."[159] In the same way, when a sage appears, one can expect a spontaneous, correlative response from Nature, whether it be changes in the weather, new configurations of the stars, or the appearance of prodigious plants and animals.[160]

Correlative thinking and the concern with portends and omens it encouraged were already widespread in the Han before the arrival of Buddhism. Nevertheless, with the arrival of Buddhism, the idea was readily adapted to Buddhist literature. After all, even according to Indian sources, the death of the Buddha was accompanied by spontaneous changes in Nature. On the death of the famous translator and pilgrim Xuanzang, it was said that white arcs of light stretched across the sky, just as had happened at the Buddha's Nirvana.[161] The arcs of light were not the work of the Buddha, nor were they the work of spirits or other beings; they were a direct, spontaneous response of Nature to a significant event. The extension of the musical principle to the religious realm had great explanatory power, and the applicability of indigenous Chinese notions of the miraculous to Buddhist figures seems never to have been questioned.

Huijiao's work is full of examples of monks who evoke miraculous responses from Nature.[162] Whenever Sengye sat down for meditation "a fragrant scent would fill the room."[163] After the cremation of the body of Huishao, a paulawnia tree sprouted up from his ashes.[164] Whenever Shengjin went out alone, blue horses would walk beside him "like guards,"[165] and so on. We also find in the *Liang Biographies* two examples of what would later become a common motif in the *Biographies*: the miraculous birth. Xuangao's mother had a marvelous dream presaging her son's birth, and at the moment of delivery the room filled with a fragrant scent and a brilliant light.[166] Yet Huijiao seems to have taken such occurrences for granted. He notes these miraculous responses of Nature in passing like a modern biographer notes his subject's academic awards and honors. As Huijiao says in the introduction to his work, "In selection for inclusion in the present work, we insist that the monk in question has achieved a level of transcendence. If there is a monk who has a small degree of resonant power (*tonggan*), then we append his biography to the end of [one of the main] biographies."[167]

With the compilation of the *Further Biographies*, however, the subject of resonance found a connoisseur of the miraculous in the person of Daoxuan. In addition to his voluminous historical works and his writings on the Vinaya, Daoxuan also compiled two fascinating works dealing with the miraculous. The first, the *Record of Spiritual Resonance Associated with the Three Jewels in China*,[168] is a collection of miracle stories. The second, posthumously entitled the *Record of Spiritual Resonance of Master of the Regulations Daoxuan*,[169] records a series of interviews Daoxuan himself claimed to have conducted with spirits. Daoxuan's fascination with such matters is also apparent in the *Further Biographies* in which he devotes an entire chapter to miracles.[170] In the chapter, the *Gantong pian*, Daoxuan recounts dozens of miracles associated with Sui Wen Di's policy in the first years of the seventh century of distributing relics throughout the empire. Typically, when a monk had escorted a relic to a stupa in a given district on imperial orders, the consecration was accompanied by strange and wondrous sights, which Daoxuan duly recorded. In large measure, it is these miracles rather than the monks connected with the relics that are the focus of these biographies.[171] To make way for these biographies, Daoxuan departed from Huijiao's schema, calling his chapter "Spiritual Resonance" (*gantong*) rather than "Divine Marvels" (*shen-yi*), a chapter that for Huijiao was devoted to monks with spiritual powers rather than to monks who evoked spontaneous responses from Nature.[172]

Zanning followed Daoxuan's division, also titling one of the chapters of the *Song Biographies* "Spiritual Resonance" rather than "Divine Marvels." As Zanning explains it, Huijiao's chapter was reserved only for monks of the highest attainments. "As modest omens and marvels of a lower grade could not possibly have been collected in full, such accounts were left out of the book." Zanning then goes on to praise Daoxuan's schema, based, he tells us, on the expression "when stimulated [*gan*], it penetrates [*tong*]." The monks described in the chapter, Zanning continues, "penetrate, and attain the nature of wisdom; they cultivate, and attain 'stimulation.' Supernormal powers [*tong*] are the fruits [of their cultivation]." Finally, after comparing Daoxuan to the great Han historian Ban Gu who introduced innovations to the historical format developed by Sima Qian, Zanning concludes that Daoxuan "was like the sages who valued the hexagrams. Did not they also add to the original lines? This being so, if they had not first 'looked upward' and 'looked downward' how could they later have penetrated [and elicited] transformations?"[173]

Here Zanning, like Daoxuan before him, bases his understanding of resonance on the "Great Treatise" of the *Book of Changes*,[174] a philosophical treatise attributed to Confucius but probably composed in the second or third century B.C.[175] Indeed the very expression *gantong* is taken from the quotation from the "Great Treatise" cited above: "When stimulated [*gan*], it penetrates [*tong*]."[176] Likewise, when Zanning refers to "the sages who valued the hexagrams," he alludes to a passage in the "Great Treatise": "[To establish the technique of the *Change*, sages] looked upward to observe the markings in the heavens and looked downward to examine the patterns on the earth; in consequence of this, [the *Change* and the superior man] know the causes of what is obscure and what is obvious."[177] In other words, the sages of antiquity who compiled the *Book of Changes* did so after discerning patterns in natural phenomena that allowed them to understand the workings of the universe. By casting Daoxuan (and by extension, him-self) in the same role as the sages who composed the *Changes*, Zan-ning places himself and Daoxuan before him in a long and reputable Chinese tradition of scholars concerned with the nature of the cosmos. In consciously applying themselves to the enterprise of collect-ing and evaluating accounts of miracles, Daoxuan and Zanning were attempting not only to propagate Buddhism and prove the truth of its claims; they were also engaged in the enterprise of uncovering the nature of miracles, the mechanism of the numinous.

Daoxuan and Zanning saw no conflict between ideas associated with the *Book of Changes* and Buddhism; the two were complemen-tary. In the treatise to his chapter on resonance, Daoxuan laments that while the Chinese prognosticators of the past knew something of deter-mining fate, they did not understand the principle on which fate is based, namely, karma. Daoxuan then goes one step further, stating that not only is fate tied to karma, but further, karma is tied to the mind.[178] Here we reach a level of abstraction that, though useful for determining Daoxuan's understanding of destiny, is less helpful for interpreting the biographies he purports to explain.

While we can assume that most Chinese took the concept of spiri-tual resonance for granted, many were left unconvinced by arguments like these for the role of Buddhism in this mechanism. For example, in an attempt to determine whether or not the prominent monk Falin could "resonate" with Guanyin, Emperor Tang Taizong is said to have given the monk seven days to pray to Guanyin for rescue, after which time, if no response ensued, he was to be executed. Falin deftly avoided the test, saying cleverly that in this instance it was more proper for him to pray to the emperor than to pray to the bodhisattva.[179] In a similar test, according to the *Shishuo xinyu*, when the son of Buddhist layman Ruan Yu took ill, Ruan "prayed on his behalf to the Three [Jewels] (the Buddha, the [Law], and the Saṅgha), not slackening by day or by night, for he felt that *if his utmost sincerity had any power to move*, he would surely receive help. But in the end the child did not recover, whereupon Ruan bound himself to an external hatred of the Buddha, and all the devotion of his present and past lifetimes was totally wiped out."[180]

Monks and the Spirit-World

As in these last two examples, Buddhist miracles were usually associ-ated with Buddhist "agents," Buddhas, bodhisattvas, and so on. In the first example, the emperor tested Falin by asking him to pray to the bodhisattva Guanyin. In the second example, layman Ruan appealed to a wider array of agents by praying to the "Three Jewels." While the

Biographies are of only limited value for telling us which deities were important for Buddhist laypeople, they do give us a good idea of which deities—from Buddhas, to local gods—were most important for monks. But before returning to the biographies themselves, we need to look at one more abstract theory, the source of some of the most erudite and difficult discussion in Buddhist literature: the theory of the different "bodies" of a Buddha.

While there were a number of different theories attempting to delineate the different aspects, or "bodies," of a Buddha, the most commonly held theory in China maintained that a Buddha exists in three different aspects. At the highest level, a Buddha exists in a "Body of the Law" (*fashen*). This is the Buddha as Absolute, a transcendent and ineffable state. Little can be said about this aspect of the Buddha—an abstract entity, by definition beyond definition. Buddhas were also said to exist in a more concrete though exceedingly marvelous state known as the "Reward Body" (*baoshen*). In China, the most famous example of a Buddha in this state is Amitābha, who dwells in his Pure-Land, appearing to the inhabitants there as a spectacular, dazzling being. Finally, Buddhas of the past like Śākyamuni appeared in roughly human shape in the "Response Body" (*yingshen*, var. *huashen*).[181]

The three-body theory is mirrored in references to Buddhas in the hagiography. "Response Body" Buddhas play a very minor role in the biographies. While archaeological and textual evidence demonstrates that there were many images of Śākyamuni, Śākyamuni is never cited as the source of a miracle. There is a story in the *Song Biographies* of the monk Shaokang who at the age of seven spoke his first word, "Śākyamuni," when excitedly spotting an image of the Buddha on a visit to a monastery with his mother on the Buddha's birthday.[182] But the incident is not accompanied by a miracle. Indeed, there is no sense of Śākyamuni being *present* in the image at all; the emphasis of the story is on the boy's recognition. The same is true of the next "historical" Buddha, Maitreya, the Buddha to come, who is connected with only one miracle in all of the biographies.[183] Amitābha, representative of the "Reward Body," also plays only a minor, tangential role in the *Biographies*, occasionally appearing in visions to dying monks destined for rebirth in his Pure Land. Daoxuan states in his *Record of Resonance* that the Body of the Law and the Reward Body cannot be seen by humans; only the Response Body appears in the world.

Nevertheless, Daoxuan suggests that the numinous abstraction known as the Body of the Law does make itself manifest in various forms at various times.[184] Similarly, there are a few scattered references in the Liang and Song biographies of resonance issuing from the Body of the Law.[185] But aside from these poetic allusions, glorifying this most abstract of concepts, the Body of the Law is hardly mentioned. In sum, in the *Biographies*, past, future, and cosmological Buddhas have little to do with miracles; monks may long for the glorious days when Śākyamuni walked the Earth, anxiously await the coming of Maitreya, or look forward to a future life in the presence of Amitābha, but for the present life, monks looked to deities of a less imposing nature.

In his studies of religion in Sri Lanka, Edmund Leach noted the need in Sri Lankan religion for mediators, middling deities bridging the gap between the individual and the most powerful gods. Extrapolating from the local scene, Leach went on to make up a simple chart illustrating a basic structure underlying Hindu, Buddhist, and Christian pantheons. For all three religions it is possible to make basic distinctions between "great gods" (Viṣṇu, God the Father, Buddha) who are ultimate sources of power, and "mediators" (Gaṇeśa, Jesus) who render the great gods more accessible to the faithful.[186] Once recognized, the phenomenon seems so prevalent as to be obvious. In Mahāyāna Buddhism, the most important mediators are bodhisattvas, spectacular beings who, though capable of leaving the world, remain in it for the sake of ordinary people. Unlike the Buddhas, bodhisattvas are very much present in the *Biographies*, central figures in the stories of holy monks who were themselves mediators between the mundane and the numinous.

The most popular bodhisattva in the *Biographies*—especially in the *Liang Biographies* and the *Further Biographies*—is Guanyin (var. Guanshiyin, Skt. Avalokiteśvara).[187] In the *Biographies*, Guanyin often serves as the vehicle for monastic miracles. And as in the case of spells, many of these miracles involve illnesses. *The Liang Biographies* relates the story of the monk Zhu Fayi who in 372 suddenly took ill. "He then constantly recited [the name] Guanyin, whereupon he saw in a dream a man who opened his stomach and washed his intestines. When he awoke, he had recovered from the illness."[188] When the mother of the sixth-century monk Zhiqin took ill, he chanted the name of Guanyin, whereupon "Buddhas appeared on the leaves of the trees in their courtyard. Everyone in the family saw them, and the mother's illness was cured."[189]

The ability to cure illness was attributed to all manner of deities, but there are other themes in the *Biographies* associated especially with Guanyin. One of these is Guanyin's penchant for freeing monks from fetters. The monk Chaoda, for example, was falsely imprisoned under charges of possessing seditious charts and prognostications (of the fall of the throne). Imprisoned and placed in stocks, the hapless monk chanted the name of Guanyin, whereupon his fetters fell to the ground.[190] In a related theme Guanyin saves the monk Fali. In the story, after he is captured by bandits who bind him to a tree, Fali can only chant the name of Guanyin and await a certain death. But when the bandits attempt to kill him, their swords cannot so much as scratch him. The astonished bandits flee in terror, and Fali is saved.[191] Finally, already in the *Further Biographies* we see Guanyin respond to a woman's prayers for a child.[192]

All of these themes can be traced back to the twenty-fifth chapter of the *Lotus Sūtra*, one of the most popular chapters of the book. The long list of saving deeds attributed to Guanyin in the chapter include the very themes mentioned most frequently in the *Biographies*. "Even if there is a man, whether guilty or guiltless, whose body is fettered with stocks, pillory, or chains, if he calls upon the name of the bodhisattva He Who Observes the Sounds of the World [Guanshiyin], they shall all be severed and broken, and he shall straightway gain deliverance."[193] "If, again, a man who is about to be murdered calls upon the name of the bodhisattva He Who Observes the Sounds of the World, then the knives and staves borne by the other fellow shall be broken in pieces, and the man shall gain deliverance."[194] "If there is a woman, and if she is desirous and hopeful of having a son, making worshipful offerings to the bodhisattva He Who Observes the Sounds of the World, she shall straightway bear a son of happiness, excellence, and wisdom."[195] The connection between the book and the belief in the saving powers of Guanyin is made explicit in biographies like that of Daojiong, a monk known for chanting the *Lotus* who turns immediately to Guanyin when he finds himself lost and alone in a cave.[196]

In addition to the direct correlations between the stories in the *Biographies* and the injunctions in the twenty-fifth chapter of the *Lotus*, the popularity of the Guanyin chapter is attested by the continued circulation of the chapter independent of the sutra as a whole,[197] and by depictions of the chapter in Dunhuang murals.[198] A more direct source of material for the *Biographies* was a series of Chinese collections of stories compiled from the fifth through the sixth centuries, relating tales of the miraculous interventions of Guanyin.[199] At one point in the *Further Biographies*, after relating stories of monks saved from fire and bandits, Daoxuan notes, "The *Accounts of the Miracles of Guanyin* circulates independently. It is a more inclusive and expansive text, so we do not here relate [these stories] in more detail."[200]

The combination of scriptural sources, hagiography, and iconography made Guanyin by far the most popular Buddhist deity in China, at least until the Tang. The superiority accorded Guanyin is testified in the biography of the sixth-century monk Daotai. When Daotai takes ill, a friend tells him, "I have heard that chanting the name of Guanyin once is equal to worshiping all of the six million, two hundred thousand bodhisattvas." When Daotai appeals to Guanyin, sure enough, his illness is cured by morning.[201]

In later biographies, however, in addition to stories of the miracles of Guanyin, we also see the rise in popularity of the bodhisattva Mañjuśrī. In the early biographies, part of the appeal of Guanyin is his ubiquity; he can be called upon anywhere and at anytime. Mañjuśrī, on the other hand, came to be associated with a specific place: Mount Wutai. The cult to Mañjuśrī at Wutai may go back as far as the fourth century,[202] and according to later sources, received imperial support during the reign of Xiao Wen Di in the late fifth century.[203] From this time forward the cult gained in prominence, eventually becoming the premiere Buddhist pilgrimage site in all of China, depicted in the Dunhuang caves, and attracting pilgrims from as far away as Tibet.

The scriptural justification for the claim that Mañjuśrī lived on Wutai is echoed in the biography of the early seventh-century monk Tanyun who made the pilgrimage to Wutai after hearing that "Mount Wutai is the Qingliang Mountain of the *Flower Adornment Scripture*. According to tradition, this is the place in which Mañjuśrī lives. From ancient times monks have gone there to make supplications [to the bodhisattva]."[204] The passage to which Tanyun alludes is found in a chapter of the *Flower Adornment* that enumerates the (mythical) dwelling places of various bodhisattvas of different directions. In the middle of this long list is the passage, "In the Northeast there is a dwelling place of bodhisattvas known as Mount Qingliang ('Cold Mountain'). In the past, various bodhisattvas stayed there. A bodhisattva named Mañjuśrī appears there, accompanied by a myriad of other bodhisattvas for whom he preaches on the Law."[205] Because of the location (Northeast) given for the mountain, and perhaps because of the name as well (Wutai is indeed a "cold mountain"), Qingliang was identified with Wutai.

Before the rise of Wutai as a pilgrimage site, Mañjuśrī was known in China as a central figure in the *Vimalakīrti Sūtra*. Nevertheless, Mañjuśrī is not so much as mentioned in the *Liang Biographies*; it was the notion of a very tangible presence of the deity in a specific place in China that captured the imagination of monks and hagiographers. In the biography of Wuran—the monk who eventually burned himself to death after having a vision of Mañjuśrī—we have seen an example of the sort of encounter with Mañjuśrī common in the *Biographies*. The earliest example of this motif in the *Biographies* is found in the biography of the monk Sengming who claimed to have traveled to Wutai in search of Mañjuśrī in 578. In a stone valley, he comes across a stone mortar and wooden pestle, beside which sit two mysterious large men with long eyebrows who cast no shadows. The men lead the monk to a marvelous hall filled with people talking and laughing. After staying for a while, Sengming is escorted from the hall and returns home.[206]

Word that Mañjuśrī appeared to sincere and faithful monks on Mount Wutai quickly spread throughout China and beyond, drawing monks to the mountain in search of visions and spawning a plethora of accounts of encounters with the bodhisattva. *The Song Biographies* contains a dozen such stories, the most famous of which is that of Buddhapāli who after meeting Mañjuśrī stayed on with the bodhisattva and was reported to have been seen there close to a hundred years later.[207]

The success of the Mañjuśrī cult at Wutai inspired a similar cult of the bodhisattva Samantabhadra (Ch. Puxian) at Mount Emei in present-day Sichuan. If the biographies are any indication, the Samantabhadra cult came to prominence in the late Tang. Neither the *Liang* nor *Further Biographies* mention Emei in connection with Samantabhadra; when monks traveled to Emei at that time, they did so for the scenery.[208] Even in the *Song Biographies* we only see mention of the Emei cult in the biography of Xingming, a monk who lived at the end of the Tang. In this biography, Mañjuśrī "living in his golden world" on Wutai is paired with Samantabhadra who lives in a "silver world" on Emei.[209] Just as in the case of Mañjuśrī, scriptural justification for placing Samantabhadra at Emei was found in a passage in the *Flower Adornment*.[210] By the end of the tenth century when the *Song Biographies* were compiled, Zanning felt compelled to explain the appearance of an incarnation of Samantabhadra at Wutai. He explains that Samantabhadra was not encroaching on Mañjuśrī's territory, for "the holy ones are not guided by [delusions of] the self."[211] Eventually a home was found for Guanyin as well on a mountain in present-day Zhejiang Province.[212]

Why did monks feel the need to localize these deities? Part of the answer is of course that monks were the beneficiaries of pilgrimage sites. Mountains like Wutai and Emei became major Buddhist centers and important sources of prestige and financial support. Elaborate monasteries staffed with hundreds of monks were maintained in the stunningly beautiful surroundings of Emei and Wutai in part through the donations of pilgrims, but more significantly through imperial gifts. Just as important, however, the existence of well-run monasteries within the holy dwelling places of the bodhisattvas validated the monastic way of life. When Mañjuśrī was sighted on the mountain, it was often in the form of a monk, living in a monastery. Monks were somehow closer to Mañjuśrī than ordinary people; others came and went, but the monks of Wutai and Emei had a sense that they lived in a holy realm, separate from the world below.

Whether the ubiquitous Guanyin or bodhisattvas of specific locales, these deities were incontrovertible evidence of the resonance eminent monks inspire. Just as an accomplished monk may cause a plum tree to sprout and blossom in his courtyard,[213] the sincerity of a great monk causes the bodhisattvas to come to his assistance. Even more prevalent in the *Biographies* are stories of spirits or "gods" (*shen*) who cannot help but react to the character and actions of lofty monks. As Zanning put it, "Extreme suffering moves the spirits; perfect concentration shakes heaven and earth. In the world of men, these are difficult accomplishments indeed!"[214]

Of course, such "difficult accomplishments" are commonplace among the eminent monks of the *Biographies*. When a monk skilled in chanting intoned the scriptures, celestial beings were said to flock to listen to his hymns.[215] When Hongju chanted scriptures at night, spirits came to assist him. "Some would light the lamps for him, while others replenished the incense."[216] When Quanzai left his mountain dwelling, spirits served him, "some sweeping the road before him, while others attended on him at his side; some drew water for him, while others supplied him with fresh-picked fruit. People frequently saw the spirits, but Quanzai never spoke of them."[217] The spirits assist the monks in more substantial ways: supplying wood for the construction of monasteries, causing floodwaters to recede, and wreaking vengeance on those who abuse members of the *saṅgha*.[218]

Unlike the ghosts and phantoms of the *zhiguai* genre who relate long, sad stories of dissolute lives and cruel injustice, the spirits of the *Biographies of Eminent Monks* remain for the most part one-dimensional stock characters; the focus of the biographies is, after all, on monks and not the spirits who serve them.[219] Nevertheless, occasional chance references suggest that sophisticated monks did in fact have full and complicated pictures of the lives of the spirits. In general the spirits were thought of as ghosts, for they had at one time lived as men. In one story a spirit appears to the Tang monk Daoying and identifies himself as Prince Zhuangxiang, a minister who lived during the Warring States period. The prince asks Daoying for a meal, stating that he has not eaten in eighty years. He complains that he has suffered a cruel fate in the afterworld in part because in his day Buddhism had not yet come to China and he could only cultivate merit through tolerance and pardon, rather than through Buddhist rites of confession.[220]

In Daoxuan's *Record of Resonance*, Daoxuan asks the spirits he encounters to tell him their origins. One who speaks with a Sichuan

(Shu) accent tells of his life as a Chinese official, while another relates the story of his life in ancient India.[221] In a typically learned note to one of the accounts in the *Song Biographies*, Zanning comments that "ghosts and spirits consume sacrificial offerings; as these beings are physically impeded, they can only use that which has been transformed by fire. When something as gorgeous and spectacular as a stupa or monastery is burned, much of it is consumed by ghosts and spirits."[222] From passages such as these it is clear that monks like Daoxuan and Zanning had thought about the world of the spirits and considered them a suitable topic for scholastic speculation.

Not all of the spirit stories, however, were the products of erudite speculation, or even a general interest in the marvelous. More than an attempt to represent or shape the imagination, many of the stories reflect very real struggles for adherents and resources. There are dozens of stories in the *Biographies* of monks who journey into a new area in which the local inhabitants worship a local god. If in a mountain, the god usually acknowledges the superiority of the monk and relinquishes the cave to the monk, at the same time asking to hear a sermon on the Law, or better yet, to receive the precepts from the monk.[223] Rolf Stein has demonstrated that for much of Daoist history, the most intense religious struggle was not between Daoist priests and Buddhist monks, but between Daoists and local cults.[224] The same was true for Buddhism; away from the capital, monks were at least as if not more concerned with cults to local deities than they were with rival Daoists.

In the *Song Biographies*, for example, the Tang monk Huiming castigates a local god for receiving animal sacrifices. The sheepish deity appears soon thereafter, repenting of the practice, asking to receive the bodhisattva precepts, and offering to give over his temple to the monk.[225] The violence of these encounters between established cults and righteous monks is hinted at in the biography of the Chan monk Xiqian in which Xiqian arrives in a village and discovers that the villagers "show great respect for ghosts and spirits, offering many lascivious sacrifices." As in similar Daoist texts, "lascivious sacrifices" (*yinsi*) refers to offerings of animal flesh and wine. Xiqian promptly destroys the local shrines and leads away the oxen that had been prepared for sacrifice.[226]

A part of this ongoing battle was to convince potential patrons of the superiority of Buddhism to local gods, an enterprise in which narratives such as these played an important role. We read, for instance, of a family that is haunted by ghosts after converting to Buddhism and halting its customary offerings at a local temple. The family then calls in the monk Sengrong who temporarily dispels the ghosts by chanting scriptures. When the ghosts come after the monk together with a demonic army, he chants the name of Guanyin, where-upon an enormous deity appears and crushes the demon troops.[227]

The *Biographies* also disclose, however, that more than a struggle for the hearts of local inhabitants, the struggle was also over land, buildings, and precious metal. The *Liang Biographies* relates the story of an enterprising monk named Sengliang. After vowing to construct a huge Buddha image, Sengliang was in need of bronze. He had heard of a large temple to the god Wuzixu, frequented by "southern barbarians" and containing many bronze objects. Sengliang eventually convinces a hesitant local official to loan him ten boats and a hundred men to retrieve the bronze. After a brief encounter with a serpent, which Sengliang dispatches with a spell, a spirit greets the monk and agrees to give over all of the objects in the temple with the exception of one small basin.[228]

Once collected in the *Biographies of Eminent Monks*, stories like these served as justification (if any was needed) for taking over local shrines in the name of the Dharma. But assuming that many of the stories in the *Biographies* represent only one recension of stories that circulated in many forms, including oral tales, the accounts were likely also used for purposes of persuasion, in the hopes that when monks arrived at such temples they would be greeted, if not by subservient gods, then at least by cooperative patrons.

Much of the preceding discussion has focused on the *Biographies* as an expression of monastic ideas: conceptions of the nature of miracles, Buddhas, bodhisattvas, and spirits. On the basis of the *Biographies* alone it is impossible to say to what extent these ideas spread beyond monastic circles. The notion of spiritual resonance (*ganying*) seems to have been common in one form or another to all levels of Chinese society. And while it is unlikely that the average peasant was interested in the distinction between a Buddha, a bodhisattva, and a Buddhist spirit, it was enough to know that these deities existed and that monks could mediate for them. This is ultimately the message that stories of thaumaturgy in the *Biographies* convey: the monks they portray inhabit the region between this and the other world. As Zanning put it, "Those who encounter transcendent beings are themselves transcendent beings."[229] Surely the point was not lost on those who read and heard these stories. That is, in addition to its value in the economy of the imagination, resonance was important cultural capital.

Conclusion

In many respects, the image of the thaumaturge presented in the *Biographies* is that of a technician or specialist. Just as an official was one trained in the use of formalized language, bureaucratic decorum, literature, and calligraphy, the accomplished monk was expected to have mastered a series of techniques—fortune-telling skills, spell-casting, meditation—and a body of knowledge, especially knowledge about the spirit-world. Like the skills of the literati, the efficacy of these fields of knowledge and practice was for the most part taken for granted. While one might question a particular monk's abilities, the average person would no more challenge the efficacy of spells against certain types of illness than he would the need for proper literary form when submitting an appeal to a local magistrate.

In general these abilities were linked to the perceived alien character of the monk. This point is particularly evident in the case of spells, in that in the early biographies monks reputed to have mastered spells were almost always foreigners. Later, the thaumaturge was often associated with enigmatic foreign texts or the ability to recite foreign words. In the first chapter I discussed the ways in which all monks were separated from the rest of society through their clothing, diet, and day-to-day behavior. This general air of distinctiveness also contributed to the perception of monks as wonder-workers possessed of methods and expertise in what was broadly understood as the spiritual realm. Anthropologists are sensitive to the problem of exoticising magic in foreign cultures, of taking for exceptional something that the actors themselves think of as commonplace.[230] But in the case of Buddhism in medieval China, there is a danger of making a mistake in the opposite direction; Buddhist knowledge and many Buddhist monks were regarded as exotic in China, and this very exoticism contributed to their success.

Just as the literatus was thought to possess the "qualities of a gentleman" distinct from learned skills, the thaumaturge was not only an expert in a given area of knowledge; he also possessed a certain intangible quality that could not be traced to training in meditation or spell manuals. This quality of the thaumaturge resembles what social theorist Lucien Lévy-Bruhl termed "participation": when he evokes miracles, the thaumaturge does not so much manipulate Nature as actively participate in its workings.[231] This notion, which Erik Zürcher links especially to religious Daoism, is implicit in most of the accounts of miracles in the *Biographies*.[232] The union between monk and Nature is at times explicit, as in the following reference in the *Song Biographies* to the monk Yishi: "When his face was dirty he did not wash it [for long stretches of time]. When he did wash, clouds would form and rain would fall. The people of Wu foretold [the weather] by this."[233] Yishi had reached a stage of attainment in which he himself was not even aware of the influences his power exerted. Similarly, also in the *Song Biographies*, the monk Sengqie notices that after a lightening storm, tiny streaking veins appeared on one of his fingers.[234] Monks such as these did not simply influence Nature any more than clouds "influence" rain. Rather, they were participants in its transformations.

The *Biographies* were not only reflections of shared perceptions of the monk; they were also an attempt to shape opinion, to instill a particular set of monastic ideals. In each of the sections of this chapter we have seen how the hagiographers employed thaumaturgical powers as a part of a subtle rhetorical strategy. Attention is drawn to a monk's powers only to be dismissed as a matter of little consequence. The ability to read minds or travel at fantastic speeds is mere child's play—the consequence of attainments in meditation and, for an accomplished monk, nothing surprising. The ability to see into the future, manipulate water with spells, or command members of the spirit-world are similarly brushed aside in a manner so matter-of-fact as to be conspicuous. On occasion the goal is to direct our attention away from wonder-working and towards meditation or scripture. More often we are left only with a vague sense that eminent monks possessing supernormal powers were ultimately interested in higher things.

But these disingenuous injunctions to ignore what the stories themselves present so dramatically, in the final analysis, carry little weight. The need to present such stories as a "hook" for drawing attention to more stolid monastic concerns reflects a fascination with thaumaturgy among the readers of the *Biographies*; in addition one suspects that even the hagiographers themselves dismissed such powers in word alone. When Holmes Welch interviewed Chinese monks in the early part of this century, asking them why they had entered the clergy, one monk replied frankly that he wished to obtain supernormal powers.[235] Given the rich Buddhist lore in China of wonder-workers, spells, and prophecy, one is hard-pressed to find a more compelling reason to "leave the home" and embark on the distinctive life of the Buddhist monk.[236]

CHAPTER 3

Scholarship

THE ENORMOUS CORPUS of Buddhist writings on metaphysics, ethics, ritual, and history testifies to the vibrancy of Buddhist scholarship in China during the medieval period. Indeed, many if not most important thinkers in medieval China were monks. While biographies can help us sketch out the broadest outlines of the ideas of leading monks like Fazang or Kuiji, hagiography is extremely limited in this respect: detailed exposition on the relationship between conventional and ultimate truth or on the implications of the idea of the Buddha-Nature for practice are not the stuff of stories. Biographies of monks can, however, tell us something about the context in which such ideas were formulated and discussed. Did monks exchange ideas in open, critical debate? How were young monks trained? By what standards was intellect judged? To what extent was erudite scholarship valued, and to what extent was it held in suspicion? In short, what precisely was meant when a monk was referred to as "brilliant" or as possessing a "keen intellect?"

The Monk-Scholar

Before the arrival of Buddhism in China, Chinese scholarly ideals for the most part allowed for two different types of scholars: the this-worldly scholar who applied himself to affairs of state and the imposition of proper ceremony and decorum on himself and his environs; and the hermit who removed himself from polite society, explicitly rejecting public office and conventional rites, devoting himself instead to private study and self-cultivation.[1] The relationship between these two ideals was complex. To a large extent, the scholar-official defined himself in opposition not to the hermit, but to the barbarian, someone either ignorant of the proper rites or morally incapable of putting them into effect. The scholar-official's attitude toward those who, often for the loftiest of reasons, rejected these values and chose instead the life of the hermit, was more ambiguous. Rather than attack the hermit, the scholar-official preferred to quietly distance himself from him. The values of the hermit, on the other hand, depended on those of the scholar-official. One cannot decline an office unless it is offered; one cannot spurn conventional decorum unless one knows what it is.

Similarly, the ideals of the scholar-monk were closely tied to those of secular literati. Certainly the scholar-monk's vocation demanded that he be versed in the Buddhist scriptures, but this was not enough. He was also expected to have mastered the Chinese classics, even if only to lament their limitations; to do anything less was to be less than literate. As we have seen, both the Buddhist ascetic and the Buddhist thaumaturge drew on long-standing Chinese traditions. But the monk-scholar is a more extreme case; it was necessary for these monks to prove that their respect for Buddhist knowledge was born of a thorough understanding of Chinese learning and a consequent recognition of its shortcomings.

Take for example the case of the great fourth-century monk Sengzhao. Even a cursory glance at Sengzhao's writings reveals a mind steeped in the Chinese classics; Sengzhao is justly famous for his deft use of the vocabulary of philosophical Daoism to discuss Buddhist ideas. Hence it is no surprise that Sengzhao's biography emphasizes his training in the traditional fields of Chinese scholarship. Sengzhao, we are told, "came from a poor family that practiced the profession of the clerk. And so Sengzhao worked for his living as an amanuensis, during which time he read through the classics and the histories, completely exhausting the great writings of the past. He dearly loved [works that embodied] the profound and subtle, taking the *Zhuangzi* and *Laozi* as the most essential." Having established the monk's facility with these writings, the biography then turns to his discovery of Buddhism. Once, while reading the *Laozi*, Sengzhao suddenly exclaimed, "Yes it is beautiful, but what of it? When I search for the means to put my spirit to rest and lighten the burden of death, the text falls short." Only later, while reading the *Vimalakīrti* did Sengzhao find what he was looking for, exclaiming, "Only now have I found something on which I can rely." After that he became a monk and began to systematically study the Buddhist scriptures.[2]

In the *Biographies*, the relationship between Buddhist and Chinese learning is not always so explicit. Chinese learning was not simply a tool for understanding or propagating Buddhism, nor was it merely a foil for extolling the even greater profundity of Buddhist doctrine; as a part of literati culture, knowledge of Chinese history, poetry, and the classics was admired in and of itself. The biography of Daoan, for instance, recounts an incident in which the scholars of the capital were baffled by the inscription on a large bell unearthed in a nearby district. Only Daoan was able to decipher the inscription and identify the bell as a Han artifact. After this, we are told, whenever scholars had questions on matters Buddhist *or non-Buddhist*, they brought their questions to Daoan.[3] Similarly, the *Biographies* are careful to mention whether a monk could boast a lay background that included success in the civil-service examination. Lingtan, for instance, is touted as a child prodigy who passed the "children's examination" (*tongziju*) and took up an official post as a teenager before eventually deciding to abandon his position and enter the clergy.[4]

The Tang state eventually established a separate examination for those who wished to become monks, an act that one would think would have provided monks with a means of intellectual legitimation separate from the secular system. In the new system, a candidate for the clergy was required to recite a set number of Buddhist scriptures before being issued an ordination certificate.[5] But this examination was rightly seen as an attempt by the state to limit and control the size of the clergy and seems never to have attained the level of prestige among monks that the civil-service examination held for scholar-officials.

Whether or not monks approved of the ordination examination, it did affirm an aspect of Buddhist scholarship that few would deny: the importance accorded memorization. The most famous story of memorization in the *Biographies* is that of Daoan who already at the age of seven was said to be able to recite any book after two readings, an ability that won him the admiration of his village. Daoan became a novice monk at the age of twelve, but because he was an ugly child, his master thought little of him and dispatched him to work in the fields. After several years of labor, Daoan asked his master for a scripture, whereupon the monk gave him a copy of the *Bianyi Scripture*, a short work in five thousand characters.[6] That evening, when Daoan came in from the fields, he returned the book to his master and asked for another. "You haven't even read the one I gave you yesterday and you want another today?" asked the master. When Daoan replied that he had already memorized the text, the skeptical teacher gave him another. Again, Daoan returned the next evening to ask for another book. This time the master tested the young monk and found to his astonishment that Daoan had indeed memorized both texts. "After this," we are told, the master "administered the complete precepts and allowed Daoan to concentrate on his studies."[7] A similar story is told of the monk Daorong, famous disciple of Kumārajīva, who, at the age of twelve and before becoming a monk, was said to have memorized the Confucian *Analects* in an afternoon.[8]

When the Jesuit missionary Matteo Ricci came to China in the sixteenth century, Chinese literati were especially interested in techniques he had developed for memorization, techniques they hoped to apply to their own studies.[9] Although the examination system was not as important to Chinese officialdom in the medieval period as it later became, great value was placed on memorization nonetheless, and, as in the case of Ricci, one who could rapidly memorize large amounts of material was necessarily accorded a degree of respect, even if he was both a monk and a foreigner. According to the *Liang Biographies*, at the age of fifteen, the Kashmiran monk Buddhayaśas could memorize twenty- to thirty-thousand words a day. Shortly after being summoned to the capital, the red-mustachioed Buddhayaśas chanted from memory the complete *Dharmaguptakavinaya*, an enormous text, on the occasion of the establishment of a new monastery. The ruler Yao Xing, suspecting that the monk's recitation was full of errors, summoned him to the throne, gave him texts in Yao's own language[10] along with medical recipes totaling some fifty-thousand characters, and allowed him two days to memorize them in full. Needless to say, Buddhayaśas returned in two days' time and recited the texts perfectly.[11]

This story illustrates the honor accorded memorization as a skill, distinct from the content of what was being memorized. Certainly, knowledge of the Chinese classics was always taken as a base requirement for literacy, but the ability to memorize texts, whether they were in a foreign language, or medical recipes, or Buddhist books, was seen as a virtue in and of itself. Indeed brute memorization was usually seen as a skill distinct from, though related to, understanding. We read, for example, of Prajñā (Ch. Zhihui), an Indian monk who *in addition to* being able to recite enormous abhidharma texts "*also* understood their meaning."[12] The phrase, "*also* understood their meaning," following a list of texts that a great monk could recite, is common in the *Biographies*. Test or no test, memorization was a clear mark of intelligence, and while a monk who could not memorize rapidly and accurately might accrue a reputation for piety, he would never be considered a great intellect.

If memorization was an important prerequisite to scholarly endeavors, there was certainly more to monastic learning than rote repetition; truly great exegetical monks understood and analyzed what they read. The Tang monk Qianzhen, author of a number of doctrinal tracts, studied and mastered both Buddhist and non-Buddhist writings, "comprehending both the extrinsic and the intrinsic meanings [of

texts]. He examined the opaque and the subtle; he carefully re-
searched teachings and principles. He searched out the depths of wisdom from the present age to the past and compared the familiar with
the unfamiliar. He separated out the different and the similar and
brought them together under one doctrine."[13] Cheng'en, who was "by
nature fond of studying and never neglected the instruction [of his
disciples]," taught his students that "enthusiasm for learning in itself
approaches the meaning of wisdom."[14] In the admittedly formulaic
language of these descriptions, we begin to see the appeal of the life of
the scholar-monk for whom study was a lifelong vocation; not only a
means to an end but also a value in and of itself.

Much of the appeal of Buddhist thought was that it represented a
coherent, comprehensive system of analysis. Most alluring of all in
this respect was the abhidharma literature, comprised of voluminous
texts seemingly subjecting every imaginable question to systematic,
reasoned analysis. These texts speak with mesmerizing authority, responding to the most erudite of questions with meticulous, matter-of-
fact divisions and illustrations. What are the physical attributes of a
bodhisattva? First, the skin is described, then the arms and legs, next
the teeth. The bodhisattva has forty teeth, "no more, no less." The teeth
are neither thick nor thin, neither protrude out of the mouth, nor slant
into the mouth. In fact, the teeth are so uniform that to the human eye
they appear to be one tooth.[15] Human emotions, the cycle of life and
death, and the structure of the cosmos are all treated in this straightforward, confident manner. A mastery of this literature—and by the
mid-Tang so many texts of this kind had been translated that no one
person could master them all—would enable the scholar-monk to speak
on the scriptures and related matters with an easy confidence, to put
facts together "like stringing pearls."[16]

The allure of Buddhist technical literature comes through not only
in the biographies of monks, but also in the manner in which biographies are explained by their compilers. After describing the ability of
the thaumaturge Wanhui to travel great distances in a moment, Zanning carefully cites passages from the technical literature in order to
classify precisely what type of supernormal power Wanhui possessed.[17]
In short, however unsatisfactory and wearying such classifications and
enumerations may seem to us, for the medieval monk these texts provided clear authoritative answers, providing him with a tested, powerful tool for evaluating the seen and unseen world around him.

The quality of a scholar-monk was measured not only by his ability
to memorize or even by his ability to understand; monks were also
attracted to the less tangible, less *Buddhist* mastery of the arts. Any
number of biographies tell of monks skilled in grass or *li* style calligra-

phy. Indeed some, like the Tang monk Huaisu, were among the most refined and influential calligraphers of their time. Some monks may have brought Buddhist sensibilities to their calligraphy and approached the brush in the same way they approached meditation, but in general monks were drawn to calligraphy for the same reasons their secular counterparts were drawn to it: for the joy of the art and for the prestige fine calligraphy brought. The account in the *Liang Biographies* of the fifth-century monk Tanyao tells us little more about the monk than that he was a skilled calligrapher whose calligraphy was admired by the powerful officials of the time.[18] Similarly, it was on the basis of his brush that the sixth-century monk Hongyan was "admired by all of the [secular] elites of his day."[19]

Monastic attitudes toward poetry are similar to those toward calligraphy. There is only the vaguest hint in the *Biographies* of the notion that verse and calligraphy are decadent or otherwise unbecoming a monk. We read, for instance, of monks who took up poetry only after "reading in the Vinaya that it is acceptable to spend some time studying non-Buddhist disciplines."[20] In general, however, the value of poetry is taken for granted, and a fine line is always admired, whether or not it relates to Buddhism. As in the case of calligraphy, some monks treated poetry as a part of their practice, incorporating Buddhist themes into their verse. The biography of the Tang monk Zhixuan provides an example of the subtlety of Buddhist reference in the poetry of some monks. According to the biography, when Zhixuan was a child of five, before he had decided to become a monk, his grandfather ordered him to compose a poem on some flowers. The boy thought for a moment and chanted:

> Flowers blossom, the trees fill with red.
> Flowers fall, ten thousand branches empty.
> Only one petal remains.
> Tomorrow it too will follow the wind.

Though the poem contains no specifically Buddhist terminology, the frustrated grandfather sighed sadly, lamenting that the boy he had hoped would rise to high office would surely become a monk instead.[21]

While we may dismiss this story as a pious literary conceit, there is ample anecdotal evidence, not to mention extant poetry, demonstrating that capable monks frequently composed poetry that they shared among themselves and with other literati. Indeed, some of the monks whose biographies are recorded in the *Song Biographies* number among the most important poets of the Tang. But as Stephen Owen has argued, we see Buddhism in the poetry of monks like Jiaoran and Lingyi chiefly because we know they were monks; their poetry is for the most part secular, and monks like these were very much a part of the literary culture of the scholar-officials with whom they exchanged conversation and verse.[22] There are a few examples of monks who devoted their poetry almost exclusively to Buddhist concerns (most notably, Hanshan), but more typical are monks who seem intent on demonstrating their sophistication in the secular poetic tradition.

For their part, many of the literati were attracted to the cultivated monk, evoking as he did romantic images of detachment from the byzantine world in which scholar-officials found themselves. We read, for instance, of a sixth-century prince going out to the thatched *"dhūta* hut" of the monk Zhizang in order to exchange poems with him.[23] And many prominent poets from Xie Lingyun to Wang Wei maintained close friendships with the cultivated monks of their day (Wang Wei even took for his cognomen the name "Vimalakīrti") in an attempt to strike a balance between other-worldly and this-worldly aspirations. One scholar, attempting to account for the dearth of creative interpretations of the classics in the Tang when compared to Buddhist learning of the same period, has even argued that the strictures of secular learning in the Tang drove original thinkers to Buddhist thought, where their ideas were not subjected to the official scrutiny and rigid guidelines demanded of interpretations of the classics.[24]

Education

When young men in medieval China studied for a career in government, they often did so in private schools. Some scholars have argued that Buddhist methods for training monks served as the catalyst for the development from the private schools of the Han to the large academies (*shuyuan*) of the Song.[25] Because they were located in serene, isolated locations, equipped with large libraries containing secular as well as Buddhist writings, and staffed with erudite monks, large famous monasteries were considered prime locations for concentrated study. It even became common for struggling students to lodge on monastic grounds for a period of undistracted independent study (of the classics, not Buddhism) in preparation for the civil-service examinations.[26] For monks and novices interested in studying Buddhist scriptures, the monasteries were of course even more appealing.

Although monks did not as a rule receive full ordination until they were at least twenty, many began their training much earlier. The *Biographies* seldom dwell on precisely how young novices were trained, but they do occasionally provide glimpses of the process by which young monks were taught. In general, the novice chose a particular master and, if accepted, worked with him until old enough to receive ordination. Teaching styles no doubt varied, but the sort of interaction described in the biography of Daoan discussed above seems to have been the rule. That is, the master provided the novice with a scripture, told him to study or memorize it, and perhaps drilled him briefly on its contents.[27]

The *Further Biographies* provides a brief description of the teaching style of at least one monk, the sixth-century figure Jing'ai:

> Jing'ai's rules for speaking on the Law required all to be respectful before he would speak. First he would always have his disciples stand with a shoulder exposed and palms pressed together. They would maintain this position of respect for some time before he would order them to bring out his corded-chair and position themselves around him. When they had finished seating themselves with utmost respect, Jing'ai would slowly take out the scriptures. He would then point to one passage at a time, explaining its meaning in order that they might understand it. He would then ask members of his audience to explain their understanding of the line. Only when they had answered to his satisfaction would he continue with the next passage. If one of his listeners did not understand, he would explain it again. He lectured in this way every day without tire.[28]

We occasionally read that when a promising young monk reached a certain level of proficiency, his master allowed him to "follow his interests," indicating that in the first years of training, a program of study was laid out for young monks. There seems to have been quite a wide variety of texts that were emphasized, depending largely on the interests of the master. Meditative practice was also a part of the training of a young monk. The degree of emphasis on meditation versus study again seems to have varied from monastery to monastery. In the biography of his own master, Huijun, Daoxuan tells of how, at the age of twenty, he went before Huijun and expressed his interest in practicing meditation. Huijun insisted that Daoxuan first master the Regulations before concentrating on meditation. Daoxuan then proceeded to devote more than ten years to the study of the Vinaya.[29]

The relationship between a monk and his master was usually a close one, and masters were regarded by their disciples much as fathers were by their sons. As the monk Zhiwei put it, "My father and mother gave birth to my physical body, and my Dharma Master gave birth to my Dharma-body."[30] Like the traditional Chinese father, the master was expected to maintain a certain distance from his disciples. Many are described as "severe" men, "respected and feared" by their disciples.[31] Even Daoxuan, who had a fairly intimate relationship with his master, describes him as a man who "showed no emotions."[32]

The life of the scholar-monk was not all book-reading and composition, for medieval monks were great talkers, known for their charisma and eloquence. They debated with an "eloquence [as rapid] as gusting winds, [as unrelenting] as torrential rains."[33] And even allowing for hyperbole in the *Biographies*, it is clear that the sermons of a monk with a reputation for eloquence attracted all manner of people, from local commoner, to itinerant monk, to literatus, to the emperor himself. When Tanyi, an eighth-century expert in the Regulations, spoke on his specialty, it is said that pupils came "like clouds rolling in. His capacity for teaching others was unbounded, for he spoke whenever asked. Thus from start to finish he lectured on the *Regulations in Four Divisions*[34] some thirty-five times, and the *Notes on the Emendations*[35] more than twenty times."[36] Guangyi, the monk who severed his penis to avert a seductress, went on to become a figure of some renown and is said to have spoken to crowds of thousands.[37]

When Emperor Xuanzong completed a commentary of his own on the *Diamond Sūtra*, he ordered monks throughout the empire to lecture on it. At that time, commander-in-chief of the Henan Circuit Yuan Yanchong invited the monk Xuanyan to deliver a public sermon on the text. "Xuanyan thereupon expounded on the deepest of subtleties in a lecture that was in accord with the mind of [the Son of] Heaven. The blind saw the light of the Sun and Moon; the deaf heard the roar of thunder."[38] We can well imagine how cautious and contrived a lecture on the emperor's writings would have been, but other sermons were far from mechanical or perfunctory, and in general, ingenuity in public speech was admired. When later monks looked for inspiration to the biographies of their predecessors, they read, for example, the account of how the great fifth-century exegete Huiyuan struggled to develop a new style of sermon. According to the biography, Huiyuan began to deliver sermons at the age of twenty-four. He found at first that many in his audience could not understand the finer points. He would discuss Buddhist doctrine for hours on end, "but they only became more confused." He then began to draw analogies with the teachings of Zhuangzi and discovered that his audiences could finally understand. After this, his teacher Daoan encouraged him to continue to employ secular writings in his lectures.[39]

As illustrated in this last story, monks were observed and trained in the art of public speech by their masters. We see the same sort of dynamic at work in the biography of the great exegete Sengrui, who learned his craft under the tutelage of Kumārajīva. According to Sengrui's biography, when Kumārajīva had completed his translation of the *Chengshi lun*,[40] he ordered Sengrui to lecture on the text, warning him that "among the disputations [presented in this book] there are seven points at which it refutes the abhidharma [of the Sarvastivadins]. These [seven points] are obscure. If you can understand them without asking, then you deserve to be called brilliant." Sengrui then proceeded to lecture on the text, explaining each of the seven points accurately.[41] In stories like this one, we see that while young monks received guidance from their teachers, exceptional monks were expected to be able to interpret texts for themselves and to develop their own styles of exposition.

After receiving basic training and full ordination, monks were encouraged to travel for a period of time and to listen to lectures by an assortment of teachers. Ideas spread quickly from one teacher to another, and there are numerous accounts of prominent masters asking the young monks in their audience about the teachings of a rival. The competition between monks for recognition and pupils contributed to the drive for doctrinal innovation. The extremes to which this competition went are reflected in a dubious account included in the biography of the famous exegete and disciple of Xuanzang, Kuiji. In the story, soon after translating the *Treatise on Consciousness Only*,[42] Xuanzang delivered a series of private lectures to his disciples, including Kuiji. Wishing to hear these lectures for himself, the Korean monk Wŏn-ch'ŭk, who stayed at the nearby Ximing Monastery, bribed the doorkeeper and surreptitiously listened to the lectures. After several days of this, Wŏn-ch'ŭk "sounded the bell at the Ximing Monastery and, gathering together the monks, began to speak on the treatise." The disappointed Kuiji, who had apparently wanted to be the first to lecture publicly on the treatise, complained to Xuanzang who assured him that while Wŏn-ch'ŭk was the first to interpret the text in public, Kuiji understood its doctrines more fully.

Later, when Kuiji asked Xuanzang to lecture on the *Yoga Treatise*[43] for him alone, Wŏn-ch'ŭk once again managed to secretly listen and again lecture on the text before Kuiji.[44] The story reads suspiciously like the product of a squabble, not between Kuiji and Wŏn-ch'ŭk, but between their disciples. Nonetheless, even if the story is a malicious fabrication, it still reflects the value placed on innovation and even scholarly fashion among scholar-monks, a tendency that is readily understandable when we consider the constant influx of new texts from India, some of which claimed to negate those that came before them.

Even lay scholars were attracted to the excitement of challenging lectures on new scriptures and doctrines by famous foreign and Chinese monks. A story concerning the monk Saṅghadeva recounts that when he first arrived in the southern capital, Wang Xun and Wang Mi, two scholar-officials, attended one of his lectures on abhidharma. "He had just started his lecture, and the session was barely at the halfway point, when Wang Mi announced, 'It's completely clear to me already,' and forthwith, taking from among those present three or four monks who were willing to accompany him, he proceeded to another room to lecture himself."[45]

Others less sympathetic to Buddhism grew weary of all the new-fangled, abstract Buddhist theories that coursed incessantly through literati society. A story in the secular collection *Shishuo xinyu* discloses just such an attitude. In the story, when the monk Zhi Mindu was about to flee southward across the Yangtze River with a fellow monk, he commented to his friend, " 'If we go to the land east of the river with nothing but the old theory, I'm afraid we'll never manage to eat.' So together they concocted the 'Theory of Mental Nonexistence' (*xinwu yi*)."[46] This account reads suspiciously like gossip whispered from one skeptic to another, rather than an objective account of a real incident.

Nevertheless, in addition to reflecting skepticism on the part of some members of the laity toward abstract Buddhist doctrines, the story also suggests the give-and-take relationship between monks and literati at this time; major monasteries were seldom isolated from the outside world, and monks spoke to a wider audience than just their monastic brethren. With this story, we begin to stray from the topic of education to performance as monks attempted to attract followings for themselves and their ideas. The two are often closely intertwined; by nature, most all religious writings are intended at some level to edify, and it would be wrong to limit a discussion of Buddhist education to the training of young monks.

One common way in which monks propagated ideas both to laymen and to other monks was through letters. The *Biographies* are filled with references to monastic correspondence. Some are of a personal nature, as in the letter from the monk Zhu Fatai to Daoan lamenting the recent death of a fellow monk.[47] Others were part of ongoing correspondence, as in a discussion between the monk Fayun and a number of literati on the question of the mortality of the soul, all of which took place in letters.[48] In the Tang, a sophisticated postal system was constructed, including a network of postal stations, complete with runners and fresh horses on land and fleet boats on the waterways, but this system was reserved for official documents.[49] Correspondence between monks circulated instead on an informal basis, with letters passed on from one monk to another until they eventually reached their destination. It is perhaps in part because of their mobility that monks were able to exchange so many letters so freely. The biography of Huichi, in addition to recounting a number of letters between Huichi, other monks, and literati, also mentions that Huichi himself traveled all the way from Lu Shan in eastern China to Emei

Shan in the west.[50] Journeys of this length are not uncommon in the *Biographies*.

The biography of Huiyuan, which includes a number of letters, alludes to the most famous monastic correspondence in the history of Chinese Buddhism, that between Huiyuan and Kumārajīva.[51] Huiyuan, who lived in the south at Lu Shan, had never met the great Kuchean master of Mahāyāna doctrine, who lived in the north in Chang'an, but he had heard of him and held him in great esteem. And so Huiyuan wrote a series of letters to Kumārajīva asking him to resolve a number of knotty doctrinal questions concerning, among other things, the *dharmakāya* or "body of the Law." Kumārajīva responded in lengthy letters dotted with quotations from texts like the *Da zhi du lun*, which were not yet available to Huiyuan in Chinese translation.[52] This exchange is often taken as a turning point in the history of Chinese Buddhist thought, as a sign that Chinese monks had by this point attained a level of sophistication in Buddhist doctrine at which they could begin an internal analysis of Buddhist ideas without reference to Chinese concepts. The exchange between Huiyuan and Kumārajīva is also a testament to the hunger for new ideas and new books among Chinese monks and to the rapidity with which new ideas were introduced and assimilated.

Debate

Monks gained reputations not only as effective, eloquent speakers, but also for their ability to refute challenges from their audience or from rival speakers. When Daosheng debated, "even esteemed scholar-monks and famous secular scholars of the time found themselves refuted and at a loss for words—none dared challenge him."[53] When Kumārajīva spoke before the king of Kucha, "They came great distances from all directions, and none could refute him."[54] As in this last example, many rulers took an interest in hearing monks speak. Far from somber sermons, these lectures often took the form of heated debates, either between monks or among representatives of Buddhism, Daoism, and Confucianism.

The reasons for holding such public, official debates were various. In his *Brief History of the Clergy*, Zanning includes an overview of the history of the practice of debating before the emperor on the emperor's birthday. In the section, Zanning suggests that the reason emperors began to invite monks to speak at their birthdays was because of the belief that hearing the Buddha Law would bring the emperor good health and a long life.[55] Similarly, Chen Wu Di (r. 557–559) once held a debate between monks at a major monastery on the occasion of the Buddha's birthday, presumably in order to accrue merit.[56]

However, most of the formal court debates described in the *Biographies* were between representatives of Buddhism and Daoism. When Zhou Wu Di (r. 561–578) prepared for one of the first great state persecutions of Buddhism in China, he first held a debate between Buddhists and Daoists. According to the Buddhist account, when the debate went poorly for the Daoist representative, the emperor himself mounted the lecturer's platform and took the priest's place.[57] Clearly the debate was a thinly disguised pretext for the persecution that followed. Conversely, when the famous Buddhist Emperor Liang Wu Di (r. 502–549) decided to give his support to the Buddhist clergy at the expense of the Daoists, he too held a court debate. Nonetheless, one suspects that many of these formal court debates were held neither in order to accrue merit, nor for purposes of state policy, but rather for the entertainment value, for the spectacle of watching skilled orators match wits. Emperor Wenzong of the Tang (r. 827–840), for example, called no less than Bai Juyi, famous for his devotion to Buddhism, to represent the Confucian perspective.[58] With such a contestant, this particular debate was likely a very stylized affair with emphasis placed on eloquence and wit rather than reasoned, heart-felt analysis.

In general, as presented in the *Biographies*, the content of the court debates is rather disappointing, focusing often on the tired question of whether or not Buddhism was in fact founded by Laozi, with each side arguing over the dating of Laozi and Śākyamuni.[59] Needless to say, in the *Biographies*, the Buddhist argument is always superior. Other debates between Buddhists and Daoists—the *Biographies* seldom refer to debates between Buddhists and Confucians—often degenerate into name-calling and ad hominem attacks.

Accounts of court debates in the *Biographies* are frustratingly pithy —brief abstracts of highlights rather than transcriptions of what were lengthy debates. The same is true of references to debates between monks in the monasteries. Hence it is difficult to analyze the rhetoric of Buddhist debate from the hagiography. Nonetheless, there is evidence to suggest that distinctively Buddhist styles of debate were adopted during the Tang. Already in medieval times India could boast a long and rich tradition of the study of logic and rhetoric.[60] Xuanzang introduced the most influential work (in China) of one of the greatest of the Indian Buddhist logicians, Dignāga. The text, the *Yinming ru zhengli lun*,[61] lays out principles of how to construct a proper argument and how to refute a fallacious one, a branch of Buddhist thought termed *yinming* or "the elucidation of causes."

We occasionally see the influence of formal Buddhist logic on Chinese monks. In Kuiji's biography, for example, we read that after listening to Xuanzang lecture on the writings of Dignāga, Kuiji became adept in the "three branches" of analysis (*sanzhi*).[62] The *Yinming ru zhengli lun* divides a solid argument into three component parts. Rather than the ubiquitous introduction, body, and conclusion of modern English rhetoric, the monk was to begin his argument with a proposition (*zong*), followed by his reason (*yin*), and concluding with an analogy (*yu*).[63] For example, there is fire on the hill (proposition), because there is smoke (reason), just as when one sees smoke in the kitchen it is accompanied by fire (analogy). Or, the monk must not go to extremes in ascetic practice (proposition), because if the monk practices asceticism too rigorously he renders himself incapable of practice while if he abandons asceticism entirely he becomes enmeshed in worldly affairs (reason), just as the strings of a lute will not play properly if either too tight or not tight enough (analogy).

There are numerous references in the *Song Biographies* to monks after Xuanzang who devoted themselves for a time to the study of the "Elucidation of Causes," and the influence of Dignāga's ideas in the China of Xuanzang's time and the decades that followed was considerable. Nevertheless, Buddhist logic as a branch of learning was never to attain the level of prominence in China that it did in Tibet;[64] indeed, the references to debates in the *Biographies* have little to say for coolheaded reasoning. Debate in the *Biographies* is marked instead by heated, emotional attacks, often of a very personal nature.[65]

In the *Liang Biographies*, in the treatise to his chapter devoted to exegetes, Huijiao compares the use of language to the use of weapons. "Weapons are inauspicious tools, but one uses them when one has no other choice; [so too] language is not an [ideal] instrument of truth, but one employs it when one has no other choice."[66] The analogy seems an apt one, employing as it does the standard Buddhist caveat concerning the inadequacies of language and is not in itself remarkable. But when we gather accounts of debate in the *Biographies*, the prevalence of the military metaphor is striking. Huizhe "debated divinely, like a sword that few could withstand."[67] Huiyuan praised his disciple Sengche, saying his arguments were "as solid as a city wall. When an enemy attacks you, it loses its generals."[68] When Fuli debated, he was "a strong front line that could not be broken."[69] In the *Shishuo xinyu*, after Zhi Dun loses a debate to the scholar Yin Hao before a local official, the official consoles Zhi Dun saying, "This naturally is his battlefield. How can you match sword points with him?"[70]

Far from polite conversations or exchanges of ideas, these were verbal wars in which victory was glorious and defeat devastating. The *Biographies of Eminent Monks* make no attempt to disguise the fact that one of the goals of these debates was to humiliate the opponent. Zhiyuan was known as a talented orator. "There were skilled scholar-monks and laymen who challenged his teachings. In their attempts to defeat him, some would, from a hidden place, watch him [debate], hoping to detect a flaw. Then they would swagger up to his lecture mat with a look of arrogance. But in the end they would retire respectfully, their faces red with embarrassment."[71]

Or take, for example, the debate between Huiyuan and a monk named Daoheng. Hearing of the monk Daoheng who was preaching the Theory of Mental Nonexistence, Zhu Fatai, a leading fourth-century monk, ordered one of his disciples to debate the monk on this theory, which he believed to be false. The two debated fiercely all day long, neither able to defeat the other. The next day, Zhu had Huiyuan engage the monk in debate. After a time, "Daoheng realized that his own reasoning was faulty. His facial expression changed slightly, and he struck the table with the fly-whisk.[72] Before he could think of a response, Huiyuan said, 'There is no hurry and yet you're flustered. What is it you're weaving in there?'[73] Those in attendance all laughed, and the Theory of Mental Nonexistence ceased from that point on."[74] Evidently, sneering ridicule was not considered beneath even a monk of Huiyuan's stature. Notice that the passage makes no attempt to describe what precisely the doctrine in question was, or what precisely Huiyuan's objection to it was. The point here is that Huiyuan outmaneuvered and humiliated his opponent; the defeat of the man necessarily entailed the defeat of the doctrine.

This type of rhetorical move is not uncommon in the *Biographies*. After debating with an old adversary he had not seen in some time, the monk Zhi Dun remarked derisively, "You and I have been separated many years, but your interpretations and terminology haven't made any progress whatever." The opponent, the account continues, "withdrew in great embarrassment."[75] Zhi Dun, though indisputably an eminent monk, was said to have engaged in a number of petty tiffs and squabbles. When one of his lay opponents called him a "specious sophist," Zhi retorted, "Wearing a greasy cap and tattered cloth single robe, with a copy of the 'Zuo Commentary' tucked under his arm, chasing along behind Zheng Xuan's[76] carriage—I ask you, what sort of dust-and-filth bag is he anyhow?"[77]

We may be tempted to dismiss such stories as exceptional cases, indicative of the contentious intellectual environment of the Wei-Jin period, but stories of ad hominem attacks continue into the *Song Biographies*. After debating with a monk who had been more successful at attracting disciples than he, Yuankang mocked his rival with the words, "The sweet peach tree bears no fruit, while the branches of the bitter plum are weighed down to the ground." His opponent replied, "The Wheel-Turning King has a thousand sons, while the alley tramp hasn't a one." The biography notes that Yuankang's display of wit in this exchange was greatly admired and that news of his rhetorical feats even reached the ears of the emperor.[78]

Clearly the ideal of the invincible debater who humiliates his opponents through acerbic barbs clashes with any number of well-known Buddhist notions—compassion, selflessness, control of emotions, and so on. The tension between ideals of the great Buddhist orator and the meek, benign monk did not go entirely unnoticed. After witnessing the Tang monk Shending defeat an opponent in debate, a layman "sighed in admiration, saying, 'Seeing your lightening speed in debate, I realize that you have attained the level of a bodhisattva.' Shending replied, 'A bodhisattva takes no delight in victory and feels no enmity in defeat. When beaten, he does not anger; when insulted, he feels no wrath. Now when I am victorious I am delighted. When I lose I feel enmity. If someone beats me I am angered, and if someone insults me I feel wrath. Seen in this light, I am far from being a bodhisattva.' "[79]

But judging by the *Biographies*, this sort of introspection was rare indeed. In addition to the biographies of monks of the past, monks needed look no farther for a model of ferocious debate than Vimalakīrti, a man so skilled in debate that none but the reluctant Mañjuśrī dared to engage him in conversation. In short, the ideal of a skilled monastic debater was based on the model of battle rather than dialogue and took as its goal a crushing victory rather than subtle persuasion.

Limits of Scholarship

Although Daoxuan eventually came to be considered the founder of a particular school of interpretation of the Vinaya, the *Biographies* are as a whole ecumenical. Biographies of representatives of different schools of interpretation are presented side by side with little attempt to adjudicate between them, to pronounce one interpretation superior to another. Throughout the medieval period, when there was a central Buddhist administration, it was operated by the state and for the state, and hence was more concerned with administrative matters than with passing judgment on doctrinal disputes. Certainly, the Buddhist canon was regulated by the state, as witnessed by the prefaces to many translations that begin "translated on imperial edict by . . . ," and texts judged seditious or potentially socially disruptive were rigorously suppressed.[80] Nonetheless, as long as doctrinal disputes did not pose a political threat, the state administration had little interest in them. For this reason, the label of "heresy" was not as onerous in medieval China as it was in Europe at the same time. Indeed, scholars of Chinese Buddhism have been reluctant to use the term, referring to "false" teachings rather than "heterodox" ones. This is not to say that monks were necessarily more tolerant of divergent views, but rather that there was no central mechanism for determining which views were orthodox and which heterodox; such matters were left to individual monks and their followers.[81]

Nevertheless, individual monks and their followers did indeed label particular interpretations of the scriptures as not only wrong, but as vile and destructive, as views that entailed karmic retribution in the next life and social punishment in this one. For example, Sun-kyŏng, a Sillan monk, was criticized for his interpretation of an extremely difficult, technical doctrine of Xuanzang's known as "true inference of consciousness only."[82] "According to one tradition," Sun-kyŏng's biography concludes, "when Sun-kyŏng was bed-stricken and ordered his disciples to lift him to the ground, the ground split open and he fell into the earth. The people of the time said that he was reborn in hell. To this day there is a ravine about a *zhang* wide—actually it is just a crevice—that is called 'Sun-kyŏng's hell [Skt. *naraka*].' "[83] True to the inclusive spirit of the *Biographies*, Zanning in a note defends his decision to include Sun-kyŏng in the collection, stating that the monk had been slandered and was in fact a great exegete, despite his mistake in the case of Xuanzang's doctrine.

But even the generally tolerant compilers of the *Biographies* occasionally cannot disguise their disgust with propagators of "false doctrines." And judgments passed in the world of hagiography could be harsh indeed. We read, for example, of the monk Daowen, a specialist in the *Nirvāṇa Sūtra* who "became twisted in his later years, claiming that the Buddha[-nature] was not permanent. Just before his death, the root of his tongue rotted away."[84] Such stories likely had their origins in disputes among teachers or among their disciples, and may well have been motivated by animosities arising from reasons other than intellectual disagreement—personal affronts, struggles for prestige and resources, and so on. But even without this vital background, cases like those of Sun-kyŏng and Daowen are important for what they tell us about the general intellectual environment of the times, for what they tell us about the limits of intellectual and doctrinal tolerance. Unlike the monks labeled as sorcerers for using spells for evil ends, Daowen was condemned for his views themselves; there is no presumption of improper motivations behind his teachings.

The closest we come to heresy in the sense it was used in Europe is in the famous incident involving Daosheng, one of the most influential exegetes of his day, and his interpretation of the *Nirvāṇa Sūtra*. Before the arrival of the larger version of the *Nirvāṇa Sūtra*, Chinese exegetes accepted the notion of a type of person known as *icchantika*, someone so muddled, so ignorant, that he is fundamentally incapable of achieving enlightenment in this life or in any future life for eternity. According to his biography, Daosheng challenged this view during his stay in the capital, stating that even *icchantika* are capable of achieving enlightenment.[85] Because he had no scriptural support for this notion, Daosheng was branded the propagator of "false teachings," castigated in front of an assembly of monks, and driven from the capital.[86]

As in so many cases, the hagiography presents us here with the caricature of an event. Before leaving the capital, Daosheng turns to his persecutors and vows, "If my interpretation is at odds with the scriptures, may my body be covered with boils. But if my teaching does not run counter to the ultimate truth, when I die, may I sit on the 'lion's seat' [lecturer's chair] at the moment of my death." Not long after this, another, longer version of the *Nirvāṇa* was translated, providing the scriptural support for Daosheng's position. And of course he died on the lecturer's chair immediately after delivering his final sermon. Daosheng was known for his sharp, abrasive personality, and this too may have played a role in the dispute. Like so many of the events described in the *Biographies*, the actual circumstances of the *icchantika* incident elude us. Did Daosheng in fact propose his reading of the *Nirvāṇa* based solely on intuition and reasoning, or had he heard of the content of the larger version of the scripture before it was translated? Was the entire incident—including the early, perceptive interpretation, the banishment, and the heroic vow—a later legend circulated by Daosheng's supporters?

In short, the details of the fiery dispute that took place in a particular Chang'an monastery in the early years of the fifth century are just beyond our grasp; we must settle once again for inquiries into the mentalities of the recorders of the event and their audience. Happily, such inquiries are revealing in themselves. Note that Daosheng's detractors are not condemned for excessive zeal in silencing their opponent; they are condemned only for persecuting an innocent man. As in the cases above, the division between a mere disagreement and a dangerously false opinion was not based on the monk's intentions or character; in the story, Daosheng's enemies criticize him because his interpretation is "false" and not because of, say, an attempt to usurp control of a monastery. Further, public castigation before the assembly and banishment from the region were not in themselves considered excessive by the readers of the story. Again, the mistake according to the hagiographer was in finding Daosheng guilty of propagating a false teaching, not in the punishment levied against such a person. Equally important are the limits placed on punishment for doctrinal error. After leaving Chang'an, Daosheng traveled to Huqiu Shan in the east where he gathered, according to the biography, "hundreds of disciples." There was no question of corporal punishment or defrocking for a monk accused of doctrinal error; such punishments were administered only by the state for crimes against the state.

In stories of monastic disputes and rivalries, debates, slander, and enmity, we find fissures in the same *saṅgha* depicted in official edicts and memorials as a uniform block of nameless, dark-robed religious. Nevertheless, in general, even the *Biographies* paint a consistent, coherent picture of the scholar-monk, diligently poring over lengthy scrolls, methodically instructing attentive disciples, or fully engaged in debate over abstruse doctrinal matters.

In the *Song Biographies*, however, we detect hints that this image of the monk was increasingly coming under attack from another monastic ideal of a radically different sort. The new image of the scholar-monk was hardly a scholar at all. He had little patience for those lengthy scrolls and indeed was sometimes unashamedly illiterate. He debated in a manner of speaking, but in a dizzying barrage of strange terms, jokes, and images—without recourse to the old rules of logic, rhetoric, and decorum. What in the *Song Biographies* was only a hint of the rise of this figure, the Chan monk, soon became a torrent of hagiographic enterprise so powerful that it eclipsed the image of the monk presented in the *Eminent Monks* series for subsequent Chinese Buddhist history.

The Rise of the Chan Ideal

The *Shishuo xinyu* includes an account of a layman who, offended by the cantankerous Zhi Dun, composed a treatise entitled "Why a Śramaṇa is not Capable of Becoming an Eminent Gentleman" in which he argued that "the śramaṇa, although claiming to be beyond earthly ties, is, on the contrary, more than ever in bondage to his doctrine and cannot be said to be fully self-possessed in his feelings and disposition."[87] Hostile literati were not the only ones to see a tension between the monastic claim to be "beyond the world," and the practices of reading, writing, and debating scripture; this same anxiety over finding oneself "in bondage" to doctrine is also expressed with great regularity in the *Biographies*. In the treatise to the chapter on exegetes in the *Liang Biographies*, Huijiao is at pains to justify exegesis. In the treatise, Huijiao first establishes that "the ultimate principles are without words" and that "the sage acts without words." Huijiao then cites the example of Vimalakīrti who ended his great debate with Mañjuśrī by responding to a question on the nature of nonduality with "deafening silence."

Nonetheless, Huijiao continues, because of the sorry state of the world and the ignorance of ordinary people, the sage, in his compassion, has no choice but to resort to language to convey the Teaching to others. Later in the treatise, Huijiao cites the familiar Zhuangzi passage that says that just as one employs a snare only to catch a rabbit and can discard the snare after catching the rabbit, one should use words only to convey a message and not become attached to the words themselves.[88]

This sort of caveat is standard fare in Chinese Buddhist texts, but in medieval hagiography this suspicion of language for the most part gave way to the scholar-monk ideal. The definition of what constituted "attachment" to language was of course a fluid one. Certainly we read of ascetics who "had no interest in words, paper, and brush, choosing to remain instead silent, reducing desires and avoiding the burdens of the world,"[89] who "were not fond of talk and conversation," who "kept silent, refusing to serve words and discourse,"[90] but biographies such as these never challenge the scholar ideal directly. The inherent conflict between the ideal of an eloquent orator, master of scriptures, and prolific writer, and that of the silent, intuitive sage is hardly apparent in the *Biographies;* that is, not until the *Song Biographies* when we begin to get hints of strange new undercurrents in Buddhist hagiography, of new themes and motifs that were soon to dominate the genre.

The Attack on Scholarship

In the biography of Zongmi, one of the leading Buddhist exegetes of the early ninth century, Zanning includes a quotation from Zongmi's epitaph written by Pei Xiu, the monk's most famous disciple. The epitaph notes that during his lifetime Zongmi had come under attack not so much for the content of his scholarship as for engaging in scholarly activities at all. "Critics claim," the epitaph states, "that the great master did not observe *chan* practice but lectured widely on [Buddhist] scriptures and treatises, traveled about to famous cities and the great capitals, and took his task to be the promotion [of Buddhism]. Does this not show that he was a slave to his erudition?"[91] At the end of the biography, Zanning addresses the criticism again in his addendum, stating, "Now there are those in the Chan School who do not understand Zongmi and criticize him, saying that it was inappropriate for him to lecture on teachings and books." Zanning ends by dismissing such critics as men "of little learning and less knowledge," jealous of Zongmi's attainments. Earlier biographies on occasion criticize monks for arrogance, but this criticism for simply lecturing on scripture is something new. And this new attack on the traditional scholar-monk was not directed at Zongmi alone.

In his treatise to the chapter on "Practitioners of Chan," Zanning returns once again to these anonymous critics and complains of those who "never realize that to produce the mind of a bodhisattva *through the scriptures* is itself to see the Buddha nature." Instead, "When someone holds up a scripture and shows it to them, they reply, 'That is the doctrine of phenomenal appearances.'[92] Or, 'Aren't those the teachings of Mara? Let's burn it!' Then they set the scripture aside and refuse to discuss it."[93] In short, scholarship founded on scriptural exegesis was under attack. Unlike the incidents I have described previously, however, this time criticism did not come from hostile literati or Daoist priests, but from within the *saṅgha* itself.

Previous to these instances, in the *Liang* and *Further Biographies* there were accounts of monks who elected to pursue the ascetic life rather than the life of the scholar-monk, but these earlier biographies rarely mention any hostility of ascetics to their scholarly counterparts; ascetics are portrayed instead as simply following a personal preference. In the *Song Biographies*, however, this indifference to scholarship turns, on occasion, to contempt. In the story of Huineng, the "sixth patriarch" who was made famous in the *Platform Scripture*, Huineng proudly defends his illiteracy before an astonished literate nun with the statement, "It was not the Buddha's intent that we become attached to the words of Buddhist principles and treatises."[94] The same antischolastic bent is even more pronounced in the biographies of later monks in Huineng's lineage. Huanpu "did not advise [his disciples] to read the doctrines in the scriptures."[95] Zhixian, frustrated by the inadequacy of written texts, one day burned all of his copies of the "recorded sayings" of Chan masters, saying that "a painted biscuit can't satisfy your hunger."[96] Qingzhu studied Vinaya texts for a time but then abandoned them, labeling them "gradual doctrines" (*jianzong*).[97]

This new radical stance against scholasticism seems to have emerged in the eighth century in certain Chan circles, particularly that of Mazu and his followers.[98] In his writings, Zongmi criticized this branch of Chan, the so-called Hongzhou School, which he characterized as radically antinomian, as holding that, as the Buddha-nature is present in everyday activity, all forms of practice and study are irrelevant to enlightenment.[99] As we have seen, Zongmi was in turn criticized for his position. Further, between the death of Zongmi and the compilation of the *Song Biographies* one and a half centuries later, the attack on traditional scholarship gained momentum, and stories of burning books and spurning preachers proliferated. What is important for our purposes is that this attack on traditional scholarship took form not in scholarly treatises—which would of course be absurd —but in hagiography, specifically in "recorded sayings" and in genealogical biographies known as "transmission of the lamp" collections.

The first occurrence of the term "recorded sayings" (*yulu*) is in the *Song Biographies* where it refers to a new genre of Chan literature that emerged in the eighth century.[100] These texts are composed of short, often enigmatic dialogues between a master and another figure, often a disciple or another Chan master. Occasionally, a few biographical or environmental facts are given along with the dialogue, but the focus is on the exchange itself. In other words, in form these brief encounters are very much like the descriptions of debates between monks in the *Biographies*, only stripped of the larger biographical context.

The content of the dialogues in the recorded sayings, however, is entirely different from that of the debates recorded in the *Biographies*. Masters respond to questions with paradoxes, crude jokes, enigmatic gestures, shouts, and beatings, repeatedly emphasizing the theme that enlightenment is not found outside of one's own mind. The purpose of these encounters is taken to be neither persuasion nor explanation, but direct and unmediated enlightenment.[101] In these dialogues, monks not only depart from the tradition of the scholar-monk, they ridicule and disparage it. "Followers of the Way, even if you can understand a hundred sutras and treatises, you're not as good as one plain monk who does nothing," advises Linji Yixuan, the eighth-century figure at the center of one of the most famous collections of recorded sayings.[102] Layman Pang accosts a scholar-monk lecturing on the scriptures with, "Lecture-master, since there is no self and no person, who is he who's lecturing, who is he who's listening?"[103] It is said that as a youth Linji studied the Vinaya but later abandoned his studies, saying "These are mere medicines and expedients to save the world. They are not that doctrine that has been separately transmitted outside the scriptural teachings!"[104]

When tenth-century monks compiled the collection of biographies of Chan monks known as the *Zu tang ji* (*Collection of* [*Accounts from*] *the Hall of the Patriarchs*), this attack on book-learning continued. In the *Hall of the Patriarchs*, Yangshan Huiji discourages his students from reading the scriptures, insisting that "The essence of Caoxi [Huineng] has nothing to do with reading books."[105] When a monk discovers Yaoshan reading a book, he asks, "You do not usually allow us to read scriptures. How is it that you read them yourself?" To this Yaoshan replies, "I'm trying to get some sleep."[106]

In addition to ridiculing reading and lecturing, Chan literature from this period also disparages recitation, writing of commentaries, and memorization.[107] In short, the Chan accounts ridicule every element of the scholar-monk ideal that had taken shape over the centuries in traditional hagiography. It should be noted that, although this attack on mediation of all kinds focuses on the scholar-monk, some

Chan accounts also single out for ridicule meditation, self-mutilation, and the six supernormal powers.[108] In fact, examples can be found in the immense literature of the "classical period" of Chan ridiculing all of the aspects of the monastic ideal I have discussed this far, including ideals associated with scholarship, thaumaturgy, and asceticism.

These Chan dialogues are not as straightforward as a simple critique of the traditional image of the monk. The iconoclastic imagery of the encounters is often intended to be taken symbolically. Linji advises his disciples to kill their fathers and mothers, draw blood from the Buddha, and burn Buddhist scriptures, but when questioned by his disciples, explains that the "father" is ignorance; the mother, concupiscence, and so forth.[109] Other dialogues are less explicit, leaving the reader uncertain of just what the words and images symbolize or whether they are to be read symbolically at all. Throughout, the dialogues are extremely sophisticated and self-referential, playing off of traditional hagiography and increasingly in the later dialogues off of the sayings and responses of previous Chan masters.

These new genres of hagiography put the compilers of the *Song Biographies* in an awkward position. In keeping with the ecumenical nature of the *Eminent Monks* genre, Zanning included biographies of the most important Chan monks of even the most radical lineage, yet he clearly did not feel comfortable with the brash image of the iconoclastic Chan monk. The *Song Biographies* do include a few examples of "encounter-dialogues," including Huineng's famous encounter with Hongren in which Hongren greets the southerner Huineng with the statement that men from the South do not possess the Buddha nature, to which Huineng responds, "There are northern and southern men, but there is no north and south to the Buddha nature."[110] Playing on this theme, when Hengtong first meets his master, Zhaoxian, and tells him he is from Xingzhou, Zhaoxian comments, "My Way does not come from there," to which Hengtong responds, "Do you mean to imply that you, Reverend, are here?"[111] The *Song Biographies* even include the famous story of Danxia Tianran burning an image of a Buddha to keep warm.[112] Nevertheless, the accounts of Chan monks in the *Song Biographies* for the most part read like biographies of other monks, for the compilers of the *Song Biographies* were reluctant to include material from the new genres of Chan literature.

At the end of a short, conventional biography of Zhaozhou Congshen, a well-known monk in the Mazu lineage, the *Song Biographies* states that "his 'recorded sayings' circulate widely and are very popular."[113] Similarly, Linji is given only a few lines in the *Song Biographies*, though, as the *Biographies* themselves note, "his sayings circulate very widely."[114] In other words, when compiling the *Song Biographies*, Zanning had access to collections of recorded sayings but chose not to use them. Zanning's distaste for this material and the type of monk it represents is confirmed in a comment by the Song monk Huihong. In a preface Huihong notes, "When I first traveled to the Wu Region and read Zanning's *Song History of Monks*, I thought it strange that he did not include a biography of Yunmen [Wenyan] [a prominent Chan figure of the late Tang]. I asked an elderly man about this, and he said that he had once heard his teacher, who was from the Wu Region, say that he had met Zanning who explained that he had deleted Yunmen's biography because he 'was no scholar.' "[115] Apparently then, by eschewing accounts of encounter-dialogue and criticizing the antischolastic bent in some Chan circles, Zanning hoped to temper the brunt of the Chan critique and maintain an image of the scholar-monk consistent with traditional Chinese Buddhist hagiography.

The Transformation of the Genre

Earlier in my discussion of the meat-eating, wine-drinking monks, we saw a battle over the image of the monk at court with the enemies of the clergy painting the average monk as a profligate scoundrel and Buddhist hagiographers presenting the monk as either an upright holy man or as a transcendent figure beyond the ken of conventional morality. Similarly, as we saw in the second chapter, those antagonistic to Buddhism characterized Buddhist thaumaturges as evil sorcerers, while Buddhist hagiography depicts such monks as benevolent wonderworkers. Here in the case of the teacher-monk we again see a thinly veiled, and perhaps even unconscious, struggle for the image of the monk, with the *Song Biographies* attempting to paint a conventional image of the monk as scholar firmly rooted in Buddhist scholasticism and the new Chan literature presenting an image of a monk who eschews the trappings of traditional scholasticism for direct awakening. In other words, the new Chan literature represented not only an attack on traditional scholarship, but also the creation of a new image of the monk, a Chan ideal.

To a certain extent the image of the monk was influenced by portraiture and poetry. In both of these arenas the dramatic image of the Chan monk prevailed over that of the more sober scholiast. When we think of portraits of Chinese monks today we think first of paintings of the eccentric Bodhidharma or of Huineng, and when we think of Buddhist poetry, we think first of the personal, intensely religious poetry of Hanshan, rather than the more refined secular poetry of Jiaoran. But most of all, the image of the monk was shaped by hagiography, providing as it did detailed accounts of what monks (supposedly) said and did. In this arena it is clear that Zanning's efforts to tone down the radical image of the Chan monk in favor of that of a more traditional scholar-monk were not successful.

Less than twenty years after the completion of the *Song Biographies*, another collection of Buddhist biographies, the *Jingde chuandeng lu* (*Transmission of the Lamp* [*Compiled During the*] *Jingde Era*), was submitted to the throne. Although compiled by a member of the Fayan Chan lineage and exclusively devoted to Chan concerns, this collection is even longer than the *Song Biographies*. Unlike the *Song Biographies*, the *Transmission of the Lamp* is only tangentially interested in the feats of asceticism, thaumaturgy, and scholarship that so concern the *Biographies of Eminent Monks*. Rather, it is most interested in the *bon mots* of "recorded sayings" and in lineage.[116]

The *Transmission of the Lamp* traces the lineages of the monks of the early Song back through the masters of the early Tang and ancient India all the way to the seven Buddhas who preceded Śākyamuni in distant antiquity. Rather than dividing monks into categories of translators, reciters, exegetes, and so forth, the *Transmission of the Lamp* groups monks according to Chan lineages. The individual accounts in the *Transmission of the Lamp* can only loosely be described as biographies. A typical account begins with a few lines recounting the monk's family background, after which it quickly establishes the monk's lineage, and then launches into a series of "transcriptions" of encounters between the monk and his master or the monk and his own disciples. While Daoyuan, the compiler of the *Transmission of the Lamp*, relied occasionally on epitaphs or accounts in the *Eminent Monks* series, the chief source for his biographies was the recorded sayings of the late Tang. Therefore, the success of the *Transmission of the Lamp* in addition to signaling the success of a new image of the monk also signaled the success of a new genre of Buddhist hagiography.

The *Transmission of the Lamp* was not the first collection to string together recorded sayings into genealogies, but it was the first to gain widespread acceptance. Its best-known predecessors, a Chan collection known as the *Baolin zhuan* and the *Hall of the Patriarchs* with their colloquial, often coarse language, were perhaps too unrefined for literati tastes. The *Hall of the Patriarchs* seems to have been little known in China and may even have been compiled outside of China, while the *Baolin zhuan*, though occasionally cited, was often criticized for poor organization and inferior style.[117] The *Transmission of the Lamp*, on the other hand, met with immediate and sustained success.[118] Approximately twenty years after the completion of the *Transmission of the Lamp*, another, expanded version of the text was compiled, like the *Transmission of the Lamp*, on imperial edict.[119] This was followed in later years by new "lamp histories" expanding on the original, adding exchanges to the original biographies or adding biographies of monks who had lived since the completion of the original text.

In 1151, Chao Gongwu, a prominent Song bibliographer, noted that the *Transmission of the Lamp* "circulates widely throughout the world" and praised the text as "the primary source for the study of Chan."[120] The Song fascination with the lamp histories culminated in the *Wudeng huiyuan* (*Compendium of Five Lamp [Histories]*) by the Southern Song monk Puji, who brought together and edited five different lamp histories.[121] The influence of the lamp histories extended even to Confucian scholars like Zhu Xi who compiled the *Yiluo yuanyuan lu*, a collection of the sayings of Confucian scholars modeled on the lamp histories.[122]

In contrast, while the *Eminent Monks* series was continued with a *Ming Biographies of Eminent Monks*, this work was much shorter than its predecessors and seems to have had little influence. Other collections drew heavily on the *Eminent Monks* series when recounting the lives of non-Chan monks who lived before the Song. In addition, two other genres of Buddhist hagiography—Tiantai works organized chronologically and Pure-Land works, taking as their theme stories of monks rewarded for carrying out Pure-Land practices—also proliferated after the Tang and are, in some ways, more similar in style and subject matter to the *Eminent Monks* series than the Chan collections. Nonetheless, overall, the position of the *Eminent Monks* in Buddhist hagiography was superseded by the lamp histories.

Conclusion

At one point in his writings, Huihong, the twelfth-century critic of the *Eminent Monks* series, argued that the reason for the omission of certain key Chan figures from the *Eminent Monks* and the placement of the accounts of translators and exegetes before Chan masters stems from the fact that Chan masters "do not make use of brush and ink," an activity reserved for "lecturers" (*jiangshi*), a term Huihong used derisively to refer to pedants concerned only with petty technical matters.[123] This critique is in keeping with the general trend in Buddhist hagiography from the late Tang through the Song away from the traditional Buddhist scholar to the radical antischolasticism of the Chan monk. But what is curious about Huihong's critique is that Huihong was himself a "lecturer" who was well known for "making use of brush and ink." Not only did Huihong compile lengthy biographies of monks, albeit in the new Chan style, he was also an accomplished literary critic, best known to scholars of Chinese poetry as the author of the *Lengzhai yehua*, a collection of secular poetry with commentary.

Huihong's relation to traditional scholarship is indicative of the position in which Chan monks found themselves, especially after the ascendancy of the new Chan hagiography. For many such monks there was clearly a gap between the antischolar rhetoric and practice. Modern scholars of Chan have pointed out that despite the prevalence of Chan hagiography that ridicules traditional forms of practice, Chan monks continued to meditate, conduct rituals, and study scriptures.[124] Although the gap between rhetoric and practice cautions us against overemphasizing the impact of Chan rhetoric, it does not discount entirely the importance of the new Chan *exempla*. After the rise of the new hagiography, the position of the scholar-monk was much more precarious than it had been. And while many monks continued to be attracted to exegetical, doctrinal writings, they now prefaced their interest with uneasy caveats, reservations, and misgivings.

Final Reflections

THE TITLE of this book, *The Eminent Monk*, suggests that it will present a detailed portrait of the ideal monk. After following a series of motifs through the vast hagiographical corpus, we find that if we hope to encompass all of the representations of medieval Chinese monks in a single picture, we can paint this picture only in the broadest of brush strokes. On the most general level, the ideal monk of this hagiography was composed of the qualities I discussed in the first section of the first chapter ("The Monastic Distinction"). The monk was recognized by his clothing, his diet, and the habits and strictures that governed his everyday life, setting him apart from "the vulgar." This being said, it should be evident by now that when we look more closely, we see that there was more than one ideal of the monk in China; individuals entered the Order for various reasons, pursued different goals, and were perceived differently by the laity. This should come as no surprise. The social category of the monk, like that of the peasant or the official, was not narrowly defined and always allowed for a variety of gradations and intersections with other types of people. Within the category of official there were high officials and low officials, court officials and local officials, southern officials and northern officials. The same could be said for the monastic community: there were powerful monks and monastic menials, provincial monks and urban monks, southern monks and northern monks. To a certain extent, all of these distinctions are mental categories, depending on the values placed on juxtapositions and the lines drawn between them. But these sorts of distinctions—north / south, rich / poor—are the subject of another study; in this study I have focused instead on qualities clearly laden with a positive value judgment, social categories recognized as goals to be striven for, characteristics and behaviors considered worthy of the title *eminent*. One way to gain a purchase on the three themes I have discussed is to present them as ideal types.

One such ideal type, within the *sangha*, was the ascetic. Distinguished from those outside of the Order by his chastity, his diet, and his coarse, simple clothing, the ideal ascetic was devoted to a life of rigorous self-cultivation. In contrast to the secular world which placed supreme value on progeny, the ascetic renounced the possibility for sons, not to mention sexual pleasure, by living a life of sexual abstinence. In contrast to the value placed on meat and wine by peasant and official alike, the ascetic maintained a strict vegetarian diet and did not allow wine to pass his lips. The same could be said at some level of most all monks, but the ideal ascetic took the notion of asceticism a step further. Ascetic virtuosi went beyond the strictures of a vegetarian diet, renouncing all food and water for extended periods of time. Ascetic heros did not limit themselves to subduing the passions of the body; they attacked it as a source of defilement, mutilating, burning, and even killing themselves as a part of their ascetic practice. The allure of the ascetic life, however, came not only from a desire to destroy the impure body, but also from a longing to purify the self, to create a better, cleaner body, an idea expressed most clearly in the belief that monks who immolated themselves would be reborn in a pure-land and, in place of a puss-filled bag of flesh and bones, leave behind bright, shiny, numinous relics.

Another ideal type we might construct from the hagiography is that of the wonder-worker or thaumaturge. As a result of his attainments in self-cultivation, most conspicuously meditation, the ideal thaumaturge came to possess extraordinary qualities. Occasionally these qualities took the form of one or more of the "six supernormal powers" of a Buddha—magical powers, supernormal hearing, the ability to read minds, knowledge of one's previous existences, ability to discern the previous lives of others, and finally, the state of having "no outflows," a state in which one is no longer plagued by any form of defilement. But more commonly, the thaumaturge was defined by his ability to see into the future. Stories circulated of monks of the past who had known in advance of recent political and social upheavals and had predicted them in enigmatic phrases decipherable only after the events occurred. Such stories, in addition to verifying the existence of holy monks, also provided a sense of historical continuity and order. If the baffling and often cruel vagaries of history seemed incomprehensible to the ordinary person, he could rest assured that the thaumaturge had perceived the order behind the chaos even before it occurred. The ideal wonder-worker was also known for his mastery of esoteric techniques, inspiring monks to study the arts of fortune-telling and healing and to pore over spell manuals translated (or purporting to be translated) from Sanskrit. Above all, the ideal thaumaturge was one who understood the mechanism of the unseen world of spirits, gods, and ghosts and could at key moments manipulate this world.

The vast corpus of Chinese Buddhist exegetical writings testifies to the prevalence of yet another type of ideal monk: the scholar-monk. The ideal scholar-monk was an erudite master of the written word. He memorized vast quantities of texts through which he was able to classify and analyze the seen and unseen world around him. The ideal scholar-monk applied himself to Indian and Chinese learning. He was versed in the Chinese classics and so skilled in the arts of verse and calligraphy that he inspired the admiration of the scholar-officials who were considered the caretakers of these traditions. The scholar-monk was a fierce debater, who, through swift rhetoric and wit, humiliated his opponents before crowds of admiring students. And the scholar-monk was a great teacher who gathered together hundreds of disciples to absorb and carry on his teachings after his death.

Finally, juxtaposed to the scholar-monk was the Chan eccentric, an ideal figure who took shape in the mid-Tang and became by the Song one of the most memorable types of monks in Chinese Buddhism. Hinted at obliquely in the *Song Biographies of Eminent Monks*, the Chan ideal was propagated chiefly in a new brand of hagiography centering on the words and actions of Chan masters. In these texts, the enlightened Chan master lives in a constant state of awareness, exhibiting his enlightenment through enigmatic, often crude phrases and gestures. In contrast to the scholar-monk, the ideal Chan monk ridicules scriptures and literary erudition, eschews meditation, and shows little interest in the written word. Unfettered by scriptures, rituals, and meditation, the ideal Chan figure is above all unlocalizable; his awakening, unmediated.

I referred earlier to Victor Turner's idea of "root-paradigms," that is, set patterns of behavior with particular symbolic associations. Within the various ideal types I have described above were these nested systems of practice; not necessarily ways of life, but rather guidelines for short-term, very special types of conduct. In the hagiography, a monk intent on a life of especially rigorous asceticism does not practice random austerities, but follows instead set patterns of practice. One of the most common of these sets of practices was the twelve *dhūtāṅga*, namely: wearing garments made of rags from the dust-heap; wearing only the three garments of a monk; deriving food only from begging; begging from door to door; eating in only one sitting a day; eating with only one bowl and only accepting one serving of food; living in the forest; sitting under a tree; residing in an unsheltered place; staying in a cemetery; taking any seat provided; and never lying down, even to sleep. These practices were not carried out universally by the Chinese *saṅgha*, but when monks decided to follow the life of the more severe ascetic, even if only for a short period of time, the *dhūtāṅga* provided an established, ordered map for action. Supported by canonical texts and propagated in stories of biographies of monks, these practices provided parameters to the ascetic life-style, standards against which monks could measure themselves.

Another of these root-paradigms was the practice of self-mutilation and ritual suicide. As in the case of *dhūtāṅga*, the forms of self-mutilation practiced in the hagiography are based on scripture, most notably the *Lotus Sūtra*. Monks do not mutilate themselves at random but according to established methods of self-sacrifice. Similarly, when monks burn themselves to death in the *Biographies*, it is as a part of an involved ritual of anointment and scriptural recitation that was pregnant with meaning. Although there were men both within and without the *saṅgha* who condemned the practice of mutilation, mutilation and ritual suicide were supported by a pervasive belief in the efficacy of such practices for self-purification and the accumulation of merit. The symbolic significance of the signs of these practices—the missing finger, the bright red characters of a scripture copied in blood, the stele marking the relics of a monk who had burned himself to death— were instantly recognized as Buddhist forms of self-sacrifice. Although those who did not share Buddhist beliefs condemned or ridiculed self-mutilation, those who did hold these beliefs responded to the mutilated monk with the respect and reverence these beliefs entailed.

We have also seen the outlines of the root-paradigm of prophecy in the *Biographies*. Monks were routinely attributed the ability to foresee the future, and many actively pursued the techniques and learning associated with prophecy and fortune-telling. The massive body of literature either coming from India or purporting to come from India presented Chinese monks with contradictory views on the propriety of monastic fortune-telling. Despite the occasional condemnation of fortune-telling in the canonical literature, Chinese monks seem to have had no compunction about practicing fortune-telling as long as they received no money for their services. Although some monks were undoubtedly influenced by mantic arts developed in India, for the most part prophecy and fortune-telling followed indigenous Chinese practices dating back to the Han Dynasty and earlier. Related to the practice of fortune-telling was that of geomancy, particularly the selection and positioning of graves—a practice in which many monks engaged, and a sphere in which monks served a lay need for religious professionals.

Finally, in the later biographies of Chan monks, we see the emergence and development of the root-paradigm of encounter-dialogue. In the hagiography, the exchange between a Chan master and his disciple did not follow the conventional rules of debate or instruction depicted in the earlier hagiography. The rules of encounter-dialogue were more elusive, their parameters constantly changing. This was an extremely self-conscious genre of hagiography, a genre that required adherence to the basic structure of master-disciple exchange, but at the same time demanded constant innovation within this structure. Once Huineng's reply to the statement that men from the South do not possess the Buddha Nature became known, other monks were expected to reply to the same question differently, but in such a way as to reveal their understanding of the original exchange. This dynamic reached its extreme in the dozens of increasingly enigmatic replies to sets of questions such as, "Why did Bodhidharma come from the West?" repeated endlessly in the Chan literature.

We can discern these ideal types and root-paradigms in the hagiography, but must keep in mind that the hagiography is not a direct, unmediated reflection of monastic values. In other words, the writers of the biographies, and the compilers who collected them into the *Eminent Monks* series shaped the presentation of monastic ideals. When we place the hagiography in historical context, we see that the biographies often played a role in contests for the image of the monk. That is, the biographies were not only products of the detached musings of religious thinkers, but were also responses to very real threats to the monastic community.

The clearest example of this sort of "image-war" is in the contrast between the depiction of monks in the *Biographies* and the image of the monk in anti-Buddhist court polemic. In memorials to the throne calling for official measures against the *saṅgha* and in the edicts these memorials provoked, we can perceive the attempt on the part of critics to create an image of the monk as a depraved tax-evader. Far from a spiritual figure, the monk (and nun), according to these accounts, was enmeshed in worldly desire, a glutton and a lecher who used the begging bowl and tonsure as a disguise in order to better carry out his self-serving depravities. With these attacks as background, we can readily understand the need leading monks felt for biographies of upright ascetics who scrupulously avoid all contact with women, meat, and wine. I have further argued that the curious accounts in the *Biographies* of monks who do drink wine and eat meat were in fact added to the collection to combat this image problem, for the behavior of these monks is shown in the *Biographies* to stem from the loftiest of goals. Consequently, the biographies send the message that most monks are upright ascetics, and that even monks who appear to be breaking the monastic code may in fact be operating on a high spiritual plane incomprehensible to ordinary men.

A similar instance of Buddhist hagiography attempting to wrest control of the image of the monk from his detractors is in the portrayal of spells in the *Biographies*. According to the Tang legal code, the use of incantations was a punishable offense. At the same time, however, certain emperors actively supported the translation of Buddhist spell manuals. In short, the distinction between wonder-working and sorcery was a fluid one, depending largely on the circumstances in which a spell was used. If a spell was used to cure a princess, the monk who cast it was hailed as a benevolent thaumaturge. In times of political crisis, however, any use of incantations drew the charge of sedition, for spells were believed to have the power to imprecate and destroy their targets. Not surprisingly, spells in the Buddhist hagiography are all of a benign nature, used to cure illness, bring water in times of drought, and drive away evil spirits. The spells cast by rivals to Buddhism, on the other hand, whether visiting Brahmans from India or Daoist priests, are either condemned as destructive and evil or dismissed as ineffective.

In the last chapter I discussed a contest for the image of the monk within the *saṅgha* in different genres of Buddhist hagiography. Whereas the scholar-monk is depicted in the *Eminent Monks* series as a knowledgeable sage worthy of emulation, in the Chan hagiography the scholar-monk is portrayed as a pedant mired in insignificant technicalities and his own ego. Conversely, the radical Chan monk was criticized by Zongmi and others as hedonistic, as abandoning scriptures and practice for self-indulgence, a critique echoed obliquely in the *Song Biographies*. In the Chan hagiography, on the other hand, the same figure is depicted as an enlightened master who has transcended mundane attachments to doctrine and practice for unmediated enlightenment.

In practice, the lines that divide the ascetic from the thaumaturge, or the practice of self-mutilation from the study of spells, were permeable. Most monks at various times in their lives pursued different and even contradictory goals. But when we attempt to be more precise about the impact of hagiography and the ideals it propagated on actual monks, we must set aside the abundance of materials available for the study of ideals and attempt to make sense of bits and pieces of scattered information: archaeology, third-party descriptions of monks, and occasional offhand comments in the hagiography itself hinting that the average monk may have fallen far short of the monastic ideal. Some evidence suggests that many monks ignored the prohibition on wine or circumvented it through casuistry, justifying wine-drinking as a form of medication. Sophisticated ridicule of scriptures and meditation in Chan recorded-sayings betrays a knowledge of scripture and meditation, suggesting that even the Chan monks who claimed to have transcended traditional forms of study and practice, did in fact engage in them.

In addition to the problem of the gap between ideal and practice, the sheer bulk and orderliness of monastic hagiography can easily mislead us. As we read through lively stories conveniently collected in the canon in uniform language, the power of the monastic vision leads us to exaggerate its importance. Leading scholars of Chinese religion have warned that in practice Buddhism was nothing so orderly as a progression of teachings through distinct lineages from masters to disciples, that the canon that contains these biographies represents a censored, "clean" version of the history of Buddhism. Naturally enough, women, farmers, merchants, and craftsmen have little place in biographies of monks. The danger, then, is in taking monastic ideals for Buddhism as a whole, as in any number of popular presentations of Buddhism that characterize Buddhism with a few lines about meditation, renunciation, and emptiness—concerns closely tied to the monastic ideal. This being said, though we may not wish to place monks at the center of medieval Chinese Buddhism, they themselves did just that. That is, monks thought of the monastic life as the authentic Buddhist way of life and encouraged their followers to think the same way. It is the strength of this vision, the idea of the eminent monk expressed so vividly in the hagiography that accounts in large measure for the successful introduction and expansion of the monastic institution in China.

Abbreviations

GSZ   Huijiao 惠皎, *Gaoseng zhuan* 高僧傳 (*The Liang Biographies*), eds. Tang Yongtong 湯用彤 and Tang Yixuan 湯一玄 (Beijing: Zhonghua shuju, 1992), with reference to *T* 2059, v. 50. References are to the *juan* number, followed by the number of the biography within the *juan*, followed by the *Taishō* page number.

SBBY   *Sibu beiyao* 四部備要.

SBCK   *Sibu congkan* 四部叢刊.

SSZ   Zanning 贊寧, *Song gaoseng zhuan* 宋高僧傳 (*The Song Biographies*), ed. Fan Xiangyong 范祥雍 (Beijing: Zhonghua shuju, 1987), with reference to *T* 2061, v. 50. References are to the *juan* number, followed by the number of the biography within the *juan*, followed by the *Taishō* page number.

T   J. Takakusu 高楠順次郎 and K. Watanabe 渡辺海旭, eds., *Taishō shinshū daizōkyō* 大正新修大藏經 (Tokyō: Taishō issaikyō kankōkai, 1924–1932).

XSZ   Daoxuan 道宣, *Xu gaoseng zhuan* 續高僧傳 (*The Further Biographies*), with reference to *T* 2060, v. 50. References are to *juan* number, followed by the number of the biography within the *juan*, followed by the *Taishō* page number.

XZJ   *Xu zangjing* 續藏經 (Taibei: Xinwenfeng, 1968–1970), a reprint of Nakano Tatsue 中野達慧, ed., *Dai Nihon zoku-zōkyō* 大日本續藏經 (Kyoto: Zōkyō shoin, 1905–1912).

Notes

Introduction

1. I treat the various sources for this story in detail in the second section of chapter 1.

2. Xuyun, *Empty Cloud: The Autobiography of the Chinese Zen Master*, translated by Charles Luk (Longmead: Element Books, 1988), p. 1. I have removed some of the translator's interpolations.

3. Xuyun, *Empty Cloud*, pp. 38–39.

4. Reference to scholarship on Christian hagiography is instructive. The secondary literature on Christian hagiography is immense, and new works appear each year. Most of these works adopt one of five approaches. (1) For a classic example of the attempt to separate legend from a factual core, see Hippolyte Delehaye, *The Legends of the Saints* (New York: Fordham University Press, 1962). (2) For an eloquent example of the value of fabulous biographies apart from the question of historicity, see Peter Brown, "The Saint as Exemplar in Late Antiquity," *Representations* 1. 2 (Spring 1983): pp. 1–25. (3) Donald Weinstein and Rudolph Bell, *Saints & Society: The Two Worlds of Western Christendom, 1000–1700* (Chicago: University of Chicago Press, 1982) is innovative and controversial for its use of statistical analysis of biographies of saints. (4) Richard Kieckhefer, *Unquiet Souls: Fourteenth Century Saints and Their Religious Milieu* (Chicago: University of Chicago Press, 1984) is a good example of the use of hagiography to trace a shift in religious mentality over time. (5) Finally, Kenneth Woodward, *Making Saints—Inside the Vatican: Who Become Saints, Who Do Not, and Why* (London: Chatto and Windus, 1990) is a fascinating meditation on the process by which saints are selected, in this case by the Vatican.

In recent years, scholars of Chinese religion have begun to examine Chinese hagiography for what it can tell us about mentalities. See for example Franciscus Verellen, "Luo Gongyuan: Légende et culte d'un saint taoïste," *Journal Asiatique* 275. 3–4 (1987): pp. 282–332; Robert Campany, "Notes on the Devotional Uses and Symbolic Functions of Sūtra Texts as Depicted in Early Chinese Buddhist Miracle Tales and Hagiographies," *Journal of the International Association of Buddhist Studies* 14. 1 (1991): pp. 28–72; and Mu-chou Poo, "The Images of Immortals and Eminent Monks: Religious Mentality in Early Medieval China (4–6 c. A.D.)," *Numen* 42 (1995): pp. 172–196.

5. Huijiao completed his work during the Liang Dynasty (in approximately 530). I will subsequently refer to this text as the *Liang Biographies* to distinguish it from its successors. In addition to the 257 major biographies, there are also 242 subordinate biographies, that is, short biographies appended to some of the major ones. At this time there is no complete English translation of the *Liang Biographies*. English translations by the late Arthur Link have recently begun to appear along with Japanese annotation by Hirai Shun'ei in the journal *Komazawa daigaku Bukkyō gakubu ronshū* 49 (Mar. 1991): pp. 1–15; 23 (Oct. 1992): pp. 1–14; 24 (Oct. 1993): pp. 1–35; 25 (Oct. 1994): pp. 11–25.

6. See Arthur Wright, "Biography and Hagiography: Hui-chiao's *Lives of Eminent Monks,*" in *Silver Jubilee Volume* (Kyoto University: Jimbun kagaku kenkyū-sho, 1954), pp. 407–408. This article includes a translation of Huijiao's preface. A few fragments from the *Mingseng zhuan* do survive in a thirteenth-century Japanese copy preserved as *Meisōdenshō* in *XZJ* v. 134. Cf. Wright, "Biography and Hagiography," p. 410.

7. *GSZ* 14 (419a); Wright, "Biography and Hagiography," p. 408.

8. *GSZ* 5.12 (356b–c).

9. *Fangguang [banruo] jing* (Skt. *Pancaviṃśatisāhasrikāprajñapāramitā*) *T* 221, v. 8.

10. In addition to the 485 major biographies, the *Further Biographies* also contains 219 appended biographies.

11. More precisely, the *Song Biographies* contains 531 major biographies and 125 appended biographies.

12. *GSZ* 14.1 (418b); Wright, "Biography and Hagiography," pp. 403–404.

13. *SSZ* 0.2 (709c).

14. Compiler of the *Records of the Three Kingdoms* (*Sanguo zhi*).

15. Compiler of the *Records of the Historian* (*Shiji*). *SSZ* 0.2 (709b–c).

16. As Robert Campany notes, concern for the preservation of historical documents was also a motivating force behind the compilation of "anomaly accounts" (*zhiguai*). See Campany, *Strange Writing: Anomaly Accounts in Early Medieval China* (New York: State University of New York Press, 1996), pp. 143–146.

17. *SSZ* 18.5 (821c).

18. *GSZ* 14.4 (422c).

19. Cf. Makita Tairyō, "*Kōsōden* no seiritsu," *Tōhō gakuhō* 44 (1973):

p. 103. For Yuan Di's remark, see *Jinlouzi* 6, "Jushu pian" 2.18a–b (*Siku quanshu* edn.).

20. On Daoxuan's life and his proselytizing efforts, see Shi Guodeng, *Tang Daoxuan* Xu gaoseng zhuan *pipan sixiang chutan* (Taibei: Dongchu chubanshe, 1992), and Robin Wagner, "Buddhism, Biography and Power: A Study of Daoxuan's Continued Lives of Eminent Monks" (Ph.D. dissertation, Harvard University, 1995).

21. See Albert Dalia, "The 'Political Career' of the Buddhist Historian Tsan-ning," in David Chappell, ed., *Buddhist and Taoist Practice in Medieval Chinese Society* (Honolulu: University of Hawai'i Press, 1987), pp. 146–180.

22. See *SSZ* 0.1 (709a) for Zanning's comments, *GSZ* 5.1 (352a) for those of Huijiao.

23. *SSZ* 0.1 (709b).

24. *XSZ* 6.5 (471b).

25. *SSZ* 23.*T* (862a). The quotation is from *Shijing* no. 335.

26. *SSZ* 0.2 (710a).

27. In Huijiao's preface and in the *Further* and *Song Biographies*, this chapter is entitled *yishen*, which can also be translated as "Those Who Sacrificed Themselves."

28. Strangely, Zanning asserts that Daoxuan changed the category of "Hymnodists" (*jingshi*) to "Chanters and Reciters" (*dusong*), even though it would seem that Daoxuan's "Chanters and Reciters" section was an outgrowth of Huijiao's "Chanters" section, while Daoxuan's "Miscellaneous Sermonists" seems to have been inspired by Huijiao's "Hymnodists" chapter (Cf. *XSZ* 30.*T* [705c5]). Perhaps there was some confusion about just how the categories of chanting and psalmody were defined. Cf. *SSZ* 25.*T* (872b) for Zanning's comments.

29. The *zan* for the last two categories are not extant. Cf. Wright, "Biography and Hagiography," p. 391.

30. Wright, "Biography and Hagiography," pp. 390–392.

31. The discussion of sources in Wright, "Biography and Hagiography" is still excellent, but the most comprehensive overview of the sources of the *Liang Biographies* is Makita Tairyō, "*Kōsōden* no seiritsu," *Tōhō gakuhō* 44 (1973): pp. 101–125, and 48 (1975): pp. 229–259, in which Makita traces thirty different sources for the *Liang Biographies*. Zheng Yuqing's *Gaoseng zhuan yanjiu* (Taibei: Wenjin chubanshe, 1990), pp. 7–40, covers much of the same ground and contains some emendations to Makita's work. For a nuanced, detailed analysis of the ways in which the compilers of the *Eminent Monks* series used two types of sources, see Koichi Shinohara, "Two Sources of Chinese Buddhist Biographies: Stupa Inscriptions and Miracle Stories," in Phyllis Granoff and Koichi Shinohara, eds., *Monks and Magicians: Religious Biographies in Asia* (Oakville: Mosaic Press, 1988), pp. 119–229. For discussion of the sources of the *Further Biographies*, see Shi Guodeng, *Tang Daoxuan*, pp. 43–92. I am currently at work on a com-

plete translation of the *Song Biographies* which will include a more extensive discussion of the sources for this work.

32. *GSZ* 14.1 (418c); Wright, "Biography and Hagiography," p. 405.

33. In an important study of medieval Chinese miracle tales, Kominami Ichirō demonstrates that many of these tales, collected by literati, originated in oral stories told by monks. "Rikuchō Zui Tō shōsetsu no tenkai to Bukkyō shinkō," in Fukunaga Kōshi, ed., *Chūgoku chūsei no shūkyō to bunka* (Kyoto: Kyoto daigaku jimbun Kagaku kenkyū-sho, 1982), pp. 415–500.

34. Shinohara, "Two Sources of Chinese Buddhist Biographies," p. 125; Kenneth Chen, "Inscribed Stelae during the Wei, Chin, and Nanch'ao," in Lawrence G. Thompson, ed., *Studia Asiatica: Essays in Asian Studies in Felicitation of the Seventy-fifth Anniversary of Professor Ch'en Shou-yi* (San Francisco: Chinese Materials Center, 1975), pp. 75–84.

35. Shinohara, "Two Sources of Chinese Buddhist Biographies," p. 124.

36. This approach to the writing of history was not limited to Buddhist biography, but was true of secular history as well. Cf. Denis Twitchett, "Problems of Chinese Biography," in Arthur Wright and Denis Twitchett, eds., *Confucian Personalities* (Stanford: Stanford University Press, 1962), pp. 24–42.

37. *Meisōdenshō* 23, *XZJ*, v. 134.11b–12a.

38. This daunting hagiological quandary is not limited to Chinese or Buddhist material. As Kenneth Woodward puts it, "To cite an extreme example, one may ask whether Joan of Arc (1412–1431) reflects the religious mentality of fifteenth-century France, or the priorities—spiritual or political—of the Holy See in 1920, when she was finally canonized." *Making Saints*, p. 388.

39. *Tang huiyao* 49 (Taibei: Shijie shuju, 1968), pp. 860–861, quoted in Kenneth Chen, *The Chinese Transformation of Buddhism* (Princeton: Princeton University Press, 1973), p. 105. On book-selling in the Tang, see Denis Twitchett, *Printing and Publishing in Medieval China* (New York: Frederic Beil, 1983), p. 17.

40. The *Fahua ganying zhuan*. Jōjin, *San Tendai Godaisan ki* 3.57, in *Dai Nihon Bukkyō zensho* (Tokyo: Kōdansha, 1970–1973), v. 115.

41. Cf. Yan Gengwang, "Tangren xiye shanlin siyuan zhi fengshang," in *Yan Gengwang shixue lunwen xuanji* (Taibei: Lianjing chuban shiye, 1991), pp. 271–316.

42. *XSZ* 0.1 (425b2–3).

43. *Liangchu qingzhong yiben T* 1895, v. 45.842b12. In addition, Tang poets made occasional reference to the *Biographies of Eminent Monks*. See for example "Chunri shangfang jishi" by Wang Wei, *Quan Tang shi* (1960; rpt. Beijing: Zhonghua Shuju, 1985), 126.1278, and "Wan bo Xunyang wang Lu shan" by Meng Haoran, *Quan Tang shi* 160.1645.

44. See, for example, the biography of Mingche, *XSZ* 6.13 (473a).

45. The Yuan Dynasty work *Shishi jigu lüe* (*T* 2037, v. 49) and the Ming work *Shenseng zhuan* (*T* 2064, v. 50), for instance, rely heavily on the *Biographies of Eminent Monks* series.

46. *Siku quanshu zongmu* (Taibei: Yiwen yinshuguan, n.d.; facsimile reproduction of the Dadong shuju edition), 145.7 (2859). For a modern assessment of the style of the *Liang Biographies*, see Su Jinren, "Liang Shi Huijiao ji qi *Gaoseng zhuan,*" *Shijie zongjiao yanjiu* (1981.1), pp. 133–140.

47. Yang Shoujing, *Riben fangshu zhi* (Linsuyuan edn., 1897), 16.1a.

48. *Zongtong biannian*, *XZJ*, v. 147, 19.140b.

49. In reference to the biography of Chengguan. Cf. *Huayan xuantan huixuan ji*, *XZJ* v. 12.5a.

50. "Ti Fojian sengbao zhuan," in *Shimen wenzi chan*, *SBCK* v. 112, 26.4a, cited in Chen Yuan, *Zhongguo fojiao shiji gailun* (1962; rpt. Beijing: Zhonghua shuju, 1988), p. 135. For a comparison between the historiography of Huihong and Zanning, see Abe Shōichi, "Sō kōsoden to *Zenrin sōhōden*—Hoku-Sō no Sannei to Dokō no sōshikan," in *Rekishi ni okeru minshū to bunka—Sakai Tadao sensei koki shukuga kinen ronshū* (Tokyo: Sakai Tadao sensei koki shukuga kinen no kai, 1982), pp. 297–312.

51. Huihong, "Ti xiu sengshi," *Shimen wenzi chan*, 25.10b–11a. Thirteenth-century monk Zhipan repeats Huihong's comments in his *Fo zu tong ji* 43, *T* 2035, v. 49.400a. I have been unable to locate Huang Tingjian's comments in Huang's extant works.

52. *Yixue.* The first two sections of the *Biographies* are reserved for translators and exegetes. Apparently, Huihong considered translators to be exegetes as well.

53. Huihong, *Linjian lu*, *XZJ*, v. 148, A.294a. Zhijue is better known as Yongming Yanshou. On Huihong's criticism of Zanning's treatment of Yanshou, see Albert Welter, *The Meaning of Myriad Good Deeds: A Study of Yung-ming Yen-shou and the Wan-shan t'ung-kuei chi* (New York: Peter Lang, 1993), pp. 64–65, 92–93.

Chapter 1: Asceticism

1. Luis Gomez, "BUDDHISM: Buddhism in India," in Mircea Eliade, gen. ed., *Encyclopedia of Religion* (New York: Macmillan and Free Press, 1987), v. 2, p. 356.

2. *Xi jing fu*, in *Wen xuan SBBY* C102.1, 2.17a, translated in David R. Knechtges, *Wen xuan*, "Volume One: Rhapsodies on Metropolises and Capitals" (Princeton: Princeton University Press, 1982), p. 237. In this last line, my translation differs slightly from that of Knechtges. For a discussion of the significance of this line for our understanding of Han Buddhism, see Arthur Wright, *Buddhism in Chinese History* (Stanford: Stanford University Press, 1959), pp. 21–22; and Erik Zürcher, "Han Buddhism and the Western Region," in W. L. Idema

and E. Zürcher, eds., *Thought and Law in Qin and Han China* (Leiden: E. J. Brill, 1990), pp. 158–182.

3. Our first explicit accounts of Chinese monks date from some time later. Cf. Erik Zürcher, *The Buddhist Conquest of China* (Leiden: E. J. Brill, 1959), pp. 24, 28.

4. Zhan Ji is known variously as Zhan Huo, Liu Hui, and Liuxia Hui. Cf. Knechtges, *Wen xuan*, p. 236, and Martin J. Powers, *Art and Political Expression in Early China* (New Haven: Yale University Press, 1991), pp. 214–215.

5. On this point see the first four chapters of R. H. Van Gulik, *Sexual Life in Ancient China* (1961; rpt. Leiden: E. J. Brill, 1974), especially page 50. This was not a uniquely Chinese reaction; when confronted with chaste ascetics, ancient Indians expressed similar concerns. Cf. Wendy Doniger O'Flaherty, *Asceticism and Eroticism in the Mythology of Siva* (London: Oxford University Press, 1973), pp. 68–70.

6. Cf. Van Gulik, *Sexual Life*, pp. 137, 195–196.

7. *GSZ* 2.1 (330a).

8. *GSZ* 2.1 (331c).

9. *GSZ* 2.1 (332c).

10. *GSZ* 3.*T* (345c23).

11. *Mishasai wu fen jieben* (Skt. **Mahīśāsakavinaya*) *T* 1422, v. 22.196a, and *Si fen lü* 1 (Skt. **Dharmaguptakavinaya*) *T* 1428, v. 22.570c. As I focus here on the Chinese perception of India, I limit myself to Indian texts that found their way to China and were translated into Chinese there. However, many interesting parallels can be found in Pāli sources. In *Buddhist Monastic Life According to the Texts of the Theravāda Tradition* (Cambridge: Cambridge University Press, 1990), Mohan Wijayaratna gives a concise summary of early Buddhist views on, among other things, chastity, food, and clothing according to Pāli sources. For a detailed survey and analysis of Buddhist interdictions concerning sex in East Asia as well as in India, see Bernard Faure, *Sexualités bouddhiques* (Paris: Le Mail, 1994), pp. 63–88.

12. That is, *saṃghāvaśeṣa*. Cf. *Si fen lü T* 1428, v. 22.196a–b.

13. Cf. Peter Brown, *The Body and Society: Men, Women, and Sexual Renunciation in Early Christianity* (New York: Columbia, 1988), pp. 401–403.

14. According to the *Chang ahan jing* (Skt. *Dīrghāgama*), this is the case in the heaven known as Trāyastriṃśa (Cf. *T* 1, v. 1.133c). Other texts claim that the inhabitants of other heavens have sex by variously embracing, holding hands, or speaking with one another. In the highest heavens, as there is no longer a distinction between male and female, all of this is unnecessary. Cf. Xiao Dengfu, *Han Wei Liuchao Fo Dao liang jiao zhi tiantang diyu shuo* (Taibei: Xuesheng shuju, 1989), pp. 45–49.

15. From "Zhihuo jie," included in *Guang hongming ji* 7, *T* 2103, v. 52.131c.

16. Cf. *Zizhi tongjian* (1956; rpt. Beijing: Zhonghua shuju, 1987), 124.3923; and Kenneth Chen, *Buddhism in China* (Princeton: Princeton University Press, 1964), p. 149.

17. The chief sources for this incident are *Xin Tang shu* (1975; rpt. Beijing: Zhonghua shuju, 1986), 83.3648, 96.3858; and *Zizhi tongjian* 199.6279. On these accounts and Bianji in general, see Chen Yuan, "*Da Tang Xiyu ji* zhuanren Bianji" in Wu Ze, ed., *Chen Yuan shixue lun zhu xuan* (Shanghai: Shanghai renmin chubanshe, 1981), pp. 266–287.

18. Cf. Faure, *Sexualités bouddhiques*, pp. 160–169. Western parallels abound. See Graciela S. Daichman, *Wayward Nuns in Medieval Literature* (Syracuse University Press, 1986). Daichman argues that the accounts of wayward nuns in medieval European literature were rooted in genuine promiscuity in the convents.

19. "Tian di yinyang jiao huan da le fu," in Ye Dehui, ed., *Shuangmei jing'an congshu* 1.7b. My translation differs from that of Van Gulik, *Sexual Life*, p. 207.

20. There are many Indian stories in which an ascetic achieves great powers through years of sexual abstention only to lose them all in an evening encounter with a temptress. Cf. O'Flaherty, *Asceticism and Eroticism*, pp. 40–82. Chinese stories of (non-Buddhist) eremites, on the contrary, are more likely to emphasize the abilities of the adept to have sex even at an advanced age. See, for example, the biography of Wang Zhen in *Hou Han shu* (Beijing: Zhonghua shuju, 1965), 82.2750–51.

21. In "Sengshi suo zai Zhongguo shamen jianshou yinjie de yi xie shili," Cao Shibang collected accounts from the *Biographies* and other Chinese Buddhist sources related to proscriptions on male-female relations in the *saṅgha*. *Huagang foxue xuebao* 5 (1982): pp. 275–288. The case of the murder of the fifth-century monk Tanwuchen (Skt. Dharmakṣema) is a particularly revealing example of the distinction between secular and Buddhist sources. According to the secular *Wei shu*, Tanwuchen was murdered when it was discovered that he was teaching sexual techniques to palace women. The account of Tanwuchen in the *Liang Biographies*, however, makes no such mention. Cf. Naomi Gentetsu, "*Kōsōden* seiritsu-jō no mondaiten—Donmushin no jirei o tōshite," *Tōyō shien* 26. 27 (Mar. 1986): pp. 63–82. Naomi rejects the story of Tanwuchen's illicit sexual activity as apocryphal.

22. *XSZ* 16.21 (559c).

23. *XSZ* 9.8 (497b).

24. *XSZ* 19.2 (579c). In the early years of the Song, emperor Taizu promulgated an edict specifically forbidding nuns from going to monks to receive ordination. Cf. *Da Song sengshi lüe* A, *T* 2126, v. 54.238c.

25. *XSZ* 20C.5 (605c).

26. *XSZ* 9.8 (497b).

27. See, for instance, the biographies of Wuzuo *SSZ* 30.10 (897a) and Yanqiu, appended to *SSZ* 28.3 (884c).

28. *Biqiuni zhuan*, *T* 2063, v. 50. Translated by Kathryn Ann Tsai, *Lives of the Nuns: Biographies of Chinese Buddhist Nuns from the Fourth to Sixth Centuries* (Honolulu: University of Hawai'i Press, 1994). Below I make only very occasional reference to nuns. This is because of the scarcity of hagiography about nuns. Unlike the *Liang Biographies*, the *Lives of Nuns* was not followed by sequels in later times.

29. Biographies of Zhixian, *Biqiuni zhuan* p. 935b (Tsai, *Lives*, p. 22); Kang Minggan, p. 935c (Tsai, *Lives*, p. 24); Zhisheng, p. 942c (Tsai, *Lives*, p. 74); Huixu, p. 944a (Tsai, *Lives*, p. 81).

30. *Biqiuni zhuan*, p. 945b; Tsai, *Lives*, pp. 88–89.

31. Cf. Owen Chadwick, *Western Asceticism* (Philadelphia: The Westminster Press, 1958), pp. 71–72. This account was the basis for Tolstoy's short story "Father Sergius."

32. *SSZ* 4.12 (729a).

33. *SSZ* 26.3 (873a–c).

34. Cf. the biography of Tanlun, *XSZ* 20b.2 (598c).

35. *Song shu* (Beijing: Zhonghua shuju, 1974), 93.2280. There are numerous post-Han references in the dynastic histories to men who swore off sex (*jue fangshi*) or refused to marry. But the tendency of court historians to downplay Buddhist elements makes it difficult to determine whether or not these men were influenced by Buddhist notions of chastity.

36. Cf. Ying-shih Yü, "Han," in K. C. Chang, ed., *Food in Chinese Culture* (New Haven: Yale University Press, 1977), pp. 74–75; and Edward Schafer, "T'ang" on page 98 of the same volume.

37. The symbolic importance of meat was not new with the Han. In his discussion of the importance of meat in the Zhou, Mark Lewis points out that one term for the Zhou aristocracy was "the meat eaters." Mark Lewis, *Sanctioned Violence in Early China* (Albany: State University of New York Press, 1990), pp. 29–30.

38. Cf. Yü, "Han," pp. 55–70.

39. *Han shu* (Beijing: Zhonghua shuju, 1962), 72.3089.

40. *Hou Han shu*, 52.1724.

41. *Han shu*, 99.4050.

42. Cf. *San guo zhi* (Beijing: Zhonghua shuju, 1959), 39.979, and *Han shu*, 68.2940, in which a prince is criticized for eating meat during the mourning period. In a note to this account, the Tang scholar Yan Shigu specifies that the term *su shi* refers specifically to a vegetarian diet, and not simply "plain" or "common" food.

43. In an article on the origins of vegetarianism in Indian Buddhism, Shimoda Masahiro argues that vegetarianism emerged in Indian Buddhism not so much as a product of Buddhist ethical or doctrinal beliefs, as a response to a pre-Buddhist Indian tradition that considered meat—along with garlic and onions—impure. Shimoda is responding in part to an article by David Reugg in which Ruegg

attempted to link the emergence of Buddhist vegetarianism to the doctrine of the *tathāgatagarbha*. See Shimoda Masahiro, "Higashi Ajia Bukkyō no kairitsu no tokushoku—nikushoku kinshi no yurai o megutte," *Tōyō gakujutsu kenkyū* 29. 4 (Dec. 1990): pp. 98–110.

44. On vegetarianism in early Chinese Buddhism, see Richard Mather, "The Bonze's Begging Bowl: Eating Practices in Buddhist Monasteries of Medieval India and China," *Journal of the American Oriental Society* 101. 4 (Oct.–Dec. 1981): pp. 417–424; and Suwa Yoshizumi, "Chūgoku Bukkyō ni okeru saishoku shugi shisō no keisei ni kansuru kanken—Bukkyō denrai Ryōsho ni itaru jiki," *Nihon Bukkyō gakkai nenpō* 43 (Mar. 1978): pp. 73–99.

45. *T* 1428, v. 22.866c, 868b–869a, 872a–b.

46. *T* 1425, v. 22.487a.

47. Cf. *Da banniepan jing T* 374, v. 12.386, though the text is not entirely consistent on this point. Cf. Mather, "The Bonze's Begging Bowl": p. 421. Besides the *Nirvāṇa*, the most prominent text to call for total vegetarianism was the *Laṅkavatārasūtra*. Cf. Yasui Kōsai, "*Nyūryōgakkyō* ni okeru nikushoku no kinshi," *Ōtani gakuhō* 43.2 (Dec. 1963): pp. 1–13. For a concise summary of different views on meat-eating in Chinese Buddhism, see Michihata Ryōshū, *Chūgoku Bukkyō shisōshi no kenkyū* (Tokyo: Heirakuji shoten, 1983), pp. 275–291.

48. *Biqiuni zhuan* 4, p. 945a; Tsai, *Lives*, p. 87.

49. Michihata, *Chūgoku Bukkyō shisōshi*, p. 289.

50. Mather dates the switch to strict vegetarianism to the fifth century. Cf. Mather, "The Bonze's Begging Bowl": pp. 421–423.

51. *GSZ* 12B.20 (408c).

52. *Nan shi* (Beijing: Zhonghua shuju, 1975), 70.1722.

53. *XSZ* 11.11 (513c).

54. *XSZ* 7.6 (480b).

55. *Biqiuni zhuan* 2, p. 938c; Tsai, *Lives*, pp. 45–46.

56. *XSZ* 27.2 (679b).

57. *XSZ* 15.*T* (549a).

58. *XSZ* 21.6 (609b).

59. *XSZ* 20B.1 (597c).

60. *GSZ* 3.7 (341a).

61. On Liang Wu Di's campaign, see Michihata, *Chūgoku Bukkyō shisōshi*, pp. 292–308; and Yan Shangwen, "Liang Wu Di 'Huangdi pusa' linian de xingcheng ji zhengce de tuizhan" (Ph.D. dissertation, Taiwan Normal University, 1989), pp. 203–232.

62. *Song shu*, 93.2292.

63. *Jiu Tang shu*, 187.4889; *Xin Tang shu*, 191.5511 and *SSZ* 20.13 (839c).

64. Suwa cites examples of the pre-Buddhist Chinese practice of vegetarianism during mourning as one of the reasons for the success of complete vegetarianism in Chinese Buddhism. The other factors Suwa enumerates for this success are the Buddhist prohibition against

killing, fear of karmic retribution, the emphasis on benevolence in Confucianism, and the pre-Buddhist dietary practice of hermits and Daoists. Cf. Suwa, "Saishoku shugi shisō."

65. *Chen shu* (Beijing: Zhonghua shuju, 1972), 20.282.

66. *Jiu Tang shu* (Beijing: Zhonghua shuju, 1975), 177.4593.

67. *Nan Qi shu* (Beijing: Zhonghua shuju, 1972), 41.732. See also *Guang hongming ji* 26, *T* 2103, v. 52.293a–b.

68. *SSZ* 11.1 (771c–772a).

69. *GSZ* 7.20 (372a–b). Similarly, according to Tibetan tradition, when the infamous Glan-dar-ma carried out a persecution of Buddhism, he had a picture of a monk drinking wine painted on the gates of one of the most prominent monasteries. Cf. *History of Buddhism* (Chos-hbyung) by Bu-ston, translated from Tibetan by E. Obermiller (Heidelberg: 1931), p. 198.

70. *GSZ* 13C.9 (417a).

71. Michihata Ryōshū devotes a lengthy chapter of a book on the bodhisattva precepts to Buddhism and wine. In the chapter, he collects material from Indian sources (in Chinese translation) as well as Chinese discursive writing and biographies relating to the question of whether or not monks should be allowed to drink wine in certain circumstances. *Daijō bosatsukai no tenkai*, vol. 7, *Chūgoku Bukkyōshi zenshū* (Tokyo: Kabushiki kaisha Shoen, 1986), pp. 381–542.

72. In "Sengshi suo zai Zhongguo shamen jianshou jiegui huo Tianzhu chuantong de ge lei shili," a follow-up article to the one mentioned above, Cao Shibang culls material from the *Biographies* relating to the maintenance of the Vinaya in China, including the prohibition on wine, the five-strong flavors, and so on. *Zhonghua foxue xuebao* (1988. 2), pp. 325–357.

73. *XSZ* 2.4 (437a).

74. *GSZ* 6.1 (361a–b); Zürcher, *Buddhist Conquest*, p. 253.

75. Sengyuan, *SSZ* 4.17 (731a).

76. Mingjie, *XSZ* 25B.38 (665c).

77. For an overview of monastic clothing in China, see Zhou Shujia, "Hanzu sengfu kao lüe," in *Zhou Shujia foxue lunzhu ji* (Beijing: Zhonghua shuju, 1991), pp. 718–725; and Kawaguchi Kōfū, "Kesa-shi ni okeru Dōsen no chii—rokumono o chūshin ni," *Shūkyō kenkyū* 47. 2 (Jan. 1974): pp. 97–121.

78. *Da Song sengshi lüe* A, pp. 237c–238a.

79. Cf. *Nanhai jigui neifa zhuan* 2, *T* 2125, v. 54.214a. Translated by J. Takakusu as *A Record of the Buddhist Religion as Practiced in India and the Malay Archipelago* (London: Claredon Press, 1896), p. 67.

80. Cf. Nakamura Hajime, *Bukkyōgo daijiten* (Tokyo: Tokyo shoseki, 1975), p. 455c. The robes could also be worn one over the other in cold weather.

81. See, for example, the biography of Jingduan, *XSZ* 18.7 (576c).

82. In Tang times pronounced **lippat*, according to Edwin Pulley-

blank, *Lexicon of Reconstructed Pronunciation in Early Middle Chinese, Late Middle Chinese, and Early Mandarin* (Vancouver: University of British Columbia Press, 1991). Skt. **repa?* cf. Yijing, *Nanhai jigui* 2, p. 214c (Takakusu, *A Record of the Buddhist Religion*, pp. 69–70).

83. *SSZ* 4.6 (727c). See also, *Sengshi lüe*, A, p. 238a. The ending quotation is actually a reference to the *Zuo zhuan*, "Xigong," 24, in *Shisan jing zhusu* (Beijing: Zhonghua Shuju, 1979), 15.116b; James Legge, trans., *The Ch'un-ts'ew with the Tso Chuen* (Hong Kong: Hong Kong University Press, 1960), p. 193a in which Mao no.151 is quoted in part.

84. On this practice, see Huang Minzhi, "Songdai de ziyi shihao" (which includes discussion of the Tang and Five Dynasties period) included in her *Songdai fojiao shehui jingji shi lunji* (Taibei: Xuesheng shuju, 1989), pp. 443–510.

85. Cf. *Zizhi tongjian*, 204.6469; Huang, *Songdai fojiao*, p. 444; Antonino Forte, *Political Propaganda and Ideology in China at the End of the Seventh Century* (Napoli: Istitut Universitario Orientale, 1976), p. 11.

86. The vagaries of state policy concerning the purple robe is the focus of Huang's article mentioned above.

87. *SSZ* 20.1 (842b).

88. *SSZ* 25.16 (870a–b) and *Quan Tang shi*, 795.8960.

89. *SSZ* 7.13 (749c).

90. In the late fourth century, the prominent Christian theologian Augustine took a similar stand on silk robes, which he considered inappropriate for a "man of the cloth." Cf. Peter Brown's *Augustine of Hippo* (Berkeley: University of California Press, 1967), p. 410.

91. *XSZ* 27.12 (684b–c).

92. *Nanhai jigui* 2, pp. 212c–213a. (Takakusu, *A Record of the Buddhist Religion*, p. 58). See also, Kawaguchi, "Kesa-shi ni okeru," p. 110.

93. Pierre Bourdieu, *Distinction: A Social Critique of the Judgement of Taste* (Cambridge: Harvard University Press, 1984), p. 57.

94. See, for example, Daoyue *XSZ* 25B.20 (662a), Changda *SSZ* 16.8 (807c) and Weijin *SSZ* 17.17 (818b).

95. *SSZ* 24.14 (864c).

96. Cf. Jing'ai, *XSZ* 23.3 (627b). The hair-shirt (*cuiyi*) was made of animal hair, such as wool. Cf. Daoxuan's *Sifen lü shanfan buque xingshi chao* C.3, *T* 1804, v. 40.131a27.

97. Qiyin *SSZ* 30.8 (896b), and Sengming *XSZ* 25B.34 (665a), respectively.

98. *XSZ* 6.12 (473a).

99. *SSZ* 7.1 (745b).

100. *Sengshi lüe* B, pp. 245a–b.

101. Cf. Jacques Gernet, *Buddhism in Chinese Society: An Economic History from the Fifth to the Tenth Centuries*, translated from the French by Franciscus Verellen (New York: Columbia University Press, 1995), p. 207. For a survey of begging in Buddhism, focusing on

Indian canonical material, see Jean Rahder, "Bunne," in *Hōbōgirin: Dictionnaire encyclopédique du bouddhisme d'après les sources chinoises et japonaises* (Paris: Adrien Maisonneuve, 1927–1983), pp. 158–169. For China, see Mather, "The Bonze's Begging Bowl": pp. 418–419.

102. *XSZ* 20.2 (589a).

103. *GSZ* 12B.5 (407a).

104. *GSZ* 11.3 (395c).

105. Cf. Cao Shibang, "Zhongguo sengshi suo zai chiwu de shijian he miandui de nanti," *Huagang foxue xuebao* 6 (July 1983): pp. 327–344; Mather, "The Bonze's Begging Bowl": pp. 417–418.

106. For an introduction to *dhūtāṅga* (Ch. *toutuo*), see Mochizuki Shinkō, ed., *Bukkyō daijiten* (Tokyo: Sekai seiten kankō kyōkai, 1958–1963), p. 2335a. The most common set of *dhūtāṅga* in Chinese texts is a list of twelve: wearing garments made of rags from the dust-heap; wearing only the three garments; deriving food only from begging; begging from door to door; eating in only one sitting a day; eating with only one bowl, and only accepting one serving of food; living in the forest; sitting under a tree; residing in an unsheltered place; staying in a cemetery; taking any seat provided; and never lying down, even to sleep. See also, Nalinaksha Dutt, *Early Monastic Buddhism* (Calcutta: Calcutta Oriental Book Agency, 1960), pp. 153–158, and Buddhaghośa's *The Path of Purification* (*Visuddhi Magga*), translated from the Pāli by Bhikkhu Nānamol (Kandy: Buddhist Publication Society, 1975), pp. 59–83.

107. Cf. the biography of Yunwen *SSZ* 16.12 (809a).

108. *Lanruoshe*, cf. Facong *XSZ* 16.9 (555a–b) and Zhizang *XSZ* 5.12 (467a).

109. *SSZ* 20.12 (839a).

110. Daoqi *SSZ* 29.21 (893c).

111. *XSZ* 16.15 (557c).

112. That is, the *Sifen lü shanfan buque xingshi chao*. For what follows, see C.3, p. 130c.

113. *XSZ* 18.4 (575a).

114. *XSZ* 20.5 (606a).

115. *XSZ* 20B.1 (597c).

116. Appended to the biography of Sengke (Huike), *XSZ* 16.6 (552c).

117. *XSZ* 20B.7 (606c).

118. *XSZ* 17.6 (569a).

119. On the abstention from grain in Daoism, see Henri Maspero, *Taoism and Chinese Religion* (Amherst: The University of Massachusetts Press, 1981), pp. 333–335. Most examples of this practice are found in the first *Biographies of Eminent Monks*, e.g. Fotucheng *GSZ* 9.1 (387a), Shegong *GSZ* 10.5 (389b), Sengcong *GSZ* 11.12 (398c), and Huiyuan *GSZ* 13.2 (410a). For an interesting account of a man who first underwent various austerities under a Daoist master before becoming a Buddhist monk, see Zhikuang, *XSZ* 25B.9 (658c). See also

Baochang, *Biqiuni zhuan* 2, biography of Guangjing, p. 939b; Tsai, *Lives*, p. 51.

120. *XSZ* 25B.18 (661b).

121. *XSZ* 21.13 (612b).

122. *XSZ* 17.7 (569a).

123. Similar ceremonies involving the Famen relic were carried out no less than seven times during the Tang in accordance with a tradition that the relic should be displayed once every thirty years. The relic was rediscovered along with a number of invaluable artifacts in the base of a stupa at Famen Si in 1982. For a detailed history of the relic and the monastery that housed it, see Chen Jingfu, *Famen si* (Xian: San qin chubanshe, 1988).

124. *Duyang zabian* C (Shanghai: Jicheng shuju, 1939), 2835.22. Translation, with minor emendations, from Kenneth Chen, *Buddhism in China*, p. 281. See also Tang Yongtong, *Sui Tang fojiao shi gao* (Beijing: Zhonghua shuju, 1982), pp. 32–33.

125. *Tang huiyao* 47, p. 838. Parts of this passage are translated in Kenneth Chen, *The Chinese Transformation of Buddhism*, p. 268.

126. *SSZ* 23.T (862a).

127. A metaphor for his own body as we will see below.

128. *Zhuangzi* 6.24; Burton Watson, *The Complete Works of Chuang Tzu* (New York: Columbia University Press, 1968), p. 80: "The Great Clod burdens me with form, labors me with life, eases me in old age, and rests me in death. So if I think well of my life, for the same reason I must think well of my death."

129. *San ye*, body, speech, and mind.

130. The three assemblies to be held by Maitreya, the future Buddha, on the day of his descent at the "dragon-flower" (*puṣpanāga*) tree.

131. Reading the *Qingliang shan zhi "xinshi"* for the *SSZ* "Ji shi," which makes no sense. Cf. *Qingliang shan zhi*, 4.6b–8a, in Du Jiexiang, gen. ed., *Zhongguo fosishi zhi hui kan* (Taibei: Danqing tushu gongsi, 1985), 3. 29.

132. Yao Wang (Skt. Bhaiṣajyarāja).

133. *SSZ* 23.3 (855c–856b).

134. Cf. D. S. Macgowan, "Self-immolation by Fire in China," *The Chinese Recorder* 19.10 (Oct. 1888): pp. 445–451, 508–521; Jacques Gernet, "Les suicides par le feu chez les Bouddhistes Chinois du Vᵉ au Xᵉ siècle," *Mélanges publiés par l'Institute des Hautes Études Chinoises* (1960): pp. 527–558; Jean Filliozat, "La mort volontaire par le feu et la tradition bouddhique Indienne," *Journal Asiatique* 251 (1963): pp. 21–51; and Jan Yün-hua, "Buddhist Self-immolation in Medieval China," *History of Religions* 4. 2 (1964–1965): pp. 243–268.

135. These examples are from the *Liu du ji jing* (Skt.*Ṣaṭpāramitā-saṃgraha*), *T* 152, v. 3.1c–2b translated into French in Édouard Chavannes, *Cinq cents contes et apologues extrait du tripitaka Chinois* (Paris: Société Asiatique, 1910), pp. 11, 15–17.

136. *SSZ* 23.11 (858b).

137. *SSZ* 23.1 (855b).
138. *SSZ* 23.4 (856b).
139. *SSZ* 21.12 (847c).
140. *SSZ* 23.18 (870a).
141. *GSZ* 12.3 (404b).
142. *GSZ* 12.2 (404a).
143. *GSZ* 12.4 (404b–c).
144. *SSZ* 23.5 (856c).
145. *SSZ* 23.4 (856b).
146. *SSZ* 14.3 (792a).
147. *SSZ* 7.7 (747a) and 23.14 (859a).
148. *SSZ* 25.16 (870b).
149. *SSZ* 26.11 (877b).
150. Holmes Welch, *The Practice of Chinese Buddhism 1900–1950* (1967; rpt. Cambridge: Harvard University Press, 1973), pp. 323–325; and J. Prip-Moeller, *Chinese Buddhist Monasteries* (1937; rpt. Hong Kong: Hong Kong University Press, 1982), pp. 320–324.
151. *SSZ* 26.14 (877a).
152. *SSZ* 12.17 (783a–b). Huiji is better known in Chan sources as Yangshan.
153. Significantly, this incident is not recounted in the *XSZ*, the earliest source we have on Huike, in which his arm is cut off by bandits, but only appears in the somewhat later *Chuan fa baoji*. Cf. Philip Yampolsky, *The Platform Sutra of the Sixth Patriarch* (New York: Columbia University Press, 1967), p. 11.
154. *SSZ* 23.10 (858a).
155. In the biography of Sengxin, *XSZ* 26.28 (673b).
156. *SSZ* 21.5 (845b).
157. Victor Turner, "Religious Paradigms and Political Action: Thomas Becket at the Council of Northampton," in *Dramas, Fields, and Metaphors: Symbolic Action in Human Society* (Ithaca: Cornell University Press, 1974), pp. 60–97.
158. For example, the *Yuedeng sanmei jing* (Skt. *Samādhirāja[candrapradīpasūtra]*) *T* 639, 640, 641, v. 15; *Pusa shan jie jing T* 1582, v. 30 (Skt. *Bodhisattvabhūmi*), especially chapter 10, v. 30.979c–982b. The most significant source for the practice of blood-writing was the *Fan wang jing T* 1484, v. 24.1009a19.
159. Leon Hurvitz trans., *Scripture of the Lotus Blossom of the Fine Dharma* (New York: Columbia University Press, 1976), p. 298.
160. Huishao *GSZ* 12.6 (404c), Sengyu *GSZ* 12.7 (405a), and Sengqing *GSZ* 12.8 (405b).
161. *XSZ* 27.10 (684a).
162. *SSZ* 23.9 (857b–c).
163. *SSZ* 23.10 (857c).
164. *SSZ* 23.7 (857a).
165. *Da Tang Dajianfu si gu dade Kang Zang fashi wen bei* by Yan Chaoyin, appended to *Fazang heshang zhuan XZJ*, v. 134.261a.

166. On the body as a source of defilement, see Jan, "Buddhist Self-immolation." In an article on self-immolation in Chinese Buddhism and in Daoism, Myōjin Hiroshi argues that in both religions the practice of self-immolation was a means of purification necessary before one could ascend to a higher realm: in the Buddhist case, to a pure-land; in Daoism, to the world of the sylphs. See Myōjin Hiroshi, "Chūgoku Bukkyōto no shōshin to Dōkyō," *Waseda daigaku daigakuin bungaku kenkyūka kiyō* 11 (1984): pp. 41–50.

167. *SSZ* 23.*T* (861b13).

168. Biography of Jing'ai, *XSZ* 23.3 (628a2).

169. Biography of Wenshuang, *SSZ* 21.12 (847c).

170. The stupa containing the remains of the Tang monk Saṅgha (Sengqie), for example, was the site of a self-immolation by a nun, and later by a monk. Cf. *SSZ* 18.6 (822a–823b) and *SSZ* 23.22 (860c–862a).

171. Robert Sharf, "The Idolization of Enlightenment: On the Mummification of Ch'an Masters in Medieval China," *History of Religion* 32. 1 (Aug. 1992): pp. 1–31; Bernard Faure, *The Rhetoric of Immediacy: A Cultural Critique of Chan / Zen Buddhism* (Princeton: Princeton University Press, 1991), pp. 132–178; Faure, "Dato" in *Hōbōgirin* (forthcoming); and T. Griffith Foulk and Robert H. Sharf, "On the Ritual Use of Ch'an Portraiture in Medieval China," *Cahiers d'Extrême-Asie* 7 (1993–1994): pp. 163–169.

172. *SSZ* 23.8 (857b).

173. *Si ta ji T* 2093, v. 51.1023c.

174. *Nanhai jigui neifa zhuan* 4, p. 231c; Takakusu, *A Record of the Buddhist Religion*, p. 197.

175. *XSZ* 27.3 (680c).

176. "Suzhou Zhongyuansi Fahuayuan shibijing beiwen," *Quan Tang wen* (Beijing: Zhonghua shuju, 1985), 678. 2a.

177. "Tang Huzhou Dayunsi gu chanshi Yugong beiming bingxu," *Quan Tang wen*, 918. 4b.

178. *GSZ* 12.*T* (406a).

179. For a brief discussion of Huijiao's views on self-immolation, see Mizuo Gensei, "Shashin ni tsuite—Ekō no tachiba," *Indo Bukkyō-gaku kenkyū* 22 (Mar. 1963): pp. 174–175, in which the author argues that Huijiao's praise of self-sacrifice was in part a critique of the selfishness and decadence of aristocratic society in the Southern Dynasties.

180. See for example *Si fen lü* (Skt. *Dharmaguptakavinaya*), pp. 575c–577b; *Mishasai wu fen jieben* (Skt. *Mahīśāsakavinaya*), p. 196a.

181. *Nanhai jigui neifa zhuan* 4, p. 231a–b; Takakusu, *A Record of the Buddhist Religion*, pp. 195–196.

182. The core doctrinal texts of Nikāyan Buddhism.

183. Tandu (Skt. *dānapāramitā*).

184. [*Dasheng*] *zhuangyan* [*jing*] *lun* (Skt. *Mahāyānasūtrālaṁkāra*) *T* 1604, v. 31.650a. The wording is slightly different from the quotation given here.

185. Yet another prominent monk to take a stand on self-immolation was the tenth-century exegete Yongming Yanshou, who praised self-immolation as an act of piety. Cf. Welter, *The Meaning of Myriad Good Deeds*, pp. 154–156.

186. Edwin Reischauer, *Ennin's Travels in T'ang China* (New York: Ronald Press, 1955), p. 223.

187. On the theme of violence and officialdom in an earlier period of Chinese history, see Lewis, *Sanctioned Violence*.

188. Hongzhen *SSZ* 23.15 (859b); Pujing *SSZ* 23.17 (859c). Likewise, the fifth-century nun Huiyao requested official permission to burn herself, but was denied it. Baochang, *Biqiuni zhuan* 2, p. 941b; Tsai, *Lives*, p. 65.

189. Cf. Hongzhen *SSZ* 23.15 (859b), *Zizhi tongjian*, 292.9527; and *Liao shi* (Beijing: Zhonghua shuju, 1974), 16.188.

190. Hu Shih, "The Indianization of China: A Case Study in Cultural Borrowing," in *Independence, Convergence, and Borrowing in Institutions, Thought, and Art* (Cambridge: Harvard University Press, 1937), pp. 219–247.

191. *Chen shu*, 36.494; *Nan shi* 65.1584.

192. See for example, *Jiu Tang shu*, 162.4244, 190.5050.

193. *Xin Tang shu*, 195.5591.

194. *Xin Tang shu*, 195.5591. It was thought that the flesh of the child was a particularly efficacious medicine for the parent. This practice, which may have been reinforced by pre-Buddhist Chinese medical conceptions, seems nevertheless to have been the product of Buddhist influence. Our earliest references to a child feeding his own flesh to a sick parent are from the Tang. The practice became quite common in later times. See Qiu Zhonglin, "Buxiao zhi xiao—Tang yilai gegu liaoqin xianxiang de shehuishi chutan," *Xin shixue* 6.1 (Mar. 1995): pp. 49–94.

195. Biography of Jianzong, appended to the biography of Congjian, *SSZ* 12.7 (779c).

196. Cf. "Bi xiaoyi," in *Pi Zi wen sou* (1959; rpt. Beijing: Zhonghua shuju, 1965), p. 86.

197. *Song shi* (Beijing: Zhonghua Shuju, 1977), 456.13405.

198. Yue Guang, known for his "pure conversation" (*qingtan*) has a biography at *Jin shu* (Beijing: Zhonghua shuju, 1974), 43.1243.

199. *Chu sanzang jiji*, *T* 2145, v. 55.98b.

200. The classic study on the subject of wine and literati in the Six Dynasties is Lu Xun's, "Wei-Jin fengdu ji wenzhang yu yao ji jiu zhi guanxi," in "Eryi ji," *Lu Xun quanji* (Beijing: Renmin wenxue chubanshe, 1981), v. 3, pp. 501–529. See also "Wenren yu jiu" by Wang Yao in his *Zhonggu wenxueshi lun* (Beijing: Beijing daxue chubanshe, 1986), pp. 156–175.

201. Appended to the biography of Zhu Shixing, *GSZ* 4.1 (346c).

202. *GSZ* 10.8 (390c–392b).

203. *GSZ* 10.11 (392c).

204. *GSZ* 10.15 (393c–394a).

205. Cf. the biographies of Tongjin *XSZ* 20B.11 (659b), Minggong *XSZ* 20B.12 (659c), and Xiang Sheli *XSZ* 25B.2 (657a).

206. Cf. Weigong *SSZ* 25.12 (869b) for gambling, the Grand Master of Guangling *SSZ* 19.15 (833c) for fighting and butchering.

207. In his chapter on Buddhism and wine, Michihata mentions in passing the existence of biographies of wine-drinking, meat-eating monks. He explains their presence in the *Biographies* by noting that they are "divine monks" (*shinsō*) and hence not subject to rules formulated for ordinary monks. (Cf. *Daijō bossatsukai*, p. 520). This is one of the explanations given by the hagiographers themselves as we will see below. In a book on the medieval Chinese monastic order, Moroto Tatsuo mentions these biographies briefly and admits to finding them puzzling. *Chūgoku Bukkyō seidoshi no kenkyū* (Tokyo: Heikawa shuppansha, 1990), pp. 202–207.

208. See Paul Radin's *The Trickster* (1956; rpt. New York: Schocken Books, 1972); Maclinscott Ricketts's, "The North American Trickster," *History of Religions* 4 (1965): pp. 327–350; Robert D. Pelton's, *The Trickster in West Africa: A Study of Mythic Irony and Sacred Delight* (Berkeley: University of California Press, 1980).

209. *SSZ* 20.5 (837c).

210. *SSZ* 18.1 (820b).

211. *SSZ* 22.8 (852a).

212. *SSZ* 25.8 (868c), not to be confused with the more famous pure-land patriarch of the same name.

213. *SSZ* 25.12 (869b).

214. *SSZ* 19.10 (831c–832a).

215. *SSZ* 19.10 (831c–832a).

216. *SSZ* 19.15 (833c).

217. This function is most clear in the case of Zanning's *Song Biographies*, which was compiled on imperial edict. Daoxuan's work, though compiled privately, was only one of several works completed by Daoxuan to defend the clergy in the face of opposition at court. Huijiao's relationship to the Liang establishment is more problematic because of the scarcity of relevant biographical data. Nevertheless, the assertion that Huijiao intended the *Gaoseng zhuan* to be read in part by prominent literati seems to me a safe assumption.

218. Robert Thurman, trans., *The Holy Teaching of Vimalakīrti* (University Park: Pennsylvania State University Press, 1976), p. 65.

219. Cf. *The Holy Teaching of Vimalakīrti*, p. 66: "All passions constitute the family of the Tathāgatas . . . without going out into the great ocean, it is impossible to find precious, priceless pearls. Likewise, without going into the ocean of passions, it is impossible to obtain the mind of omniscience."

220. Present-day Chengdu, Sichuan Province.

221. *XSZ* 20B.2 (657a). Apparently, the story of this monk was popular for some time, for reference is made to it in connection with another monk in the *Song Biographies*. Cf. *SSZ* 21.10 (847b), "Anonymous Biography" (*Wangming zhuan*).

222. *Guan* [*wuliangshoufo*] *jing* (Skt. *Amitāyurbuddhānusmṛti-sūtra*) *T* 365, v. 12. For the passage referred to here, see 346a12–26.

223. There are various sets of five. The most common set, from least serious to most serious, is killing one's father, killing one's mother, killing an arhat, drawing the blood of a Buddha, and finally, disrupting the harmony of a community of monks.

224. *SSZ* 24.18 (865c). In the *Wangsheng xifang jingtu ruiying zhuan T* 2070, v. 51.120b–c, and the *Fo zu tong ji T* 2035, v. 49.275b versions of the story, the king of the underworld reprimands Xiongjun for chanting superficially, but decides to give him another chance in the world of the living. After reviving, Xiongjun mends his ways, keeps the precepts, and chants diligently, after which, on his death, he goes to the pure-land.

225. *SSZ* 25.12 (869b).

226. Cf. *SSZ* 24.17 (865b) and *SSZ* 25.8 (868c).

227. For a discussion of the changing role of trickster figures in the Chan school, see Faure, *The Rhetoric of Immediacy*, pp. 115–131.

228. For Daoxuan's comments on meat-eating, see his widely-read *Sifen lü shanfan buque xingshi chao*, p. 118a. Michihata summarizes Daoxuan's comments in *Chūgoku Bukkyō shisōshi*, pp. 283–286.

229. In present-day Shaanxi Province.

230. *Jingxin di*, the first stage on the bodhisattva path. Cf. Nakamura, *Bukkyōgo daijiten*, p. 753b.

231. *Guozheng*, that is, spiritual attainments.

232. *Dui fa lun*, that is, the *Dasheng apidamo za jilun* (Skt. *Abhid-harmasamuccayavyākhyā*) *T* 1606, v. 31.

233. Cf. *Dasheng apidamo za ji lun*, p. 716c, which discusses the different ways in which different types of beings sustain themselves. Devas, for example, need only think of food to be satiated.

234. *SSZ* 21.11 (847b).

235. In addition to the *Dasheng apidamo za ji lun* passage cited by Zanning above, similar passages justifying such behavior can be found scattered throughout the *abhidharmic* literature. See for instance, the *Yuqie shidi lun* (Skt. *Yogacārabhūmiśāstra*) *T* 1579, v. 30.517c.

236. *Taiping guangji* (Beijing: Zhonghua shuju, 1961), 92.610. The story was originally taken from the *Kaitian zhuan xinji*, which is no longer extant. The same incident is recounted in the *SSZ* version of Śubhakarasiṃha's biography, though with less detail. Cf. *SSZ* 2.1 (715c–716a).

237. There is no evidence to suggest a connection between Tantrism and the meat-eating wine-drinking monks of the *Biographies*. In

fact, in one of Śubhakarasiṃha's own works, the *Wuwei Sanzang chan yao*, he specifically condemns wine-drinking and meat-eating. Cf. *T* 917, v. 18.943a2.

238. *SSZ* 5.12 (737a).

239. *SSZ* 4.1 (725b). In a note, Zanning denounces rumors of Kuiji's wine-drinking and womanizing as baseless slander. Cf. *SSZ* 24.17 Wangming (865b) for yet another such juxtaposition.

240. Cf. Luohan Wang *SSZ* 22.9 (852a).

241. Cf. Master Diandian *SSZ* 22.11(852c).

242. Cf. Shi Tongjin *XSZ* 25B.11 (659b).

243. Especially interesting is Shi Yinfeng *SSZ* 21.10 (847a) who dies in a standing posture.

244. Drawing on Mary Douglas's work on pollution and marginality, Barbara Babcock-Abrahams discusses the trickster as a marginal figure in her "'A Tolerated Margin of Mess': The Trickster and His Tales Reconsidered," *Journal of the American Folklore Institute* 2 (1975): pp. 147–186.

245. *SSZ* 0.2 (709c).

246. For a lyrical account of the layout of the capital, see Edward Schafer's "The Last Years of Ch'ang-an," *Oriens Extremus*, 10 (1963): pp. 133–179. The same concern for symmetrical compartmentalization of residents is evident in the capitals of the Northern Dynasties. This may also have been the case in the southern capital at Jiankang, though a lack of source material makes it difficult to determine whether or not the residents of Jiankang were divided into wards. Cf. Liu Shufen, *Liuchao de chengshi yu shehui* (Taibei: Xuesheng shuju, 1992), pp. 138–139, 147–148, 409–471.

247. Cf. Michihata Ryōshū, *Tōdai Bukkyō shi no kenkyū* (Kyoto: Hōzōkan, 1958), pp. 95–112.

248. Liang Wu Di's campaign extended from 518 to 523. The *Gaoseng zhuan* was completed in approximately 530, though it may have been finished much earlier. On Liang Wu Di's campaign, see Yan Shangwen, *Liang Wu Di*, pp. 203–232. On the dating of the *GSZ*, see Wright, "Biography and Hagiography."

249. *Quan Tang wen*, 445.4544.

250. *Quan Tang wen*, 133.1347, and 1345. Also in *Guang hongming ji*, p. 160c.

251. From a memorial by the Liang-dynasty official, Xun Ji. Cf. *Guang hongming ji*, p. 129c.

252. Cf. *Zizhi tongjian*, 124.3923 and Chen, *Buddhism in China*, p. 149.

253. *Jin seng dao bu shou jielü zhao*, in *Quan Tang wen*, 29.327.

254. *Guang hongming ji*, p. 126a.

255. Cf. Guo Zushen's biography in the *Nan shi*, 70.1721–22.

256. See Ennin's *Nittō guhō junrei gyōki;* Bai Huawen et al., *Ru Tang*

qiufa xunli xing ji jiaozhu (Shijiazhuang: Huashan wenyi chubanshe, 1992), 3.408. Translated by Edwin Reischauer in his *Ennin's Diary* (New York: Ronald Press, 1955), p. 321.

257. From *Tang huiyao*, 47.841. Translated by Edwin Reischauer in *Ennin's Travels*, p. 227.

258. *SSZ* 0.2 (710a).

259. Cf. Welch, *The Practice of Chinese Buddhism*, p. 16, and *The Buddhist Revival in China* (Cambridge: Harvard University Press, 1968), p. 222. For a study of a particularly famous trickster monk of later fiction, see Meir Shahar, "Fiction and Religion in the Early History of the Chinese God Jigong" (Ph.D. dissertation, Harvard University, 1992).

260. Michihata, *Daijō bosatsu kai*, pp. 510, 515, 528–530.

261. *Shi yu tie, Quan Tang wen*, 912.7a.

262. "Ti Zhang Sengyao zuiseng tu," *Quan Tang shi*, 808.9122. For discussion of a document that describes a ninth-century community in which monks ate meat and married, see Gernet, *Buddhism in Chinese Society*, p. 376 n. 35; the reference is to *Nan shi*, 70.1721–22.

263. Michihata, *Daijō bosatsu kai*.

264. Edward Gibbon, *The Decline and Fall of the Roman Empire*, ed. J. B. Bury (New York: The Heritage Press, 1946), p. 1152. This quotation is taken from chapter 37 of the *Decline and Fall*, which includes a flowing, vitriolic condemnation of Christian asceticism.

265. Hu Shih, "The Indianization of China," p. 228.

266. Friedrich Nietzsche, *On the Genealogy of Morals*, trans. Walter Kaufmann (New York: Vintage Books, 1967), especially pp. 162–163.

267. William James, *The Varieties of Religious Experience* (1902; rpt. New York: The Modern Library, 1936), p. 296.

268. Joseph Swain, *The Hellenic Origins of Christian Asceticism* (New York: 1916), p. 6.

269. Brown, *The Body and Society*, p. 222. For further discussion of the ways in which modern scholars have treated asceticism, see Geoffrey Galt Harpham, *The Ascetic Imperative in Culture and Criticism* (Chicago: University of Chicago Press, 1987).

Chapter 2: Thaumaturgy

1. See the discussion in Raoul Birnbaum, "The Manifestation of a Monastery: Shen-ying's Experiences on Mount Wu-t'ai in T'ang Context," *Journal of the American Oriental Society* 106.1 (Jan.–Mar. 1986): pp. 119–137.

2. *GSZ* 10.T (395a). For discussions of Huijiao's attitude toward "divine marvels," see Murakami Yoshimi, "*Kōsōden* no shin-i ni tsuite," *Tōhō shūkyō* 17 (Aug. 1961): pp. 1–17; and especially Naomi Gentetsu, "Jūryoku koku shidai no Bukkyō ni *tsuite: Kōsōden* no saikentō yori," *Ryūkoku-shidan* 87 (Mar. 1986): pp. 57–71.

3. *XSZ* 26.T (677b). For a discussion of Daoxuan's views on wonder-

working, see Yamazaki Hiroshi, "Tō no Dōsen no kantsū ni tsuite," in *Tsukamoto Hakushi shōju kinen Bukkyōshigaku ronshū* (Tokyo: Tsukamoto hakushi shōju kinenkai, 1961), pp. 855–868.

4. *SSZ* 29.1 (888c–889a).

5. In this respect, the *Biographies* are similar to "anomaly accounts" (*zhiguai*). See Campany, *Strange Writing*, especially pp. 199–201. Richard Kieckhefer makes a similar case for the function of some Christian hagiography in his *Unquiet Souls: Fourteenth Century Saints and Their Religious Milieu*, pp. 12–14. For a discussion of the marvelous as a literary category, see Tzvetan Todorov, *The Fantastic: A Structural Approach to a Literary Genre* (1970; English trans, Ithaca: Cornell University Press, 1973), pp. 41–57. Jacques Le Goff discusses some of the issues involved in the study of the marvelous in history in his "The Marvelous in the Medieval West," in *The Medieval Imagination* (1978; English trans, Chicago: The University of Chicago Press, 1988), pp. 27–44.

6. For more on the sensation of the marvelous and some of its many uses, see Stephen Greenblatt, *Marvelous Possessions* (Chicago: The University of Chicago Press, 1991).

7. That is, the *Fa ju jing*, (perhaps equivalent to *T* 2901, v. 85, one of the Dunhuang manuscripts, St. 2021); and the *Xianyu jing*, *T* 202, v. 4.

8. Biography of Sengjin *GSZ* 7.27 (373c–374a).

9. In the entry for "chih-kuai" (*zhiguai*) in the *Indiana Companion*, Kenneth Dewoskin characterizes *zhiguai* as stressing the "anomalous and curious," and the later genre of *chuanqi* as stressing the "marvelous and exotic." I am using the term "marvelous" in a more general sense to encompass a certain tendency in all of these writings, including miracle tales. Cf. William Nienhauser, ed., *The Indiana Companion to Traditional Chinese Literature* (Bloomington: Indiana University Press, 1986), pp. 280–284. On Chinese Buddhist miracle tales, see Donald Gjertson, *Miraculous Retribution: A Study and Translation of T'ang Lin's Ming-pao chi* (Berkeley: Asian Humanities Press, 1989), pp. 2–53.

10. Cf. Étienne Lamotte, *Le traité de la grande vertu de sagesse* (Louvain: E. Peeters, 1976), v. 4, pp. 1809–1816; Louis de la Vallée Poussin, "Le Bouddha et les abhijñās," *Le muséon* 44 (1931): pp. 335–342; Paul Demiéville, "Sur la memoire des existences anterieures," *Bulletin de l'École Française d'Extrême-Orient* 27 (1927): pp. 283–298.

11. *XSZ* 11.*T* (400b).

12. The six supernormal powers are mentioned in passing in the fifth-century collection of predominantly secular anecdotes, *Shishuo xinyu*. The sixth-century commentator to the text, Liu Jun, quotes an unidentified sutra to explain what the six powers are. Significantly, Liu is unsure of the topic, first defining the divine eye as the ability to see great distances, and later in the same note as the ability to see into the future. Cf. *Shishuo xinyu* (Beijing: Zhonghua Shuju, 1984) 4.54,

translated in Richard Mather, *A New Account of Tales of the World* (Minneapolis: University of Minnesota Press, 1976), pp. 119–120.

13. *SSZ* 14.14 (796b).

14. Appended to the biography of Yishi, *SSZ* 20.19 (841c–842a). On "earth shrinking," see the biography of Hu Gong in Wang Mo, ed., *Shenxian zhuan, Han Wei congshu* (Shanghai: Shanghai datong shuju, 1967), 12.14a–b.

15. See Hirakawa Akira, *A History of Indian Buddhism from Śākyamuni to Early Mahāyāna*, English translation by Paul Groner (Honolulu: University of Hawai'i Press, 1990), p. 198.

16. *SSZ* 21.6 (845c–846a).

17. *SSZ* 21.6 (845c).

18. Cf. Jan Nattier, *Once Upon a Future Time: Studies in a Buddhist Prophecy of Decline* (Berkeley: Asian Humanities Press, 1991).

19. Cf. Étienne Lamotte, *History of Indian Buddhism* (1958; English trans., Louvain: Peeters Press, 1988), pp. 536–537. Eighteenth-century English historians shared this fascination with prophecy, though for somewhat different reasons. Cf. Roy Porter, *Gibbon* (New York: St Martin's Press, 1988), p. 24.

20. *SSZ* 5.12 (737b).

21. *SSZ* 20.1 (836a).

22. *SSZ* 2.3 (716c).

23. *SSZ* 9.2 (760c).

24. For comparison, see Kenneth Dewoskin, *Doctors, Diviners, and Magicians of Ancient China: Biographies of Fang-shih* (New York: Columbia University Press, 1983).

25. *SSZ* 22.4 (850b).

26. *GSZ* 9.1 (383b–387a). For a detailed study and translation of the biography, see Arthur Wright, "Fo-t'u-teng, a Biography," *Harvard Journal of Asiatic Studies* 11 (1948): pp. 321–371.

27. Appended to the biography of Qingzhu *SSZ* 12.11 (781b).

28. *SSZ* 18.8 (824a).

29. *Jiu Tang shu* 91.2934; *Xin Tang shu* 120.4316.

30. *GSZ* 9.1 (383c); translated slightly differently in Wright, "Fo-t'u-teng," p. 339.

31. *SSZ* 13.17 (789a–789b).

32. Biography of the old monk of Jianfu Monastery, appended to the biography of Yishi *SSZ* 20.19 (842a).

33. *SSZ* 18.8 (823c).

34. *SSZ* 20.17 (841b).

35. Dewoskin, *Doctors, Diviners, and Magicians*, p. 41.

36. Keith Thomas, *Religion and the Decline of Magic* (New York: Charles Scribner's Sons, 1971), pp. 422–432.

37. See especially Forte, *Political Propaganda*.

38. Ch. Bukongju. Cf. *Mikkyō daijiten* (Kyoto: Hōzōkan, 1968–1970), v. 4, p. 1904c.

39. An incarnation of Avalokiteśvara (Ch. Guanyin).

40. *SSZ* 1.2 (711b–712a), translated by Chou Yi-liang in his "Tantrism in China," *Harvard Journal of Asiatic Studies* 8 (1945): pp. 272–284.

41. *SSZ* 2.1 (716a), Chou, "Tantrism": pp. 276–277. For another example of rain-making monks, see the biography of Qingxu *SSZ* 25.2 (876a–b).

42. The practice of official supplication for rain can be traced back to the oracle bones. Cf. Lin Fushi, *Handai de wuzhe* (Taibei: Daoxiang chubanshe, 1988), p. 70. For examples of Han ritual specialists performing rituals for rain at court, see Lin, *Handai de wuzhe*, pp. 15, 17, 39, 70–72, and Dewoskin, *Doctors, Diviners, and Magicians*, pp. 52, 125–126.

43. Richard J. Smith's *Fortune-tellers and Philosophers: Divination in Traditional Chinese Society* (Boulder: Westview Press, 1991) is a study of divination in the late imperial period, but also includes a brief overview of divination in earlier periods of Chinese history.

44. Cf. Welch, *The Practice of Chinese Buddhism*, p. 212.

45. Michel Strickmann, "Chinese Poetry and Prophecy: The Written Oracle in East Asia," (unpublished manuscript). Much of what follows concerning divination by bamboo sticks and Buddhist attitudes toward divination derives from this as yet unpublished manuscript.

46. *Guanding jing*, *T* 1331, v. 21.523c–528c.

47. *Chang ahan jing* (Skt. *Dīrghāgama*), pp. 84c, 89c.

48. *Chang ahan jing*, p. 78a; *Ji zhi guo jing* 22, v. 1.274a; *Za ahan jing* (Skt. *Saṃyuktāgama*), *T* 99, v. 2.151a.

49. *Mishasai bu hexi wufen lü*, p. 174b.

50. *Si fen lü*, p. 955b, elsewhere in the text, the Buddha prohibits monks from practicing any form of divination (963b).

51. *T* 1484, v. 24.1007a. Translated into French in J. J. M. Degroot, *Le code du Mahāyāna en Chine* (Amsterdam: Johannes Müller, 1893), p. 61. One of the monks interviewed by Holmes Welch in the first half of this century specifically cited this text as his reason for eschewing divination. Cf. Welch, *The Practice of Chinese Buddhism*, pp. 121, 483 n. 31. In addition to the *Āgamas* and the Vinaya, abhidharmic texts are also critical of monastic divination. Cf. *Da zhi du lun T* 1509, v. 25.79c and 247a (Lamotte, *Traité*, v. 1, p. 201, v. 3, p. 1624).

52. *GSZ* 3.12 (345a).

53. *GSZ* 8.9 (377a).

54. That is, the gorges through which the Yangtze runs in the western part of present-day Hunan Province.

55. *SSZ* 22.3 (850a).

56. Cf. the biography of Xingzun *SSZ* 22.4 (850b–c), of Shijian *SSZ* 22.8 (852a) and of Yixing *SSZ* 5.3 (732c–733c).

57. *SSZ* 29.6 (889c–890a). The Tang histories also relate stories of Hongshi performing such services for prominent officials. Cf. *Jiu Tang*

shu 191.5113; *Xin Tang shu* 204.5809. For monastic attitudes toward this practice in the Song, see Andō Tomonobu, "Hoku-Sō ki ni okeru inyōka no kikkyō kafuku setsu to Bukkyō," *Ōtani Gakuhō* 64.1 (Jun. 1984), pp. 32–44.

58. *Jinlouzi* 6, "Jushu pian," 2.17a.
59. *GSZ* 8.8 (376c).
60. *GSZ* 5.1 (352c).
61. *XSZ* 25B.22 (662b–c).
62. Cf. *Han shu* 30.1775.
63. Cf. Smith, *Fortune-tellers*, pp. 2–3.
64. Cf. *GSZ* 2.5 (334a) and *GSZ* 1.5 (324c).
65. See for example, *T* 1099, 1299, and 1307.
66. Ōmura Seigai, *Mikkyō hattatsu-shi* (1918; rpt. Taibei: Huayu chubanshe, 1986) in Lan Jifu, gen. ed., *Shijie foxue mingzhuyi cong*, v. 74–76, pp. 459–460 and 530. See also, Taira Hidemichi, "Shin-i shisō to Bukkyō kyōten," *Ryūkoku daigaku ronshū* 347 (Apr. 1954): pp. 123–141.
67. *XSZ* 25.1 (644b).
68. *GSZ* 4.10 (350b).
69. Cf. Joseph Needham, *Science and Civilisation* (Cambridge: Cambridge University Press, 1954), v. 3, pp. 365–395.
70. That is, Suzhou.
71. *SSZ* 20.19 (841c).
72. *SSZ* 18.4 (821b)
73. Howard Wechsler, *Offerings of Jade and Silk: Ritual and Symbol in the Legitimation of the T'ang Dynasty* (New Haven: Yale University Press, 1985), pp. 69–73.
74. Cf. *SSZ* 22.3 (850a–b), and 18.8 (824c).
75. In campaigns to eradicate such prophetic books, the state often linked them to monks. See Yasui Kōzan, "Kan-Gi Rikuchō ni okeru toshin to Bukkyō—tokuni sōden o chūshin toshite," in *Tsukamoto hakushi shōju kinen*, pp. 855–868.
76. *Jiu Tang shu*, 191.5088.
77. Cf. Donald Harper, "The Wu Shih Erh Ping Fang: Translation and Prolegomena" (Ph.D. dissertation, University of California at Berkeley, 1982), pp. 68–106; Ma Jixing and Li Xueqin, "Wo guo xian yi faxian de zui gu yifang—boshu *Wushier bingfang*" in *Mawangdui Hanmu yanjiu* (Hunan: Hunan renmin chubanshe, 1981), pp. 226–234; Harper, "A Chinese Demonography of the Third Century B.C.," *Harvard Journal of Asiatic Studies* 45.2 (Dec. 1985): pp. 459–498; Harper, "Wang Yen-shou's Nightmare Poem," *Harvard Journal of Asiatic Studies* 47.1 (June 1987): pp. 239–283.
78. Harper, "A Chinese Demonography": p. 495.
79. Harper, "A Chinese Demonography": p. 483.
80. Harper, "Wang Yen-shou's Nightmare Poem": p. 265.
81. Étienne Lamotte has reviewed some of the technical, doctrinal

Buddhist literature on spells, suggesting that, while spells were certainly prevalent in ancient India, they were not present in primitive Buddhism and only became important to Buddhism at a later date. Owing to the late dates of even our earliest sources, this final hypothesis is highly conjectural. Cf. Lamotte, *Traité*, v. 4, pp. 1854–1869.

82. *Wu ming* (Skt. **vidyā*). Namely, grammar, crafts, medicine, reasoning, and metaphysics (often referring specifically to Buddhism). Cf. Thomas Watters, *On Yuan Chwang's Travels in India* (London: Royal Asiatic Society, 1904), v. 1, pp. 157–159.

83. *GSZ* 3.12 (344a).

84. *GSZ* 2.7 (335c).

85. For a discussion of the issues involved, see Erik Zürcher, "A New Look at the Earliest Chinese Buddhist Texts," in Koichi Shinohara and Gregory Schopen, eds., *From Benares to Beijing: In Honour of Professor Jan Yün-hua* (Oakville: Mosaic Press, 1991), pp. 277–300. None of the twenty-nine texts Zürcher regards as genuine Han translations concerns spells. See the appendix to "A New Look."

86. Matsunaga and Ōmura cite the *Huaji tuoluoni shenzhou jing* (Skt.**Puṣpakūṭadhāraṇī[sūtra]*) *T* 1356, v. 21, translated circa 222, and the *Modeng qie jing* (Skt. **Mātaṅgīsūtra*) *T* 1300, v. 21 translated in 230, as two of the most important early spell-texts. Matsunaga Yūkei, *Mikkyō no rekishi* (1969; rpt. Kyoto: Heirakuji shoten, 1991), p. 132; Ōmura Seigai, *Mikkyō hattatsushi*, pp. 39, 51. It should be noted, however, that the early date for the later text has been challenged. Cf. Needham, *Science and Civilisation*, v. 3, p. 258.

87. *Zhou ya tong*, *Zhou du*, and *Zhou yan tong*. Cf. *Chu sanzang jiji* 4, p. 31c.

88. *Zhou shui jing*, *Longwang zhou shuiyu jing*, and *Zhou qing yu zhou zhi yu qu xieqi shenzhou*. Cf. *Chu sanzang jiji* 4, p. 31c.

89. *Kongque wang jing* (Skt. *Mahāmāyūrīvidyārājnī?*). Śrīmitra's translation of the text is not extant.

90. *GSZ* 1.10 (328a).

91. *GSZ* 10.2 (389a).

92. *GSZ* 5.13 (386c).

93. For a summary of all of the instances in which spells are used in the *Liang Biographies*, see Naomi Gentetsu, "*Kōsōden* no ju," *Tōyō shien* 33 (March 1989): pp. 32–48.

94. *GSZ* 10.4 (388b).

95. *GSZ* 9.1 (384b).

96. *GSZ* 12B.8 (407b).

97. *GSZ* 2.7 (336b).

98. *Mohe zhiguan* 8a, *T* 1911, v. 46.108a2–3, 109b. See also Paul Demiéville, "Byō" in *Hōbōgirin*, p. 257, translated into English by Mark Tatz as *Buddhism and Healing* (New York: University Press of America, 1985), pp. 81–89.

99. The *Liang Biographies* gives little evidence to suggest that

monks at this time administered medical assistance beyond spells. This is perhaps because diagnosis and the dispensation of common drugs were considered too routine to warrant inclusion in biographies of eminent monks. The secular *Shishuo xinyu*, for example, does include an account of a monk diagnosing and administering medicine to a layman. *Shishuo xinyu*, 20.10; Mather, *A New Account*, p. 301. Scattered references in later versions of the *Biographies* and in other sources also suggest that monks on occasion acted as physicians for both the clergy and lay people.

100. *GSZ* 2.7 (236a).

101. *GSZ* 3.12 (344c–345a).

102. *GSZ* 10.5 (389b). Naomi Gentetsu has suggested that this story had its origin in a state-sponsored irrigation project that relieved the populace from drought at this time. Naomi, "*Kōsōden* seiritsu," p. 71.

103. *GSZ* 9.1 (383c).

104. *GSZ* 2.1 (332c).

105. Edward Schafer pointed out a similar role in Tang literature for Persian merchants whose very foreignness made them the center of tales of the marvelous. Cf. "Iranian Merchants in T'ang Dynasty Tales," in *Semitic and Oriental Studies* (University of California Publications in Semitic Philology, 1951), v. 11, pp. 403–22.

106. *Da pin*, that is, the *Mohe banruo poluomi jing* (Skt. *Pañcaviṃśatisāhasrikā[mahā] prajñāpāramitā*). *T* 223, v. 8.

107. Cf. *XSZ* 25B.30 (664a) and *XSZ* 14.12 (537c).

108. Cf. *XSZ* 2.1 (432b) and *XSZ* 2.3 (435b). Most of the spells used in the *Further Biographies* are associated with either Mahāyāna texts (most notably the *Perfection of Wisdom*) or deities (most notably Guanyin).

109. Cf. Michel Strickmann, "The Consecration Sūtra: A Buddhist Book of Spells," in Robert E. Buswell, ed., *Chinese Buddhist Apocrypha* (Honolulu: University of Hawai'i Press, 1990), pp. 79–81.

110. *XSZ* 1.4 (428c–429a).

111. Cf. *XSZ* 8.1 (483b–484a) and *XSZ* 25.25(652a–b).

112. Cf. Lamotte, *Traité* 4.18544–1869, David Snellgrove, *Indo-Tibetan Buddhism* (Boston: Shambhala, 1987), pp. 122, 141–147.

113. Cf. the biography of Bodhiruci *XSZ* 1.4 (428a) and the biography of Jñānagupta *XSZ* 2.2 (434b). Jñānagupta is credited with a no longer extant translation of the *Huaju er tuoluoni* (Skt. *Puṣpakūṭadhāraṇī*), a version of the *Huaji tuoluoni* mentioned above, which extols the value of *dhāraṇī* for memorizing Buddhist teachings. Chinese exegetes recognized memory as one of several attributes associated with *dhāraṇī*. See in particular, Huiyuan's, *Dasheng yizhang*, 11, *T*1851, v. 44.685a–686b.

114. On "*dhāraṇī* scriptures" in the Six Dynasties, see Strickmann, "The Consecration Sūtra," pp. 79–81.

115. *XSZ* 20B.10 (601a).

116. *XSZ* 24B.1 (641b–c).

117. *XSZ* 8.14 (492a).

118. The identity of this twenty-fifth princess is unknown. Cf. Chou Yi-liang, "Tantrism in China," *Harvard Journal of Asiatic Studies* 8 (1945): p. 278.

119. *SSZ* 1.2 (711c), also translated with extensive annotation in Chou, "Tantrism in China," pp. 278–279.

120. Cf. the biographies of Shenzhi *SSZ* 25.14 (869c), Fazhao *SSZ* 21.4 (845a) and Buddhapāli *SSZ* 2.7 (717c).

121. See Liu Shufen, "Foding zunsheng tuoluoni jing yu Tangdai zunsheng jingchuang de jianli—jingchuang yanjin zhi yi," *Zhongyang Yanjiuyuan Lishi Yuyan Yanjiuso jikan* 67.1 (1996): pp. 145–194.

122. Appended to the biography of Yuanbiao *SSZ* 30.3 (895b). For the origins of this practice, see Sawada Mizuho, *Chūgoku no juhō* (Tokyo: Hirakawa shuppansha, 1984), pp. 176–177.

123. *SSZ* 24.12 (864a–b).

124. Robert Campany has contributed to this project with his "Notes on the Devotional Uses and Symbolic Functions of Sūtra Texts as Depicted in Early Chinese Buddhist Miracle Tales and Hagiographies," *Journal of the International Association of Buddhist Studies* 14.1 (1991): pp. 28–72.

125. Attention has been drawn to a passage in the *Hou Han shu* (72B.2731; Dewoskin, *Doctors, Diviners, and Magicians*, p. 69) in which a man chants Confucian classics to protect himself from a demon. This may be the result of Buddhist influence. See Naomi Gentetsu, "Ryō-Shin Nanbokuchō no kannon ōgendan ni okeru sōkyō," *Ryūkoku shidan* 89 (Apr. 1987), pp. 20–38.

126. *SSZ* 24.1 (862a–b), translated from an earlier version of the story in the *Mingbao ji* in Gjertson, *Miraculous Retribution*, pp. 188–190. As it turns out, the spirit in the room is not malevolent and claims that the previous men who stayed in the room died of fright and not through any ill-will on the spirit's part.

127. *SSZ* 25.2 (867a–b).

128. *SSZ* 24.11 (864a).

129. On use of the English word "spell" to translate *"mantra"* and *"dhāraṇī,"* see Snellgrove, *Indo-Tibetan Buddhism*, p. 143.

130. The shift in attitudes toward magic and religion in the Reformation is the subject of Thomas's influential book *Religion and the Decline of Magic*. Thomas has been criticized for, among other things, reading a rhetorical change as a substantive one. Cf. Robert W. Scribner, "Reformation and Magic," *Journal of Interdisciplinary History* 23.3 (Winter 1993): pp. 475–494; Stanley Tambiah, *Magic, Science, Religion and the Scope of Rationality* (Cambridge: Cambridge University Press, 1990), pp. 18–24; and E. P. Thompson, "Anthropology and the Discipline of Historical Context," *Midland History* 1.3 (Spring 1972): pp. 41–55. For a critique of the "exoticisation" of magic in other cultures,

see Jean-Pierre Olivier de Sardan, "Occultism and the Ethnographic 'I,' " *Critique of Anthropology* 12.1 (1992): pp. 5–25.

131. "Sengqie ge," *Quan Tang shi* 166.1720.

132. Ennin, *Nittō guhō*, 1.33, 1.147, 4.431–432; translated in Reischauer, *Ennin's Diary*, pp. 30, 114, 335. Further, in his sixth-century commentary to the *Shishuo xinyu*, Liu Jun cites a biography of Śrīmitra in which the monk is said to have chanted spells at the funeral of a layman. *Shishuo xinyu* 2.39; Mather, *A New Account*, p. 50.

133. Ennin, *Nittō guhō*, 1.84; Reischauer, *Ennin's Diary*, p. 63.

134. Huan Tan, *Xin lun*, in *Taiping yulan* (Beijing: Zhonghua shuju, 1960), 400.7b (cited in Harper, "Wang Yen-shou's Nightmare Poem," p. 269), translated by Timoteus Pokora in *Hsin-lun (New Treatise) and other Writings by Huan T'an* (Ann Arbor: The University of Michigan Center for Chinese Studies, 1975), p. 40.

135. *Tang lü suyi*, 18.12b–13a (Changsha: Shangwu yinshuguan, 1939), cited in Kenneth Chen, *The Chinese Transformation of Buddhism*, p. 101.

136. Ennin, *Nittō guhō*, 3.408; Reischauer, *Ennin's Diary*, p. 321.

137. *Jiu Tang shu*, 51.2176, 183.4725.

138. *Cefu yuangui* (Hong Kong: Zhonghua shuju, 1960; facsimile reproduction of the 1642 edition), 159.16a.

139. *Cefu yuangui* 63.22a–22b.

140. Ennin, *Nittō guhō*, 3.408; Reischauer, *Ennin's Diary*, p. 321.

141. *Zizhi tongjian* 195.6150.

142. *Longxing biannian tonglun* 16, *XZJ* v. 133.289b–290a.

143. *Fo zu tong ji*, p. 365a.

144. In addition to spells, a similar sort of apprehension toward supernormal powers surfaces at several points in the *Song Biographies* when Zanning is careful to distinguish the marvelous powers of eminent monks from those of demons and sorcerers. See the addenda to *SSZ* 17.11 (817a) and 18.8 (824c).

145. *XSZ* 25.7 (646a).

146. *Wangsheng ji T* 2072, v. 51.130b.

147. Youguang, a demon known already in the Han. Cf. Derk Bodde, *Festivals in Classical China* (Princeton: Princeton University Press, 1975), pp. 108–109, and 307.

148. *Ganying leicong zhi*, in *Shuofu* (Shanghai: Shangwu Press, 1927; facsimile reproduction of the 1647 edition), 109.2a.

149. Cf. Benedicta Ward, *Miracles and the Medieval Mind: Theory, Record and Event 1000–1215* (Aldershot: Scolar Press, 1987), pp. 3–20. See also Kenneth L. Woodward, *Making Saints*, p. 191.

150. One might also object to the word "miracle" in a Buddhist context, as the word is usually defined as a "supernatural occurrence" or "an act of God." It seems expedient, however, to redefine the word rather than rely on eyesores like "supernormal anomalies." On the applicability of the word "miracle" to China, see Franciscus Verellen, "Evidential Miracles in Support of Taoism: The Inversion of a Bud-

dhist Apologetic Tradition in Late Tang China," *T'oung Pao* 78 (1992): p. 227.

151. Needham, *Science and Civilisation*, 2.377.

152. Biography of Weizhong, *SSZ* 19.21 (836a).

153. Cf. Tambiah, *Magic, Science, Religion*, pp. 6–8.

154. *SSZ* 27.1 (878b).

155. The *SSZ* phrase is *zhi cheng suo gan*. The *Book of Documents* gives *zhi cheng gan shen*, translated by Legge as "Entire sincerity moves spiritual beings." *Shu jing* 4.25b in *Shisan jing zhusu*, p. 137, translated in James Legge, *The Shoo King* (1882; rpt. Taibei: SMC Publishing, 1991), p. 66.

156. *SSZ* 18.12 (827a).

157. For a detailed discussion of the incorporation of the concept of *ganying* into Chinese Buddhism, see Robert Sharf, "The Treasure Store Treatise (Pao-tsang lun) and the Sinification of Buddhism in Eighth-Century China" (Ph.D. dissertation, University of Michigan, 1991), pp. 162–232. See also, Campany, *Strange Writing*, pp. 322–323.

158. For the story of the blind mother, see the biography of Zanghuan *SSZ* 12.5 (778c–779a). For the story of the monk who finds his father's bones, see the biography of Daopi *SSZ* 17.18 (818c–819b). The account in *Jiu Wudaishi* (Beijing: Zhonghua shuju, 1975), 103.1366 may be a reference to the same figure.

159. Charles Le Blanc, *Huai Nan Tzu: Philosophical Synthesis in Early Han Thought* (Hong Kong: Hong Kong University Press, 1985), p. 138.

160. For an overview of miracles in the Han, see Michael Loewe, *Chinese Ideas of Life and Death: Faith Myth and Reason in the Han Period (202 ʙᴄ–ᴀᴅ 220)* (London: Allen and Unwin, 1982), pp. 80–90.

161. Biography of Minghui *SSZ* 24.4 (862c).

162. Tanaka Keishin provides a chart of the distribution of miracle stories throughout the *Liang Biographies* in his "Ryō kōsōden ni okeru shin-i," *Indogaku Bukkyōgaku kenkyū* 20.1 (1972): p. 292.

163. *GSZ* 11B.2 (401a).

164. *GSZ* 12.6 (405a).

165. Biography of Fatong *GSZ* 8.25 (382b).

166. *GSZ* 11.8 (397a). The other example is in the biography of Tandi *GSZ* 7.16 (370c).

167. *GSZ* 14 (419a16); minor emendations from Wright, "Biography and Hagiography," p. 407.

168. *Ji Shenzhou sanbao gantong lu*, *T* 2106, v. 52.

169. *Daoxuan lüshi gantong lu*, *T* 2107, v. 52, roughly equivalent to *Lüxiang gantong zhuan*, *T* 1898, v. 45.

170. On miracles and thaumaturgy in the *Further Biographies*, see Wagner, "Buddhism, Biography and Power."

171. Cf. Shinohara, "Two Sources of Chinese Buddhist Biographies," pp. 212–214 n. 95.

172. In translating the elusive term *gantong* as "spiritual reso-

nance," I follow the suggestion of Raoul Birnbaum in his "Shenying's Experiences," pp. 134–137.

173. *SSZ* 22.*T* (854b).

174. The "Great Treatise" (*da zhuan*) is also known as the "Commentary on the Attached Verbalizations" (*Xici zhuan*).

175. Cf. Willard J. Peterson, "Making Connections: 'Commentary on the Attached Verbalizations' of the *Book of Change*," *Harvard Journal of Asiatic Studies* 42.1 (June 1982): pp. 67–116.

176. A10.2–5.

177. A4.2, Peterson, "Commentary": pp. 99–100.

178. *XSZ* 26.*T* (677c).

179. *XSZ* 24.4 (638b–c).

180. *Shishuo xinyu* 33.11; Mather, *A New Account*, p. 476.

181. The discussion over the bodies of the Buddha was one of enormous complexity that engaged some of the best minds in Buddhist history. For a brief introduction to the subject, see Snellgrove, *Indo-Tibetan Buddhism*, pp. 115–116. For more detailed discussions, see "Busshin," in *Hōbōgirin* v. 3, pp. 174–185; and Robert Sharf, *The Treasure Store Treatise*, pp. 190–203.

182. *SSZ* 25.3 (867b).

183. Biography of Weizhong *SSZ* 19.21 (835c).

184. *Daoxuan lüshi gantong lu*, p. 439b.

185. Cf. The "Shenyi Treatise" *GSZ* 10.*T* (395a21), and the biography of Fazang *SSZ* 5.1 (732b9).

186. Edmund Leach, "Pulleyar and the Lord Buddha: An Aspect of Religious Syncretism in Ceylon," *Psychoanalysis and the Psychoanalytic Review* 49 (1962): pp. 80–102. Available in abridged form in *Reader in Comparative Religion: An Anthropological Approach*, William A. Less and Evon Z. Vogt, eds., (1958; rpt. New York: Harper and Row, 1972), pp. 302–313.

187. For a discussion of the role of Guanyin in miracle tales, see Robert Campany, "The Real Presence," *History of Religions* 32.3 (1993), pp. 233–272; and Naomi, "Ryō-Shin Nanbokuchō no kanno nō gendan ni okeru sōkyō." As the *Biographies* drew heavily on miracle tales for material, the function of Guanyin in the two genres is very similar.

188. *GSZ* 4.13 (350c).

189. *XSZ* 24B.5 (643a).

190. *XSZ* 25.2 (644b–c).

191. *XSZ* 25.6 (645c).

192. Cf. the biography of Jingzhi *XSZ* 20B.12 (601c–602a). Despite this persistent connection with fertility, before the Song, Guanyin was almost always considered a man. Guanyin's transformation into a woman seems to have occurred during the Song. Cf. Rolf Stein, "Avalokiteśvara / Kouan-yin—exemple de transformation d'un dieu en déesse," *Cahiers d'Extrême-Asie* 2 (1986): pp. 17–80. Guo Shaolin argues that Guanyin was generally considered a woman already in

the early Tang but provides scant evidence to support his claim. Cf. "Lun Tangdai de Guanyin chongbai," *Shijie zongjiao yanjiu* (1992.3), pp. 76–83.

193. *Miaofa lianhua jing* 6 (Skt. *Saddharmapuṇḍarīka*), *T* 262, v. 9.56c21; Hurvitz, *Lotus*, p. 312.

194. *Miaofa lianhua jing* 6, p. 56c17; Hurvitz, *Lotus*, p. 312.

195. *Miaofa lianhua jing* 6, p. 57a7; Hurvitz, *Lotus*, p. 313.

196. *GSZ* 12B.6 (407a–b).

197. That is, the *Pumenpin jing T* 315, v. 11, translated by Dharmarakṣa.

198. Caves nos. 45, 217, and 420.

199. The most substantial surviving collections of Guanyin miracle tales are the *Guangshiyin yingyan ji, Xu Guangshiyin yingyan ji,* and *Xi Guangshiyin yingyan ji.* Cf. Donald Gjertson, "Ming-pao chi," in *Indiana Companion*, pp. 628–629; Campany, *Strange Writings*, pp. 68–69, 77–78, 85–86.

200. *XSZ* 25.6 (645c).

201. *XSZ* 25.4 (645b).

202. Étienne Lamotte, "Mañjuśrī," *T'oung Pao* 48 (1961): pp. 54, 58 n. 134.

203. Biography of Tanyun *XSZ* 20.7 (592c).

204. *XSZ* 20.7 (592c).

205. *Dafang guangfo huayan jing* 30 (Skt. *[Buddha]avataṃsaka-sūtra*) *T* 278, v. 9.590a3. See also Thomas Cleary, *The Flower Ornament Scripture: A Translation of the Avatamsaka Sutra* (Boston: Shambhala Publications, 1984), p. 906. This version of the text was translated in the fifth century. The same passage, with minor variations, also occurs in the seventh-century translation of the text (*T* 279, v. 10.242b20). Based in part on comparison with a Tibetan translation of the text, Lamotte has argued that both of these passages were seventh-century interpolations by monks intent on winning support for the cult at Wutai. The argument seems farfetched to me as this conspiracy would have had to include the doctoring of the *Further Biographies* as well. Cf. Lamotte, "Mañjuśrī," pp. 61–84.

206. *XSZ* 25B.34 (644c–665a).

207. Cf. the biography of Buddhapāli *SSZ* 2.7 (717c–718b) and the biography of Fazhao *SSZ* 21.4 (844c25). For a study of the hagiography of another monk of the *Song Biographies* who encountered Mañjuśrī on Wutai, see Birnbaum, "Shenying's Experiences."

208. Cf. the biographies of Huichi *GSZ* 12.6 (407a), and Sengfu *XSZ* 16.1 (550b).

209. *SSZ* 23.9 (857b).

210. The mythical mountain Guangming Shan was identified as Emei, while the bodhisattva Xianshou (var. Xiansheng) was identified as Samantabhadra. Cf. *T* 278, v. 9.590a8; *T* 279, v. 10.241b29; Lamotte, "Mañjuśrī," p.79. See also the comments by the twentieth-century

monk Shi Yinguang in his introduction to *Emei shan zhi* (1934; rpt. Taibei: Wenhai chubanshe, 1970?), pp. 1–4.

211. In the biography of Haiyun *SSZ* 27.17 (882c).

212. Cf. Yü Chün-fang, "P'u-t'o Shan: Pilgrimage and the Creation of the Chinese Potalaka," in Susan Naquin and Chün-fang Yü, ed., *Pilgrims and Sacred Sites in China* (Berkeley: University of California Press, 1992), pp. 190–245. Campany comments on the significance of the fact that Guanyin was not yet localized in this way in the Six Dynasties. Cf. "Real Presence," p. 252.

213. Cf. the biography of Yuanjiao *SSZ* 24.13 (864b–c).

214. Biography of Shenwu *SSZ* 17.6 (824a).

215. Biography of Xuanzang *SSZ* 24.10 (863c) (distinguish from the more famous translator of the early Tang); and the "Dusong Treatise" *SSZ* 25.*T* (872a12–18).

216. *SSZ* 25.17 (870b).

217. *SSZ* 22.2 (850a).

218. Cf. the biographies of Tanyi *GSZ* 5.8 (355c), Baoda *SSZ* 21.9 (846c), and Buddhayaśas *GSZ*. 2.5 (333c).

219. Important studies on ghosts in early Chinese literature include Albert E. Dien, "The *Yüan-hun Chih* (Accounts of Ghosts with Grievances): A Sixth-Century Collection of Stories," in Tse-tsung Chow, ed., *Wen-lin: Studies in the Chinese Humanities* (Madison: University of Wisconsin Press, 1968), pp. 211–228; Anthony C. Yu, " 'Rest, Rest, Perturbed Spirit!' Ghosts in Traditional Chinese Prose Fiction," *Harvard Journal of Asiatic Studies* 47.2 (Dec. 1987): pp. 397–434; and Robert F. Campany, "Ghosts Matter: The Culture of Ghosts in Six Dynasties *Zhiguai*," *Chinese Literature: Essays, Articles, Reviews* 13 (Dec. 1991): pp. 15–34.

220. *SSZ* 18.13 (827a–b).

221. *Daoxuan lüshi gantong lu*, p. 435c.

222. See the biography of Huaixin *SSZ* 19.12 (833a).

223. On the relationship between Tang Chan and local cults, see Bernard Faure, "Space and Place in Chinese Religious Traditions," *History of Religions* 26.4 (May 1987): pp. 337–356, and Faure, *Rhetoric*, pp. 258–283.

224. Cf. "Religious Taoism and Popular Religion from the Second to Seventh Centuries," in Holmes Welch and Anna Seidel, eds., *Facets of Taoism* (New Haven: Yale University Press, 1979), pp. 53–82. This is not to say that such struggles between Daoists and Buddhists did not take place. See, for example, Verellen, "Evidential Miracles," pp. 246–255.

225. *SSZ* 26.8 (876b).

226. *SSZ* 9.9 (763c).

227. *XSZ* 25.5 (645b).

228. *GSZ* 13.8 (411a).

229. *SSZ* 22.5 (850c).

230. Cf. de Sardan, "Occultism and the Ethnographic 'I.' "

231. On the notion of "participation," see Lucien Lévy-Bruhl, *How Natives Think*, trans. Lilian Clare (New York: Washington Square Press, 1966), pp. 69–104, and Tambiah, *Magic, Science, Religion*, pp. 84–110.

232. Erik Zürcher, "Perspectives in the Study of Chinese Buddhism," *Journal of the Royal Asiatic Society* 2 (1982): pp. 171–172.

233. *SSZ* 20.19 (841c).

234. *SSZ* 18.6 (822b).

235. Welch, *Practice*, p. 260.

236. *SSZ* 18.4 (821b).

Chapter 3: Scholarship

1. On the eremitic ideal see Alan Berkowitz, "Patterns of Reclusion in Early and Early Medieval China" (Ph.D. dissertation, University of Washington, 1989).

2. *GSZ* 6.13 (365a).

3. *GSZ* 5.1 (353a); Arthur Link, "Biography of Shih Tao-an," *T'oung Pao* 46 (1958): pp. 29–31, and Zürcher, *Buddhist Conquest*, pp. 201–202.

4. *SSZ* 10.4 (767a).

5. The examination began during the reign of Zhongzong in 705. The examination underwent various changes and was enforced with varying degrees of success. See Erik Zürcher, "Buddhism and Education in T'ang Times," in Wm. Theodore de Bary and John W. Chaffee, eds., *Neo-Confucian Education: The Formative Stage* (Berkeley: University of California Press, 1989), pp. 32–35; Stanley Weinstein, *Buddhism Under the T'ang* (Cambridge: Cambridge University Press, 1987), pp. 188–189 n. 20; Michihata, *Tōdai bukkyōshi*, pp. 34–39.

6. *Bianyi jing*, perhaps an earlier, non-extant version of the *Bianyi zhangzhe zi jing* (*Skt. *Pratibhānamatipariprcchā*), *T* 544, v. 14, translated by Fachang between 500 and 515.

7. *GSZ* 5.1 (351c); Link, "Biography of Shih Tao-an," pp. 5–7.

8. *GSZ* 6.9 (363b).

9. See Jonathan Spence, *The Memory Palace of Matteo Ricci* (New York: Viking Penguin, 1984).

10. *Qiang ji*, probably a form of proto-Tibetan.

11. *GSZ* 2.5 (334b).

12. *SSZ* 2.2 (716a).

13. *SSZ* 5.11 (736c).

14. *SSZ* 6.12 (743a).

15. *Da zhi du lun* 4, p. 90c; Lamotte, *Traité*, p. 278.

16. Biography of Huichao, *XSZ* 6.1 (468a10).

17. *SSZ* 18.8. Specifically, Zanning cites *Da zhi du lun* 5, p. 97c.23; Lamotte, *Traité*, p. 328; and *Yujia shi di lun*, p. 491b.

18. Appended to the biography of Fazhen, *GSZ* 7.30 (374c).

19. *XSZ* 7.1 (476c).

20. Biography of Xuanyan, *SSZ* 29.19 (893b3).

21. *SSZ* 6.13 (743b).

22. Stephen Owen, *The Great Age of Chinese Poetry: The High T'ang* (New Haven: Yale University Press, 1981), pp. 282–295.

23. *XSZ* 5.12 (467a).

24. Mou Runsun, "Tangchu nanbei xueren lunxue zhi yiqu yu yingxiang," *Xianggang Zhongwen Daxue Zhongguo wenhua yanjiu xuebao* 1 (Sept. 1968): p. 80.

25. Cf. Zhou Yutong, *Zhongguo xuexiao zhidu* (Shanghai: Shangwu yinshuguan, 1933), pp. 69–84; Yan, "Tangren xiye shanlin siyuan zhi fengshang," pp. 315–316. Li Jun has objected that the extent to which secular schools borrowed from Buddhist models has been overestimated. Cf. "Lüe lun Wei-Jin Nanbei chao shiqi sixue de tedian," *Zhongguoshi yanjiu* 1 (1993): pp. 64–65. Erik Zürcher has also questioned the direct link between monasteries and the Song academies. Cf. "Buddhism and Education," p. 50. Whether or not the Song academies can be directly traced to monastic education, the importance of Buddhist monasteries to education of religious and secular alike in the medieval period is beyond question. On this point, see Gao Mingshi, "Tangdai sixue de fazhan," *Taida wenshizhe xuebao* 20 (1971): pp. 219–289.

26. Cf. Yan, "Tangren xiye shanlin siyuan zhi fengshang," pp. 271–316; Gao, "Tangdai sixue," pp. 260–268; Zürcher, "Buddhism and Education," pp. 35–50.

27. For an overview of the master-disciple relationship in Chinese Buddhism during the Six Dynasties period, focusing on the ordination ritual, see Suzuki Keizō, "Chūgoku ni okeru sōryo no shitei kankei ni tsuite," *Shikan* 57.8 (Mar. 1960), pp. 146–161. Suzuki notes that, while the master-disciple relationship in Buddhism shared much with its secular counterpart, one significant difference is that monks were allowed to follow more than one master.

28. *XSZ* 23.3 (626a).

29. *XSZ* 14.4 (534b).

30. *XSZ* 15.7 (541c24).

31. See for example, the biography of Sanhui, *XSZ* 14.6 (534c). While emphasizing the importance of the family metaphor, Suzuki Keizo goes so far as to argue that in the Six Dynasties the master-disciple relationship approached that of master-serf or master-slave.

32. *XSZ* 14.4 (534a29).

33. Biography of Fayun, *XSZ* 5.9 (464a6).

34. *Si fen lü* (Skt.*Dharmaguptakavinaya) *T* 1428, v. 22.

35. Daoxuan's [*Sifen lü*] *shan* [*fan*] *bu* [*que xingshi*] *chao*. *T* 1804, v. 40.

36. *SSZ* 14.20 (798c).

37. *SSZ* 26.3 (873c).

38. *SSZ* 14.11 (795b).

39. *GSZ* 6.1 (358a); Zürcher, *Buddhist Conquest*, p. 241.

40. *T* 1646, v. 32 (Skt.*Tattvasiddhiśāstra? Satyasidahiśāstra?*).

41. *GSZ* 6.11 (364b). For more on this incident see Tang Yongtong, *Han Wei Liangjin Nanbeichao fojiaoshi* (1938; rpt. Beijing: Zhonghua shuju, 1984), p. 224.

42. *Cheng weishi lun* (Skt. *Vijñaptimatratāsiddhi*[*śāstra*]?). *T* 1585, v. 31.

43. *Yujia* [*shi di*] *lun* (Skt.*Yogācāryabhūmiśāstra*). *T* 1579, v. 30.

44. *SSZ* 4.1 (725c–726a).

45. *Shishuo xinyu* 4.64; Mather, *A New Account*, pp. 124–125. A version of this story is also recorded in *GSZ* 1.13 (329a).

46. *Shishuo xinyu* 27.11; Mather, *A New Account*, p. 447.

47. Biography of Zhu Sengfu, *GSZ* 5.7 (355b).

48. *XSZ* 5.9 (464b).

49. Cf. Aoyama Sadao, *Tō Sō jidai no kōtsū to chishi chizu no kenkyū* (Tokyo: Yoshikawa kōbunkan, 1963), pp. 51–85.

50. *GSZ* 6.2 (361b–362a).

51. *GSZ* 6.1 (359b–360a).

52. The correspondence is preserved in the *Jiumoluoshi fashi dayi*, *T* 1856, v. 45. See also, Zürcher, *Buddhist Conquest*, pp. 226–229.

53. *GSZ* 7.1 (366b).

54. *GSZ* 2.1 (330c–331a).

55. *Sengshi lüe* B, p. 248a.

56. Biography of Huisheng, *XSZ* 24.2 (633b).

57. Biography of Zhixuan, *XSZ* 23.8 (631b). According to Zanning, it was not uncommon for emperors to take an active part in such debates. Cf. *Sengshi lüe*, B, p. 248b.

58. *Sengshi lüe*, B, p. 248b.

59. On the "conversion of the barbarians by Laozi," see Zürcher, *Conquest*, pp. 290–308. The *Biographies* describe court debates over this issue in Tanwuzui, *XSZ* 23.1 (624c); Zhixuan, *XSZ* 23.8 (631a); Huisheng, *XSZ* 24.2 (633b).

60. For a detailed study on the subject, see Th. Stcherbatsky's monumental *Buddhist Logic* (1932; rpt. The Hague: Mouton and Co.,1958).

61. (Skt. *Nyāyapraveśa*) *T* 1630, v. 32.

62. *SSZ* 4.1 (625c29–626b).

63. In Sanskrit, *pratijñā, hetu,* and *udāharaṇa.* Cf. Stcherbatsky, *Buddhist Logic*, pp. 279–283.

64. On debate in Tibetan Buddhism see F. Sierksma, "Rtsod-pa: The Monachal Disputations in Tibet," *Indo-Iranian Journal* 8.2 (1964), pp. 130–152; Daniel E. Perdue, *Debate in Tibetan Buddhism* (Ithaca: Snow Lion, 1992).

65. Even under the formal rules of debate in Tibetan Buddhism, Tibetan monks are known to become visibly angry and / or embarrassed during debate. (Sierksma, "Rtsod-pa," p. 134). Adherence to

logic does not, after all, preclude a personal investment in the argument.

66. *GSZ* 8.*T* (383a).

67. *XSZ* 9.5 (494a2).

68. *GSZ* 7.15 (370c16).

69. *SSZ* 17.2 (812c13).

70. *Shishuo xinyu* 4.51; Mather, *A New Account*, p. 118.

71. *SSZ* 7.1 (745a25).

72. *Zhuwei*, held by the speaker during a debate.

73. Weaving was a metaphor for the thinking process.

74. Biography of Zhu Fatai, *GSZ* 5.4 (354c); Zürcher, *Buddhist Conquest*, p. 148.

75. *GSZ* 4.8 (349a); also in *Shishuo xinyu* 4.42; Mather, *A New Account*, p. 114.

76. Famous scholar of the classics, d. 200.

77. *Shishuo xinyu* 26.21; Mather, *A New Account*, p. 437.

78. *SSZ* 4.6 (727b–c).

79. *SSZ* 29.5 (889c).

80. Cf. Zürcher, "Perspectives."

81. Cf. Antonino Forte, "The Relativity of the Concept of Orthodoxy in Chinese Buddhism," in Robert Buswell, ed., *Chinese Buddhist Apocrypha* (Honolulu: University of Hawai'i Press, 1989), pp. 239–249.

82. Cf. Nakamura, *Bukkyōgo daijiten*, p. 1383a.

83. *SSZ* 4.8 (728a).

84. *GSZ* 7.23 (373a14).

85. Walter Liebenthal, "The World Conception of Chu Tao-sheng," *Monumenta Nipponica* 12.1 / 2 (1956): pp. 95–97 (article continued in 12.3 / 4 [1957]: pp. 241–268); Tang, *Fojiao shi*, pp. 463–466.

86. *GSZ* 7.1 (366c). Walter Liebenthal, "A Biography of Chu Tao-sheng," *Monumenta Nipponica* 11.3 (1955): pp. 83–88; Tang, *Fojiao shi*, p. 443.

87. *Shishuo xinyu* 26.25; Mather, *A New Account*, p. 439.

88. *GSZ* 8.*T* (382c, 383a).

89. Biography of Faxian, *XSZ* 26.15 (670c).

90. Biography of Baoyan, *XSZ* 26.33 (674b14) and of Fazan, *XSZ* 10.13 (506c24).

91. *SSZ* 6.11 (742b10), quoted in Peter Gregory, *Tsung-mi and the Sinification of Buddhism* (Princeton: Princeton University Press, 1991), pp. 22–23.

92. *Xingzongfa*, opposed to the "doctrine of emptiness" (*kongzong*).

93. *SSZ* 13.*T* (789c).

94. *SSZ* 8.2 (754c14).

95. *SSZ* 12.2 (778b).

96. *SSZ* 13.3 (785b).

97. *SSZ* 12.11 (780c19).

98. The critique was, however, by no means limited to Mazu's lin-

eage. Cf. William Powell, *The Record of Tung-shan* (Honolulu: University of Hawai'i Press, 1986), pp. 13–14.

99. Cf. Gregory, *Tsung-mi*, pp. 236–244.

100. Yanagida Seizan, "The 'Recorded Sayings' Texts of Chinese Ch'an Buddhism," translated by John McRae in Whalen Lai and Lewis Lancaster, eds., *Early Ch'an in China and Tibet* (Berkeley: University of California Press, 1983), pp. 185–186. See also Judith Berling, "Bringing the Buddha down to Earth: Notes on the Emergence of *Yü-lu* as a Buddhist Genre," *History of Religions* 21.1 (1987): pp. 56–88.

101. Cf. Dale S. Wright, "The Discourse of Awakening: Rhetorical Practice in Classical Ch'an Buddhism," *Journal of the American Academy of Religion* 61.1 (Spring 1993): pp. 23–40. Examples of collections of recorded sayings from this, the "classical" period of Chan, include that of Dongshan Liangjie, translated by William Powell, *The Record of Tung-shan*; and that of Linji Yixuan, translated by Burton Watson, *The Zen Teachings of Master Lin-chi* (Boston: Shambala, 1993). Though the dating of these texts to late Tang times is problematic, in theme they are consistent with works datable to the Five Dynasties period and the Early Song.

102. *Zhenzhou Linji Huizhao chanshi yulu T* 1985, v. 47.502c16; Watson, *The Zen Teachings of Master Lin-chi*, p. 76.

103. *Pang Jushi yulu* B, *XZJ* v. 120.31a; Ruth Fuller Sasaki et al., *The Recorded Sayings of Layman P'ang: A Ninth-century Zen Classic* (New York: Weatherhill, 1972), pp. 72–73.

104. *Zhenzhou Linji lu*, p. 506c10; Watson, *The Zen Teachings of Master Lin-chi*, p. 127.

105. Yanagida Seizan, ed., *Zu tang ji* (Jap. *Sōdōshū*) (Kyoto: Chūbun shuppansha, 1974), 18.340.

106. *Zu tang ji*, 4.92b.

107. Dale, "The Discourse of Awakening," p. 37.

108. For self-mutilation, see the biography of Chunan in the *Jingde chuandeng lu, T* 2076, v. 51.292c8; for supernormal powers, see Faure, *The Rhetoric of Immediacy*, pp. 108–111.

109. *Zhenzhou Linji lu*, p. 502b; Watson, *The Zen Teachings of Master Lin-chi*, p. 74.

110. *SSZ* 8.2 (754c).

111. *SSZ* 12.16 (783a).

112. *SSZ* 11.4 (773b).

113. *SSZ* 11.13 (775c).

114. *SSZ* 12.6 (779b4).

115. "Ti Xun Shangren sengbao zhuan," *Shimen wenzi chan*, 26.6a.

116. For a comparison of the *Song Biographies* and the *Transmission of the Lamp*, see Ishii Shūdō, *Sōdai zenshūshi no kenkyū* (Tokyo: Daitō shuppansha, 1987), pp. 45–60.

117. Cf. Chen Yuan, *Zhongguo fojiao shiji*, p. 106.

118. On the emergence and success of "Lamp" or "Flame" histories,

see T. Griffith Foulk, "Myth, Ritual, and Monastic Practice in Sung China," in Patricia Ebrey and Peter Gregory, eds., *Religion and Society in T'ang and Sung China* (Honolulu: University of Hawai'i Press, 1993), pp. 147–208.

119. The *Tiansheng guang deng lu*, by Li Zunxu, completed in 1038.

120. *Zhaode junzhai dushu zhi* (Taibei: Guangwen shuju, 1967; facsimile reproduction of 1884 Changsha edition), 16.22a (951).

121. Cf. Chen Yuan, *Zhongguo fojiao shiji*, p. 98–102.

122. Other examples of Confucian "lamp histories" include Huang Zongxi's, *Ming ru xue an*, selections of which are translated in Julia Ching, ed., *The Records of Ming Scholars* (Honolulu: University of Hawai'i Press, 1987), and Wan Sitong's *Rulin zongpai*.

123. "Ti Fojian seng bao zhuan," *Shimen wenzi chan*, 26.4a; and *Linjian lu* A, p. 294a.

124. Chün-fang Yü, "Ch'an Education in the Sung," in de Bary, ed., *Neo-Confucian Education*, pp. 79–88; Carl Bielefeldt, *Dōgen's Manuals of Zen Meditation* (Berkeley: University of California Press, 1988), p. 96; Gregory, *Tsung-mi*, p. 22; Faure, *Rhetoric*, pp. 61–63.

Glossary

Characters for the names of books and their authors can be found under "Works Cited."

Ācārya Xiang 香闍梨
Anlin 安廩
Bai Juyi 白居易
Bai Minzhong 白敏中
Bai Xingjian 白行簡
Baocheng 褒城
Baoda 寶達
baofu 抱腹
Baolin zhuan 寶林傳
baoshen 報身
Baoyan 寶嚴
bashiyi 八十一
bayue shiyiri 八月十一日
Beidu 杯度
Bianji 辯機
biantan 編坦
Bianyi jing 辯意經
bu ke siyi 不可思議
Bukongju 不空鉤
Ce 策
Chan Master Na 那禪師
Changda 常達
changdao 唱導

Changyu 常遇
Chaoda 超達
Chen Shou 陳壽
Chen Shuling 陳叔陵
cheng yinyang 成陰陽
Cheng'en 乘恩
Chengguan 澄観
chenwei 讖緯
Chiren 癡人
chuanfa baoji 傳法寶記
Chuji 處寂
Chujin 楚金
Chunan 楚南
ci 此
Congjian 從諫
Cui Xuanwei 崔玄暐
Cui Yuan 崔瑗
cuiyi 毳衣
Da pin 大品
da zhuan 大傳
Daibing 代病
Danxia Tianran 丹霞天然
Daoan 道安

187

Daobian 道辯

Daoheng 道恒

Daoji 道積

Daojiong 道問

Daolin 道林

Daopi 道丕

Daoqi 道齊

Daorong 道融

Daosheng 道生

daoshu 道術

Daotai 道泰

Daowen 道溫

Daoxiu 道休

Daoxuan 道宣

Daoying 道英

Daoyuan (born in pure-land) 道願

Daoyuan (Song monk) 道原

Daozhe 道哲

Daozhou 道舟

Deshao 德韶

Diandian 點點

Dinglan 定蘭

Dongshan Liangjie 洞山良价

Do-yuk 道育

Du Kang 杜康

Duan Chengshi 段成式

Dui fa lun 對法論

Dusong pian 讀誦篇

duweina 都維那

Emei 峨嵋

Faan 法安

Fachang 法場

Facong 法聰

Fahua ganying zhuan 法華感應傳

Fajin 法進

Fakan 法侃

Fali 法力

Falin 法琳

Famen Monastery 法門寺

fangshi 方士

Fanxian 梵仙

Faqing 法慶

Faren 法忍

fashen 法身

Fatong 法通

Faxi 法喜

Faxian 法顯

Faxiang 法響

Fayan 法眼

Fayuan (fortune-teller) 法瑗

Fayuan (vegetarian) 法願

Fayun (letter-writer) 法雲

Fayun (spell-caster) 法運

Fazan 法瓚

Fazang 法藏

Fazhao 法照

Fazhen 法珍

Fazong 法宗

feng zhao 奉詔

Fotucheng 佛圖澄

Fu Jian 符堅

Fu Yi 傅奕

Fuli 復禮

Gantong 感通

Gantong pian 感通篇

ganying 感應

Gao Pian 高駢

Gaoyang Princess 高陽公主

gongyang 供養

Guangjing 光静

Guangling 廣陵

Guangming Shan 光明山

Guangshiyin yingyan ji 光世音應驗記

Guangyi 光儀

Guanshiyin 觀世音

Guo Zushen 郭祖深

guofu yi 裹腹衣

Guozheng 果證

Haiyun 海雲

Hanshan 寒山

He Yin 何胤

he 褐

hei 黑

Heluojie 訶羅竭

Hengchao 恒超

Hengtong 恒通

Hongchu 鴻楚

Hongju 鴻莒

Hongren 弘忍

Hongshi 弘師

Hongxiu 鴻休

Hongyan 洪偃

Hongyin 洪諲

Hongzhen 洪真

Hongzheng 洪正

Hongzhou 洪州

Housenghui 後僧會

Hu Gong 壺公

hua heshang 花和尚

Huaijun 懷濬

Huaisu 懷素

Huaixin 懷信

Huanpu 寰普

huashen 化身

Huayan Monastery 華嚴寺

hufa 護法

Huichao 慧超

Huichi 慧持

Huihong 惠洪

Huiji 慧寂

Huijiao 慧皎

Huijing 慧精

Huijun 慧頵

Huikai 慧開

Huike 慧可

Huikuan 惠寬

Huilin Monastery 慧林寺

Huimi 慧彌

Huiming 惠明

Huimu 慧木

Huineng 慧能

Huishao 慧紹

Huisheng 慧乘

Huishi 慧實

Huitong 慧通

Huixiang 惠祥

Huixu 慧緒

Huiyao 慧耀

Huiyu 慧瑜

Huiyuan (mentioned in connection with Daoist diet) 慧元

Huiyuan (prominent Six Dynasties monk) 慧遠

Huizan 慧瓚

Huizhe 慧哲

Huizhu 慧主

huotou jin'gang zhou 火頭金剛咒

Huqiu shan 虎丘山

Ji shi 季士

jia heshang 假和尚

jiang 絳

jiangshi 講師

jianzong 漸宗

Jianzong 鑑宗

Jiaoran 皎然

Jin'gangzhi 金剛智

Jing 涇水

Jing'ai 静藹

jingchuang 經幢

Jingduan 静端

jingjin 精進

jingshi 經師

jingxin di 淨心地

Jingxiu 淨秀

Jingzhi 静之

Jingzhou 涇州
jiu 韮
jiurou seng 酒肉僧
Jiyang 棘陽
jue fangshi 絕方室
kaiguang 開光
Kaitian zhuan xinji 開天傳信記
Kang Minggan 康明感
kongzong 空宗
Kuaiji 會稽
Kuiji 窺基
kuxing 苦行
lai heshang 癩和尚
Lanruoshe 蘭若舍
Layman Bao 鮑居士
Layman Pang 龐居士
Lengzhai yehua 冷齋夜話
Li Yuan 李源
libo 立播
Linchuan 臨川
Lingtan 靈坦
Lingyi 靈一
Lingyu 靈裕
Linji Yixuan 臨濟義玄
Liu Hui 柳惠
Liu Jun 劉峻
Liuxia Hui 柳下惠
Longwang zhou shuiyu jing
    龍王咒水浴經
Lu Shan 廬山
lun 論
Luohan Wang 羅漢王
Master of the Regulations
    Quan 詮律師
Mazu 馬祖
Mingche 明徹
Minggong 明恭
Minghui 明慧
Mingjie 明解
minglü 明律

Mount Tai 泰山
Musang 無相
nabo 納播
Nantuo 難陀
Nanyang 南陽
Niu Xiantong 牛仙童
Pei Xiu 裴休
Peng Yan 彭偃
Pi Rixiu 皮日休
Puji (Song monk) 普濟
Puji (Tang monk) 普寂
Pujing 普静
Puman 普滿
Puming 普明
Puxian 普賢
Puyuan 普圓
Qian Liu 錢鏐
Qian Renfeng 錢仁奉
Qiang ji 羌籍
Qianzhen 潛真
qiaoke 僑客
qing 青
Qingcheng 青城
Qingguan 清觀
Qingliang Mountain 清涼山
qingtan 清談
Qingxu 清虛
Qingzhu 慶諸
Qiyin 棲隱
qizai tongzai 奇哉痛哉
Quanqing 全清
Quanzai 全宰
Ruan Yu 阮裕
Rulin zongpai 儒林宗派
ruyi 如意
san mi 三密
san ye 三業
Sanhui 三慧
sanzhi 三支
Sengche 僧徹

Sengcong 僧從

Sengfan 僧範

Sengfu (martyr) 僧富

Sengfu (pilgrim to Emei) 僧副

Sengjie 僧竭

Sengjin 僧瑾

Sengke 僧可

Sengliang 僧亮

Sengming 僧明

Sengqie 僧伽

Sengqing 僧慶

Sengrong 僧融

Sengrui 僧叡

Sengshan 僧善

Sengxin 僧昕

Sengyai 僧崖

Sengye 僧業

Sengyu 僧瑜

Sengyuan 僧瑗

Sengzang 僧藏

Sengzhao 僧肇

Shandao 善導

Shangzuo 上座

Shanwuwei 善無畏

Shaokang 少康

Shaolin Monastery 少林寺

Shaoshuo 邵碩

shatai 沙汰

Shegong 涉公

Shen Daoqian 沈道虔

shen 神

Shending 神鼎

Shengjin 聖進

shentong 神通

Shenwu 神悟

Shenxuan 神喧

shenyi 神異

shenzu 神足

Shi Le 石勒

Shi Tongjin 釋童進

Shi Xiongjun 釋雄俊

Shi Yinfeng 釋隱峰

Shide 拾得

Shijian 師簡

shinsô 神僧

shiyimian Guanyin zhou 十一面
        觀音咒

Shouxian 守賢

shushu 數術 (var. 數数)

shuyuan 書院

si da 四大

Sima Bao 司馬寶

sixiang 四相

sizhu 寺主

songjing 誦經

Su E 蘇鱷

su shi 素食

Sucaoshi 束草師

suizeng 隨增

Sun-kyǒng 順景

Suzhou 蘇州

suzhutong 宿住通

Tancheng 曇稱

Tandi 曇諦

Tanjie 曇戒

Tanlun 曇倫

Tante 檀特

Tanwuchen 曇無讖

Tanwuzui 曇無最

Tanxuan 曇選

Tanyao 曇瑤

Tanyi (preacher) 曇一

Tanyi (spell-caster) 曇翼

Tanyi (finger-burner) 曇義

Tanyun 曇韻

Tanzhi 曇智

taxintong 他心通

Teng Yongwen 滕永文

tianer 天耳

tianyan 天眼

tonggan 通感

Tongjin 童進

tongziju 童子舉

Toutuo Monastery 頭陀寺

toutuo 頭陀

tuoluoni 陀羅尼

Ŭisang 義湘

Wan Jingru 萬敬儒

Wan Sitong 萬斯同

Wang Gu 王固

Wang Mang 王莽

Wang Mi 王彌

Wang Senggui 王僧貴

Wang Wei 王維

Wang Xun 王珣

Wang Zhen 王真

Wangming zhuan 亡名傳

wangshen 亡身

Wei Chuhou 韋處厚

Weigong 惟恭

Weijin 惟勁

Weimojie 維摩詰

Weizhong 惟忠

Wen'gang 文綱

Wenshuang 文爽

Wǒn-ch'ŭk 圓測

Wu ming 五明

Wu 吳

Wudeng huiyuan 五燈會元

wuloutong 無漏通

Wuran 無染

Wuyuan 吳苑

Wuzixu 伍子胥

Wuzuo 無作

Xi chan pian 習禪篇

Xi Guangshiyin yingyan ji 繫光
世音應驗記

xi 系

Xiang Sheli 香闍梨

Xiansheng 賢勝

Xianshou 賢首

Xiaogan Monastery 孝感寺

xiaogan 孝感

xichan 習禪

Xichen 息塵

Xici zhuan 繫辭傳

xie 薤

Xie Hui 謝晦

Xie Lingyun 謝靈運

Ximing Monastery 西明寺

xingfu 興福

Xingjian 行堅

Xingming 行明

Xingzhi Jueshou 行智覺壽

Xingzhou 邢州

xingzhuang 行狀

Xingzongfa 性宗法

Xingzun 行遵

xinshi 信士

xinwu yi 心無義

Xiqian 希遷

Xu Guangshiyin yingyan ji 續光
世音應驗記

Xuanchang 玄暢

Xuangao 玄高

Xuanjue 玄覺

Xuanyan (lectured before
Xuanzong) 玄儼

Xuanyan (poet-monk) 玄晏

Xuanzang 玄奘

Xun Ji 荀濟

Xuyun 虛雲

Yan Shigu 顏師古

Yancong 彥琮

yangliu 楊柳

Yangshan 仰山

Yangshan Huiji 仰山慧寂

Yangzhou 揚州

Yanqiu 彥球

Yantou Huo 嵒頭豁

Yao Wang 藥王

Yao Xing 姚興

Yaoshan 藥山

Yi Prefecture 益州

yijie 義解

Yijing 義淨

yijing 譯經

Yiluo yuanyuan lu 伊洛淵源錄

Yin Hao 殷浩

Yin Hong 殷洪

yin 因

yingshen 應身

yinming 因明

yinsi 淫祀

yishen 遺身

Yishi 義師

Yixing 一行

Yixue 義學

Yongan 永安

Yongjia 永嘉

Yongming Yanshou 永明延壽

Youguang 遊光

Yu Fadao 于法道

Yu Fakai 于法開

yu 喻

Yuan Yanchong 元彥沖

Yuanbiao 元表

Yuanhui 元慧

Yuanjiao 元皎

Yuankang 元康

Yue Guang 樂廣

yulu 語錄

Yunmen Wenyan 雲門文偃

Yunmen 雲門

Yunwen 允文

zake shengde 雜科聲德

zan 贊

Zanghuan 藏奐

Zanning 贊寧

zao 皂

Zengren 增忍

Zhan Huo 展獲

Zhan Ji 展季

Zhang Heng 張衡

Zhang Quanyi 章全益

Zhangqiu Zituo 章仇子陀

Zhao Hua 趙華

Zhaoxian 招賢

Zhaozhou Congshen 趙州從諗

zhen weishi liang 真唯識量

Zhenbian 貞辯

Zheng Xuan 鄭玄

Zheng Yue 鄭說

Zhengzhi 證智

zhi cheng gan shen 至誠感神

zhi cheng suo gan 至誠所感

Zhi Dun 支遁

Zhi Mindu 支愍度

zhiguai 志怪

Zhihui 智慧

Zhihuo jie 滯惑解

Zhikuang 智曠

Zhiqin 智勤

Zhisheng (monk) 智生

Zhisheng (nun) 智勝

Zhiwei 智徽

Zhiwen 智文

Zhixian (text-burner) 智閑

Zhixian (nun) 智賢

Zhixiang 植相

Zhixuan (monk who subdues fox-spirit) 志玄

Zhixuan (Tang exegete) 知玄

Zhixuan (debater) 智炫

Zhiyi (Keeper of Ape) 智一

Zhiyi (Tiantai exegete) 智顗

Zhiyuan 志遠

Zhizang 智藏

Zhongliang 中梁

Zhou (dynasty) 周

zhou (spell) 咒

Zhou du 咒毒

Zhou qing yu zhou zhi yu qu
  xieqi shenzhou 咒請雨咒止雨
  取血氣神咒

Zhou shui jing 咒水經

Zhou Xuzhi 周續之

Zhou ya tong 咒牙痛

Zhou yan tong 咒眼痛

Zhou Yong 周顒

Zhu Ci 朱泚

Zhu Fakuang 竺法曠

Zhu Fatai 竺法汰

Zhu Fayi 竺法義

Zhu Sengfu 竺僧敷

Zhu Shixing 朱士行

Zhu Shouchang 朱壽昌

Zhu Shulan 竺叔蘭

Zhu Tanyou 竺曇猷

Zhu Tao 朱滔

Zhu Xi 朱熹

Zhuangxiang 莊襄

Zhuhong 朱宏

Zhuo Qian 卓潛

Zhuo 卓

Zhuwei 塵尾

zibai 緇白

ziyi (purple robe) 紫衣

ziyi (black-robed ones) 緇衣

zong 宗

zongchi 總持

Zongmi 宗密

zuodao 左道

Works Cited

Primary Sources

"Bi xiao yi" 鄙孝議. Pi Rixiu 皮日休. In *Pi Zi wen sou* 皮子文藪. 1959. Reprint. Beijing: Zhonghua shuju, 1965, pp. 86–87.

Bianyi zhangzhe zi jing 辯意長者子經 (*Skt. Pratibhānamatipari-pṛcchā). *T* 544, v. 14.

Biqiuni zhuan 比丘尼傳. Baochang 寶昌, *T* 2063, v. 50.

Cefu yuangui 冊府元龜. Facsimile reproduction of the 1642 edition. Hong Kong: Zhonghua Shuju, 1960..

Chang ahan jing 長阿含經 (Skt. *Dīrghāgama*). *T* 1, v. 1.

Chu sanzang jiji 出三藏記集. Sengyou 僧祐. *T* 2145, v. 55.

"Chunri shangfang jishi" 春日上方即事. Wang Wei 王維. *Quan Tang shi* 126.1278.

Da banniepan jing 大般涅槃經 (Skt. *Mahāparinirvāṇasūtra*). *T* 374, v. 12.

Da Song sengshi lüe 大宋僧史略. Zanning 贊寧. *T* 2126, v. 54.

Da Tang Dajianfu si gu dade Kang Zang fashi wen bei 大唐大薦福寺故大德康藏法師文碑. Yan Chaoyin 閻朝隱. Appended to *Fazang heshang zhuan* 法藏和尚傳 *XZJ*, v. 134.

Da zhi du lun 大智度論. *T* 1509, v. 25.

Dafang guangfo huayan jing 大方廣佛華嚴經 30 (Skt. [*Buddha*]-*avataṃsakasūtra*). *T* 278, v. 9.

Daoxuan lüshi gantong lu 道宣律師感通錄. Daoxuan 道宣. *T* 2107, v. 52.

Dasheng apidamo zaji lun 大乘阿毗達磨雜集論 (*Skt. *Abhidharma-samuccayavyākhyā*). *T* 1606, v. 31.

Dasheng yizhang 大乘義章. Huiyuan 慧遠. *T* 1851, v. 44.

Dasheng zhuangyan jing lun 大乘莊嚴經論 (Skt. *Mahāyānasūtrālaṃ-kāra*). *T* 1604, v. 31.

Duyang zabian 杜陽雜編. Su E 蘇鶚. Shanghai: Jicheng shuju, 1939.

Fa ju jing 法句經. *T* 2901, v. 85.

Fan wang jing 梵網經. *T* 1484, v. 24.

Fo zu tong ji 佛祖統記. Zhipan 志磐. *T* 2035, v. 49.

Ganying leicong zhi 感應類從志. Zanning 贊寧. In *Shuofu* 説浮, v. 109. Facsimile reproduction of the 1647 edition. Shanghai: Shangwu Press, 1927.

Guan wuliangshoufo jing 觀無量壽佛經 (Skt. **Amitāyurbuddhānu-smṛtisūtra*). *T* 365, v. 12.

Guanding jing 灌頂經. *T* 1331, v. 21.

Guang hongming ji 廣弘明集. Daoxuan 道宣. *T* 2103, v. 52.

Han shu 漢書. Beijing: Zhonghua shuju, 1962.

Hou Han shu 後漢書. Beijing: Zhonghua shuju, 1965.

Huaji tuoluoni shenzhou jing 華積陀羅尼神咒經 (Skt. **Puṣpakūṭad-hāraṇi [sūtra]*). *T* 1356, v. 21.

Huayan xuantan huixuan ji 華嚴縣談會玄記. Purui 普瑞. *XZJ*, v. 12.

Ji Shenzhou sanbao gantong lu 集神州三寶感通錄. Daoxuan 道宣. *T* 2106, v. 52.

Ji zhi guo jing 寂志果經. *T* 22, v. 1.

Jin seng dao bu shou jielü zhao 禁僧道不守戒律詔. *Quan Tang wen*, 29.327.

Jin shu 晉書. Beijing: Zhonghua shuju, 1974.

Jingde chuandeng lu 景德傳燈錄. *T* 2076, v. 51.

Jinlouzi 金樓子 (*Siku quanshu* edn.).

Jiu Wudaishi 舊五代史. Beijing: Zhonghua shuju, 1975.

Jiumoluoshi fashi dayi 鳩摩羅什法師大義. *T* 1856, v. 45.

Junzhai dushu zhi 郡齋讀書志. Chao Gongwu 晁公武. Facsimile reproduction of 1884 Changsha edn. (Taibei: Guangwen shuju, 1967.

Liangchu qingzhong yiben 量處輕重儀本. Daoxuan 道宣. *T* 1895, v. 45.

Liao shi 遼史. Beijing: Zhonghua shuju, 1974.

Linjian lu 林間錄. Huihong 惠洪. *XZJ*, v. 148.

Liu du ji jing 六度集經 (Skt. **Ṣaṭpāramitāsaṃgraha*). *T* 152, v. 3.

Longxing biannian tonglun 隆興編年通論. Zuxiu 祖琇. *XZJ*, v. 133.

Lüxiang gantong zhuan 律相感通傳. Daoxuan 道宣. *T* 1898, v. 45.

Miaofa lianhua jing 妙法蓮華經 6 (Skt. *Saddharmapuṇḍarīka*). *T* 262, v. 9.

Ming ru xue an 明儒學案. Huang Zongxi 黃宗羲.

Mingseng zhuan 名僧傳. Fragments preserved in thirteenth-century Japanese copy, *Meisōdenshō* 名僧傳抄. *XZJ*, v. 134.

Mishasai wu fen jieben 彌沙塞五分戒本 (Skt. **Mahīśāsakavinaya*). *T* 1422, v. 22.

Modeng qie jing 摩登伽經 (Skt. **Mātaṅugīsūtra*). *T* 1300, v. 21.

Mohe banruo poluomi jing 摩訶般若波羅密經 (Skt. *Pañcaviṃśātisā-hasrikā [mahā] prajñāpāramitā*). *T* 223, v. 8.

Mohe sengqi lü 摩訶僧祇律 (Skt. **Mahāsāṃghikavinaya*). *T* 1425, v. 22.

Mohe zhiguan 摩訶止觀. Zhiyi 智顗. *T* 1911, v. 46.

Nan shi 南史. Beijing: Zhonghua shuju, 1975.

Nanhai jigui neifa zhuan 南海寄歸內法傳. Yijing 義淨. *T* 2125, v. 54.

Nittō guhō junrei gyōki (*Ru Tang qiufa xunli xing jī jiao zhu*) 入唐求法巡禮行記校註. Ennin 圓仁. Bai Huawen 白化文 et al., eds. Shijiazhuang: Huashan wenyi chubanshe, 1992.

Pang Jushi yulu 龐居士語錄. *XZJ*, v. 120.

Pumenpin jing 普門品經. *T* 315, v. 11.

Pusa shan jie jing 菩薩善戒經 (Skt. *Bodhisattvabhūmi*). *T* 1582, v. 30.

Qingliang shan zhi 清凉山志. In *Zhongguo fosi shizhi hui kan* 中國佛寺史志彙刊, v. 3, gen. ed. Du Jiexiang 杜潔祥. Taibei: Danqing tushu gongsi 丹青圖書公司, 1985.

Quan Tang shi 全唐詩. 1960. Reprint. Beijing: Zhonghua shuju, 1985.

Quan Tang wen 全唐文. Beijing: Zhonghua shuju, 1985.

San guo zhi 三國志. Beijing: Zhonghua shuju, 1959.

San Tendai Godaisan ki 參天台五台山記. Jōjin 成尋. In *Dai Nihon bukkyō zensho* 大日本佛教全書, v. 115. Tokyo: Kōdansha, 1970–1973.

"Sengqie ge" 僧伽歌. Li Bai 李白. *Quan Tang shi*, 166.1720.

Shenseng zhuan 神僧傳. *T* 2064, v. 50.

Shenxian zhuan 神仙傳. In *Han Wei congshu* 漢魏叢書, ed. Wang Mo 王謨. Shanghai: Shanghai datong shuju, 1967.

"Shi yu tie" 食魚帖. Huaisu 懷素. *Quan Tang wen*, 912.7a.

Shimen wenzi chan 石門文字禪. Huihong 惠洪. *SBCK* edn.

Shishi jigu lüe 釋氏稽古略. Juean 覺岸. *T* 2037, v. 49.

Shishuo xinyu 世説新語. Liu Yiqing 劉義慶. Ed. Xu Zhen'e 徐震堮. Beijing: Zhonghua shuju, 1984.

Shu jing 書經. In *Shisan jing zhusu* 十三經注疏. Beijing: Zhonghua shuju, 1979.

Si fen lü 四分律 1 (Skt. **Dharmaguptakavinaya*). *T* 1428, v. 22.

Si fen lü shanfan buque xingshi chao 四分律刪繁補闕行事鈔. Daoxuan 道宣. *T* 1804, v. 40.

Si ta ji 寺塔記. Duan Chengshi 段成式. *T* 2093, v. 51.

Siku quanshu zongmu 四庫全書總目. Facsimile reproduction of the Dadong shuju edition. Taibei: Yiwen Yinshuguan, n.d.

Song shi 宋史. Beijing: Zhonghua shuju, 1977.

Song shu 宋書. Beijing: Zhonghua shuju, 1974.

"Suzhou Chongyuansi Fahuayuan shibijing beiwen" 蘇州重元寺法華院石壁經碑文. Bai Juyi 白居易. *Quan Tang wen*, 678.2a.

Taiping guangji 太平廣記. Beijing: Zhonghua shuju, 1961.

Tang huiyao 唐會要. Taipei: Shijie shuju, 1968.

"Tang Huzhou Dayunsi gu chanshi Yugong beiming bingxu" 唐湖州大雲寺故禪師瑀公碑銘并序. *Quan Tang wen*, 918.4b.

Tang lü suyi 唐律疏義. Changsha: Shangwu yinshuguan, 1939.

"Ti Fojian sengbao zhuan" 題佛鑑僧寶傳. Huihong 慧洪. *Shimen wenzi chan* 26.4a.

"Ti xiu sengshi" 題修僧史. Huihong 慧洪. *Shimen wenzi chan*, 25.10b–11a.

"Ti Xun Shangren sengbao zhuan" 題珣上人僧寶傳. Huihong 慧洪. *Shimen wenzi chan*, 26.6a.

"Ti Zhang Sengyao zuiseng tu" 題張僧繇醉僧圖. Huaisu 懷素. *Quan Tang shi*, 808.9122.

"Tian di yinyang jiao huan da le fu" 天地陰陽交歡大樂賦. Bai Xingjian 白行簡. In *Shuangmei jing'an congshu* 雙梅景闇叢書, ed. Ye Dehui 業德輝, 1.7b.

Tiansheng guang deng lu 天聖廣燈錄. Li Zunxu 李遵勗.

"Wan bo Xunyang wang Lu shan" 晚泊潯陽望廬山. Meng Haoran 孟浩然. *Quan Tang shi*, 160.1645.

Wangsheng ji 往生集. Zhuhong 袾宏. *T* 2072, v. 51.

Wangsheng xifang jingtu ruiying zhuan 往生西方淨土瑞應傳. *T* 2070, v. 51.

Wen xuan 文選. *SBBY* edn.

Wuwei Sanzang chan yao 無畏三藏禪要. *T* 917, v. 18.

Xianyu jing 賢愚經. *T* 202, v. 4.

Xin lun 新論. Huan Tan 桓譚. In *Taiping yulan* 太平御覽, v. 400. Beijing: Zhonghua shuju, 1960.

Xin Tang shu 新唐書. 1975. Reprint. Beijing: Zhonghua shuju, 1986.

Yinming ru zhengli lun 因明入正理論 (Skt. *Nyāyapraveśa*). *T* 1630, v. 32.

Yuedeng sanmei jing 月燈三昧經 (Skt. *Samādhirājā [candrapradī-pasūtra]*). *T* 639, 640, and 641, v. 15.

Yuqie shidi lun 瑜伽師地論 (*Skt. Yogacāryabhūmiśāstra*). *T* 1579, v. 30.

Za ahan jing 雜阿含經 (Skt. *Saṃyuktāgama*). *T* 99, v. 2.

Zhaode junzhai dushu zhi 昭德郡齋讀書志. Chao Gongwu 晁公武. Facsimile reproduction of 1884 Changsha edn. Taibei: Guangwen shuju, 1967.

Zhenzhou Linji Huizhao chanshi yulu 鎮州臨濟慧照禪師語錄. *T* 1985, v. 47.

Zizhi tongjian 資治通鑑. 1956. Reprint Beijing: Zhonghua shuju, 1987.

Zongtong biannian 宗統編年. Jiyin 紀蔭. *XZJ*, v. 147.

Zu tang ji 祖堂集 (Jap. *Sōdōshū*). Ed. Yanagida Seizan 柳田聖山. Kyoto: Chūbun shuppansha, 1974.

Secondary Sources

Abe, Shōichi 阿部肇一. "*Sō kōsōden to Zenrin sōhōden*—Hoku-Sō no Sannei to Dokō no sōshikan" 宋高僧傳と禪林僧寶傳—北宋の贊寧と德洪の僧史観. In *Rekishi ni okeru minshū to bunka—Sakai Tadao sensei koki shukuga kinen ronshū* 歷史における民眾と文化—酒井忠夫先生古稀祝賀記念論集. Tokyo: Sakai Tadao sensei koki shukuga kinen no kai, 1982.

Andō, Tomonobu 安藤智信. "Hoku-Sō ki ni okeru inyōka no kikkyō kafuku setsu to Bukkyō"北宋期における陰陽家の吉凶禍福説と 仏教. Ōtani gakuhō 大谷学報 64. 1 (June 1984): pp. 32–44.

Aoyama, Sadao 青山定雄. Tō Sō jidai no kōtsū to chishi chizu no kenkyū 唐宋時代の交通と地誌地図の研究. Tokyo: Yoshikawa kōbunkan, 1963.

Babcock-Abrahams, Barbara. "'A Tolerated Margin of Mess' : The Trickster and His Tales Reconsidered." Journal of the American Folklore Institute 2 (1975): pp. 147–186.

Berkowitz, Alan. "Patterns of Reclusion in Early and Early Medieval China" Ph.D. dissertation, University of Washington, 1989.

Berling, Judith."Bringing the Buddha Down to Earth: Notes on the Emergence of Yü-lu as a Buddhist Genre." History of Religions 21. 1 (1987): pp. 56–88.

Bielefeldt, Carl. Dōgen's Manuals of Zen Meditation. Berkeley: University of California Press, 1988.

Birnbaum, Raoul. "The Manifestation of a Monastery: Shen-ying's Experiences on Mount Wu-t'ai in T'ang Context." Journal of the American Oriental Society 106.1 (January–March 1986): pp. 119–137.

Bodde, Derk. Festivals in Classical China. Princeton: Princeton University Press, 1975.

Bourdieu, Pierre. Distinction: A Social Critique of the Judgement of Taste. Cambridge: Harvard University Press, 1984.

Brown, Peter. Augustine of Hippo. Berkeley: University of California Press, 1967.

———. "The Saint as Exemplar in Late Antiquity." Representations 1. 2 (Spring 1983): pp. 1–25.

———. The Body and Society: Men, Women, and Sexual Renunciation in Early Christianity. New York: Columbia, 1988.

Bu-ston. History of Buddhism (Chos-hbyung). Trans. E. Obermiller. Heidelberg: 1931.

Buddhaghośa. The Path of Purification (Visuddhi Magga). Trans. Bhikkhu Nānamol. Kandy: Buddhist Publication Society, 1975.

Campany, Robert. "Notes on the Devotional Uses and Symbolic Functions of Sūtra Texts as Depicted in Early Chinese Buddhist Miracle Tales and Hagiographies." Journal of the International Association of Buddhist Studies 14. 1 (1991): pp. 28–72.

———. "Ghosts Matter: The Culture of Ghosts in Six Dynasties Zhiguai." Chinese Literature: Essays, Articles, Reviews 13 (December 1991): pp. 15–34.

———. "The Real Presence." History of Religions 32. 3 (1993): pp. 233–272.

———. Strange Writing: Anomaly Accounts in Early Medieval China. Albany: State University of New York Press, 1996.

Cao, Shibang 曹仕邦 . "Sengshi suo zai Zhongguo shamen jian-shou yinjie de yi xie shili" 僧史所載中國沙門堅守淫戒的一些實例 . *Huagang foxue xuebao* 華岡佛學學報 5 (1982): pp. 275–288.

———. "Zhongguo sengshi suo zai chiwu de shijian he miandui de nanti" 中國僧史所載持午的實踐和面對的難題 . *Huagang foxue xuebao* 華岡佛學學報 6 (July 1983): pp. 327–344.

———. "Sengshi suo zai Zhongguo shamen jianshou jiegui huo Tianzhu chuantong de ge lei shili" 僧史所載中國沙門堅守戒規或天竺傳統的各類實例 . *Zhonghua foxue xuebao* 中華佛學學報 (1988. 2): pp. 325–357.

Chadwick, Owen. *Western Asceticism*. Philadelphia: The Westminster Press, 1958.

Chavannes, Édouard. *Cinq cents contes et apologues extrait du tripitaka Chinois*. Paris: Société Asiatique, 1910.

Chen, Jingfu 陳景富 . *Famen si* 法門寺 . Xian: San qin chubanshe, 1988.

Chen, Kenneth. *Buddhism in China*. Princeton: Princeton University Press, 1964.

———. *The Chinese Transformation of Buddhism*. Princeton: Princeton University Press, 1973.

———. "Inscribed Stelae during the Wei, Chin, and Nan-ch'ao." In *Studia Asiatica: Essays in Asian Studies in Felicitation of the Seventy-fifth Anniversary of Professor Ch'en Shou-yi*, ed. Lawrence G. Thompson. San Francisco: Chinese Materials Center, 1975. Pp. 75–84.

Chen, Yuan 陳垣 . "*Da Tang Xiyu ji* zhuanren Bianji" 《大唐西域記》撰人辯機 . In *Chen Yuan shixue lun zhu xuan* 陳垣史學論著選, ed. Wu Ze 吳澤 . Shanghai: Shanghai renmin chubanshe, 1981. Pp. 266–287.

———. *Zhongguo fojiao shiji gailun* 中國佛教史籍概論. 1962. Reprint. Beijing: Zhonghua shuju, 1988.

Ching, Julia, ed. *The Records of Ming Scholars*. Honolulu: University of Hawai'i Press, 1987.

Chou, Yi-liang 周一良 . "Tantrism in China." *Harvard Journal of Asiatic Studies* 8 (1945): pp. 241–332.

Cleary, Thomas. *The Flower Ornament Scripture: A Translation of the Avatamsaka Sutra*. Boston: Shambhala Publications, 1984.

Daichman, Graciela S. *Wayward Nuns in Medieval Literature*. Syracuse University Press, 1986.

Dalia, Albert. "The 'Political Career' of the Buddhist Historian Tsan-ning." In *Buddhist and Taoist Practice in Medieval Chinese Society*, ed. David Chappell. Honolulu: University of Hawai'i Press, 1987. Pp. 146–180.

de la Vallée Poussin, Louis. "Le Bouddha et les abhijñās." *Le muséon* 44 (1931): pp. 335–342.

de Sardan, Jean-Pierre Olivier. "Occultism and the Ethnographic 'I': The Exoticizing of Magic from Durkheim to 'Postmodern' Anthropology." *Critique of Anthropology* 12. 1 (1992): pp. 5–25.

Degroot, J. J. M. *Le code du Mahāyāna en Chine*. Amsterdam: Johannes Müller, 1893.

Delehaye, Hippolyte. *The Legends of the Saints*. New York: Fordham University Press, 1962.

Demiéville, Paul. "Sur la memoire des existences anterieures." *Bulletin de l'École Française d'Extrême-Orient* 27 (1927): pp. 283–298.

———. "Byō." In *Hōbōgirin: Dictionnaire encyclopédique du Bouddhisme d'après les sources chinoises et japonaises*. Tokyo: Maison Franco-Japonaise, 1929–. Pp. 224–270. Also in *Buddhism and Healing*. English trans. Mark Tatz. New York: University Press of America, 1985. Pp. 81–89.

Dewoskin, Kenneth. *Doctors, Diviners, and Magicians of Ancient China: Biographies of Fang-shih*. New York: Columbia University Press, 1983.

———. "Chih-kuai." In *The Indiana Companion to Traditional Chinese Literature*, ed. William Nienhauser. Bloomington: Indiana University Press, 1986. Pp. 280–284.

Dien, Albert E. "The *Yüan-hun Chih* (Accounts of Ghosts with Grievances): A Sixth-Century Collection of Stories." In *Wen-lin: Studies in the Chinese Humanities*, ed. Tse-tsung Chow. Madison: University of Wisconsin Press, 1968. Pp. 211–228.

Dutt, Nalinaksha. *Early Monastic Buddhism*. Calcutta: Calcutta Oriental Book Agency, 1960.

Faure, Bernard. "Space and Place in Chinese Religious Traditions." *History of Religions* 26. 4 (May 1987): pp. 337–356.

———. *The Rhetoric of Immediacy: A Cultural Critique of Chan / Zen Buddhism*. Princeton: Princeton University Press, 1991.

———. *Sexualités bouddhiques*. Paris: Le Mail, 1994.

———. "Dato." In *Hōbōgirin: Dictionnaire encyclopédique du bouddhisme d'après les sources chinoises et japonaises*. Paris: Adrien Maisonneuve. Forthcoming.

Filliozat, Jean. "La mort volontaire par le feu et la tradition bouddhique Indienne." *Journal Asiatique* 251 (1963): pp. 21–51.

Forte, Antonino. *Political Propaganda and Ideology in China at the End of the Seventh Century*. Napoli: Istitut Universitario Orientale, 1976.

———. "The Relativity of the Concept of Orthodoxy in Chinese Buddhism." In *Chinese Buddhist Apocrypha*, ed. Robert Buswell. Honolulu: University of Hawai'i Press, 1989. Pp. 239–249.

Foulk, T. Griffith. "Myth, Ritual, and Monastic Practice in Sung China." In *Religion and Society in T'ang and Sung China*, ed. Patricia Ebrey and Peter Gregory. Honolulu: University of Hawai'i Press, 1993. Pp. 147–208.

Foulk, T. Griffith, and Robert H. Sharf. "On the Ritual Use of Ch'an Portraiture in Medieval China." *Cahiers d'Extrême-Asie* 7 (1993–1994): pp. 149–219.

Gao, Mingshi 高明士. "Tangdai sixue de fazhan" 唐代私學的發展. *Taida wenshizhe xuebao* 台大文史哲學報 20 (1971): pp. 219–289.

Gernet, Jacques. *Buddhism in Chinese Society: An Economic History from the Fifth to the Tenth Centuries*. Translated from the French by Franciscus Verellen. New York: Columbia University Press, 1995.

———. "Les suicides par le feu chez les Bouddhistes Chinois du Vᵉ au Xᵉ siècle." *Mélanges publiés par l'Institute des Hautes Études Chinoises* (1960): pp. 527–558.

Gibbon, Edward. *The Decline and Fall of the Roman Empire*. Ed. J. B. Bury. New York: The Heritage Press, 1946.

Gjertson, Donald. "Ming-pao chi." In *The Indiana Companion to Traditional Chinese Literature*, ed. William Nienhauser. Bloomington: Indiana University Press, 1986. Pp. 280–284.

———. *Miraculous Retribution: A Study and Translation of T'ang Lin's Ming-pao chi*. Berkeley: Asian Humanities Press, 1989.

Gomez, Luis. "BUDDHISM: Buddhism in India." In *Encyclopedia of Religion*, gen. ed. Mircea Eliade. New York: Macmillan and Free Press, 1987.

Greenblatt, Stephen. *Marvelous Possessions*. Chicago: University of Chicago Press, 1991.

Gregory, Peter. *Tsung-mi and the Sinification of Buddhism*. Princeton: Princeton University Press, 1991.

Guo, Shaolin 郭紹林. "Lun Tangdai de Guanyin chongbai" 論唐代的觀音崇拜. *Shijie zongjiao yanjiu* 世界宗教研究 (1992. 3): pp. 76–83.

Harper, Donald. "The Wu Shih Erh Ping Fang: Translation and Prolegomena." Ph.D. dissertation, University of California, Berkeley, 1982.

———. "A Chinese Demonography of the Third Century B.C." *Harvard Journal of Asiatic Studies* 45. 2 (December 1985): pp. 459–498.

———. "Wang Yen-shou's Nightmare Poem." *Harvard Journal of Asiatic Studies* 47. 1 (June 1987): pp. 239–283.

Harpham, Geoffrey Galt. *The Ascetic Imperative in Culture and Criticism*. Chicago: University of Chicago Press, 1987.

Hirai, Shun'ei 平井俊栄, and Arthur Link. "Kōsōden no chūshaku teki kenkyū" 高僧傳の注釈的研究. *Komazawa daigaku Bukkyō gakubu ronshū* 駒沢大学仏教学部論集 49 (March 1991): pp. 1–15; 23 (October 1992): pp. 1–14; 24 (October 1993): pp. 1–35; 25 (October 1994): pp. 11–25.

Hirakawa, Akira. *A History of Indian Buddhism From Śākyamuni to Early Mahāyāna*. Trans. Paul Groner. Honolulu: Univerisity of Hawai'i Press, 1990.

Hu, Shih. "The Indianization of China: A Case Study in Cultural Borrowing." In *Independence, Convergence, and Borrowing in Institutions, Thought, and Art*. Cambridge: Harvard University Press, 1937. Pp. 219–247.

Huang, Minzhi 黃敏枝. "Songdai de ziyi shihao" 宋代的紫衣師號. In *Songdai fojiao shehui jingji shi lunji* 宋代佛教社會經濟史論集. Taibei: Xuesheng shuju, 1989. Pp. 443–510.

Hurvitz, Leon, trans. *Scripture of the Lotus Blossom of the Fine Dharma*. New York: Columbia University Press, 1976.

Ishii, Shūdō 石井修道. *Sōdai zenshūshi no kenkyū* 宋代禪宗史の研究. Tokyo: Daitō shuppansha, 1987.

James, William. *The Varieties of Religious Experience*. 1902. Reprint. New York: The Modern Library, 1936.

Jan, Yün-hua. "Buddhist Self-immolation in Medieval China." *History of Religions* 4. 2 (1964–1965): pp. 243–268.

Kawaguchi, Kōfū 川口高風. "Kesa-shi ni okeru Dōsen no chii—roku mono o chūshin ni" 袈裟史における道宣の地位—六物を中心に. *Shūkyō kenkyū* 宗教研究 47. 2 (January 1974): pp. 97–121.

Kieckhefer, Richard. *Unquiet Souls: Fourteenth Century Saints and Their Religious Milieu*. Chicago: University of Chicago Press, 1984.

Knechtges, David R. *Wen xuan*, "Volume One: Rhapsodies on Metropolises and Capitals." Princeton: Princeton University Press, 1982.

Kominami, Ichirō 小南一郎. "Rikuchō Zui Tō shōsetsu no tenkai to Bukkyō shinkō" 六朝隋唐小説の展開と仏教信仰. In *Chūgoku chūsei no shūkyō to bunka* 中国中世の宗教と文化, ed. Fukunaga Kōshi 福永光司. Kyoto: Kyoto daigaku jimbun kagaku kenkyū-sho, 1982. Pp. 415–500.

Lamotte, Étienne. *Le traité de la grande vertu de sagesse*. Louvain: E. Peeters, 1976.

———. "Mañjusrī." *T'oung Pao* 48 (1961): pp. 1–96.

———. *History of Indian Buddhism*. 1958. English trans. Louvain: Peeters Press, 1988.

Le Blanc, Charles. *Huai Nan Tzu: Philosophical Synthesis in Early Han Thought*. Hong Kong: Hong Kong University Press, 1985.

Le Goff, Jacques. "The Marvelous in the Medieval West." In *The Medieval Imagination*. 1978, English trans. Chicago: The University of Chicago Press, 1988.

Leach, Edmund. "Pulleyar and the Lord Buddha: An Aspect of Religious Syncretism in Ceylon." *Psychoanalysis and the Psychoanalytic Review* 49 (1962): pp. 80–102. Available in abridged form in *Reader in Comparative Religion: An Anthropological Approach*, ed. William A. Less, Evon Z. Vogt. 1958. Reprint. New York: Harper and Row, 1972. Pp. 302–313.

Legge, James. *The Ch'un-ts'ew with the Tso Chuen*. Hong Kong: Hong Kong University Press, 1960.

————. *The Shoo King*. 1882. Reprint. Taibei: SMC Publishing, 1991.

Lévy-Bruhl, Lucien. *How Natives Think*. Trans. Lilian Clare. New York: Washington Square Press, 1996.

Lewis, Mark. *Sanctioned Violence in Early China*. Albany: State University of New York Press, 1990.

Li, Jun 李軍. "Lüe lun Wei-Jin Nanbei chao shiqi sixue de tedian" 略論魏晉南北朝時期私學的特點. *Zhongguoshi yanjiu* 中國史研究 (1993.1): pp. 61–67.

Liebenthal, Walter. "A Biography of Chu Tao-sheng." *Monumenta Nipponica* 11. 3 (1955): pp. 64–96.

————. "The World Conception of Chu Tao-sheng." *Monumenta Nipponica* 12. 1/2 (1956): pp. 95–97; 12. 3/4 (1957): pp. 241–268.

Lin, Fushi 林富士. *Handai de wuzhe* 漢代的巫者. Taibei: Daoxiang chubanshe, 1988.

Link, Arthur, "Biography of Shih Tao-an." *T'oung Pao* 46 (1958): pp. 1–48.

Link, Arthur, and Hirai Shun'ei 平井俊榮. "Kōsōden no chūshaku teki kenkyū" 高僧傳の注釈的研究. *Komazawa daigaku Bukkyō gakubu ronshū* 駒沢大学仏教学部論集 49 (March 1991): pp. 1–15; 23 (October 1992): pp. 1–14; 24 (October 1993): pp. 1–35; 25 (October 1994): pp. 11–25.

Liu, Shufen 劉淑芬. *Liuchao de chengshi yu shehui* 六朝的城市與社會. Taibei: Xuesheng shuju, 1992.

————. "Foding zunsheng tuoluoni jing yu Tangdai zunsheng jingchuang de jianli" 佛頂尊勝陀羅尼經與唐代尊勝經幢的建立. *Zhongyang Yanjiuyuan Lishi Yuyan Yanjiusuo jikan* 中央研究院歷史語言研究所集刊. 67. 1 (1996): pp. 145–194.

Loewe, Michael. *Chinese Ideas of Life and Death: Faith Myth and Reason in the Han Period (202 BC–AD 220)*. London: Allen and Unwin, 1982.

Lu, Xun 魯迅. "Wei-Jin fengdu ji wenzhang yu yao ji jiu zhi guanxi" 魏晉風度及文章與藥及酒之關係. In *Eryi ji* 而已集. Vol. 3, *Lu Xun quanji* 魯迅全集. Beijing: Renmin wenxue chubanshe, 1981. Pp. 501–529.

Ma, Jixing 馬繼興, and Li Xueqin 李學勤. "Wo guo xian yi faxian de zui gu yifang—boshu *Wushier bingfang*" 我國現已發現的最古醫方—帛書《五十二病方》. In *Mawangdui Hanmu yanjiu* 馬王堆漢墓研究. Hunan: Hunan renmin chubanshe, 1981. Pp. 226–234.

Macgowan, D. S. "Self-immolation by Fire in China." *The Chinese Recorder* 19. 10 (October 1888): pp. 445–451; 508–521.

Makita, Tairyō 牧田諦亮. "Kōsōden no seiritsu" 高僧傳の成立. *Tōhō gakuhō* 東方学報 44 (1973): pp. 101–125; 48 (1975): pp. 229–259.

Maspero, Henri. *Taoism and Chinese Religion*. Amherst: The University of Massachusetts Press, 1981.

Mather, Richard. *A New Account of Tales of the World*. Minneapolis: University of Minnesota Press, 1976.

———. "The Bonze's Begging Bowl: Eating Practices in Buddhist Monasteries of Medieval India and China." *Journal of the American Oriental Society* 101. 4 (October–December 1981): pp. 417–424.

Matsunaga, Yūkei 松長有慶. *Mikkyō no rekishi* 密教の歴史. 1969. Reprint. Kyoto: Heirakuji shoten, 1991.

Michihata, Ryōshū 道瑞良秀. *Tōdai Bukkyōshi no kenkyū* 唐代仏教史の研究. Kyoto: Hōzōkan, 1958.

———. *Chūgoku Bukkyō shisōshi no kenkyū* 中国仏教思想史の研究. Tokyo: Heirakuji shoten, 1983.

———. *Daijō bosatsukai no tenkai* 大乘菩薩戒の展開. Vol. 7, *Chūgoku Bukkyōshi zenshū* 中国仏教史全集. Tokyo: Kabushiki kaisha shoen, 1986.

Mikkyō daijiten 密教大辞典. Kyoto: Hozokan, 1968–1970.

Mizuo, Gensei 水尾現誠. "Shashin ni tsuite—Ekō no tachiba" 捨身について—慧皎の立場. *Indo Bukkyōgaku kenkyū* 22 (March 1963): pp. 174–175.

Mochizuki, Shinkō 望月信亨, ed. *Bukkyō daijiten* 仏教大辞典. Tokyo: Sekai seiten kankō kyōkai, 1958–1963.

Moroto, Tatsuo 諸戸立雄. Chūgoku Bukkyō seidoshi no kenkyū 中国仏教制度史の研究. Tokyo: Heikawa shuppansha, 1990.

Mou, Runsun 牟潤孫. "Tangchu nanbei xueren lunxue zhi yiqu yu yingxiang" 唐初南北學人論學之異趣與影響. *Xianggang Zhongwen Daxue Zhongguo wenhua yanjiu xuebao* 香港中文大學中國文化研究學報 1 (September 1968): pp. 50–89.

Murakami, Yoshimi 村上嘉実. "Kōsōden no shin-i ni tsuite" 高僧傳の神異について. *Tōhō shūkyō* 東方宗教 17 (August 1961): pp. 1–17.

Myōjin, Hiroshi 明神洋. "Chūgoku Bukkyōto no shōshin to Dōkyō" 中国仏教徒の焼身と道教. *Waseda daigaku daigakuin bungaku kenkyūka kiyō* 早稲田大学大学院文学研究科紀要 11 (1984): pp. 41–50.

Nakamura, Hajime 中村元. *Bukkyōgo daijiten* 仏教語大辞典. Tokyo: Tokyo shoseki, 1975.

Naomi, Gentetsu 直海玄哲. "*Kōsōden* seiritsu-jō no mondaiten— Donmushin no jirei o tōshite" 『高僧傳』成立上の問題—曇無讖の事列を通して. *Tōyō shien* 東洋史園 26. 27 (March 1986): pp. 63–82.

———. "Kōsōden no ju" 「高僧傳」の咒. *Tōyō shien* 東洋史園 33 (March 1989): pp. 32–48.

———. "Ryō Shin Nanbokuchō no kannon ōgendan ni okeru sōkyō 兩晉南北朝の觀音応驗譚に於ける誦経. *Ryūkoku shidan* 89 (April 1987): pp. 20–38.

Nattier, Jan. *Once Upon a Future Time: Studies in a Buddhist Prophecy of Decline*. Berkeley: Asian Humanities Press, 1991.

Needham, Joseph. *Science and Civilisation*. Cambridge: Cambridge University Press, 1954.

Nienhauser, William. *The Indiana Companion to Traditional Chinese Literature.* Bloomington: Indiana University Press, 1986.

Nietzsche, Friedrich. *On the Genealogy of Morals.* Trans. Walter Kaufmann. New York: Vintage Books, 1967.

O'Flaherty, Wendy Doniger. *Asceticism and Eroticism in the Mythology of Siva.* London: Oxford University Press, 1973.

Ōmura, Seigai 大村西崖. *Mikkyō hattatsu-shi* 密教發達志. 1918. Reprint. Vols. 74–76, *Shijie foxue mingzhu yicong* 世界佛學名著譯叢. Gen. ed. Lan Jifu 藍吉富. Taibei: Huayu chubanshe, 1986.

Owen, Stephen. *The Great Age of Chinese Poetry: The High T'ang.* New Haven: Yale University Press, 1981.

Pelton, Robert D. *The Trickster in West Africa: A Study of Mythic Irony and Sacred Delight.* Berkeley: University of California Press, 1980.

Perdue, Daniel E. *Debate in Tibetan Buddhism.* Ithaca: Snow Lion, 1992.

Peterson, Willard J. "Making Connections: 'Commentary on the Attached Verbalizations' of the *Book of Change.*" *Harvard Journal of Asiatic Studies* 42. 1 (June 1982): pp. 67–116.

Pokora, Timoteus. *Hsin-lun (New Treatise) and Other Writings by Huan T'an.* Ann Arbor: The University of Michigan Center for Chinese Studies, 1975.

Poo, Mu-chou. "The Images of Immortals and Eminent Monks: Religious Mentality in Early Medieval China (4–6 c. A.D.)." *Numen* 42 (1995): pp. 172–196.

Porter, Roy. *Gibbon.* New York: St Martin's Press, 1988.

Powell, William. *The Record of Tung-shan.* Honolulu: University of Hawai'i Press, 1986.

Powers, Martin J. *Art and Political Expression in Early China.* New Haven: Yale University Press, 1991.

Prip-Moeller, J. *Chinese Buddhist Monasteries.* 1937. Reprint. Hong Kong: Hong Kong University Press, 1982.

Pulleyblank, Edwin. *Lexicon of Reconstructed Pronunciation in Early Middle Chinese, Late Middle Chinese, and Early Mandarin.* Vancouver: University of British Columbia Press, 1991.

Qiu, Zhonglin 邱仲麟. "Buxiao zhi xiao—Tang yilai gegu liaoqin xianxiang de shehuishi chutan" 不孝之孝—唐以來割股療親現象的社會史初探. *Xin shixue* 新史學 6. 1 (March 1995): pp. 49–94.

Radin, Paul. *The Trickster.* 1956. Reprint. New York: Schocken Books, 1972.

Rahder, Jean. "Bunne" 分衛. In *Hōbōgirin: Dictionnaire encyclopédique du bouddhisme d'après les sources chinoises et japonaises.* Paris: Adrien Maisonneuve, 1927–1983. Pp. 158–169.

Reischauer, Edwin. *Ennin's Travels in T'ang China.* New York: Ronald Press, 1955.

———. *Ennin's Diary.* New York: Ronald Press, 1955.

Ricketts, Maclinscott. "The North American Trickster." *History of Religion* 4 (1965): pp. 327–350.

Sasaki, Ruth Fuller. *The Recorded Sayings of Layman P'ang: A Ninth-century Zen Classic*. New York: Weatherhill, 1972.

Sawada, Mizuho 沢田瑞穂. *Chūgoku no juhō* 中国の咒法. Tokyo: Hirakawa shuppansha, 1984.

Schafer, Edward. "Iranian Merchants in T'ang Dynasty Tales." In Vol. 11, *Semitic and Oriental Studies*. University of California Publications in Semitic Philology, 1951. Pp. 403–422.

———. "The Last Years of Ch'ang-an." *Oriens Extremus* 10 (1963): pp. 133–179.

———. "T'ang" In *Food in Chinese Culture*, ed. K. C. Chang. New Haven: Yale University Press, 1977. Pp. 85–140.

Scribner, Robert W. "Reformation and Magic." *Journal of Interdisciplinary History* 23. 3 (Winter 1993): pp. 475–494.

Shahar, Meir. "Fiction and Religion in the Early History of the Chinese God Jigong." Ph.D. dissertation, Harvard University, 1992.

Sharf, Robert. "The Idolization of Enlightenment: On the Mummification of Ch'an Masters in Medieval China." *History of Religion* 32. 1 (August 1992): pp. 1–31.

———. "The *Treasure Store Treatise (Pao-tsang lun)* and the Sinification of Buddhism in Eighth-Century China." Ph.D. dissertation, University of Michigan, 1991.

Sharf, Robert, and T. Griffith Foulk. "On the Ritual Use of Ch'an Portraiture in Medieval China." *Cahier d'Extrême-Asie* 7 (1993–1994): pp. 149–219.

Shi, Guodeng 釋果燈. *Tang Daoxuan* Xu gaoseng zhuan *pipan sixiang chutan* 唐道宣《續高僧傳》批判思想初探. Taibei: Dongchu chubanshe, 1992.

Shi, Yinguang 釋印光. Emei shan zhi 峨嵋山志. 1934. Reprint. Taibei: Wenhai chubanshe (1970).

Shimoda, Masahiro 下田正弘. "Higashi Ajia Bukkyō no kairitsu no tokushoku—nikushoku kinshi no yurai o megutte" 東アジア仏教の戒律の特色—肉食禁止の由來をあぐって. Tōyō gakujutsu kenkyū 東洋学術研究 29. 4 (December 1990): pp. 98–110.

Shinohara, Koichi. "Two Sources of Chinese Buddhist Biographies: Stupa Inscriptions and Miracle Stories." In *Monks and Magicians: Religious Biographies in Asia*, ed. Phyllis Granoff and Koichi Shinohara. Oakville: Mosaic Press, 1988. pp. 119–229.

Sierksma, F. "Rtsod-pa: The Monachal Disputations in Tibet." *Indo-Iranian Journal* 8. 2 (1964): pp. 130–152.

Smith, Richard J. *Fortune-tellers and Philosophers: Divination in Traditional Chinese Society*. Boulder: Westview Press, 1991.

Snellgrove, David. *Indo-Tibetan Buddhism*. Boston: Shambhala, 1987.

Spence, Jonathan. *The Memory Palace of Matteo Ricci*. New York: Viking Penguin, 1984.

Stcherbatsky, Th. *Buddhist Logic.* 1932. Reprint. The Hague: Mouton and Co., 1958.

Stein, Rolf. "Religious Taoism and Popular Religion from the Second to Seventh Centuries." In *Facets of Taoism,* ed. Holmes Welch and Anna Seidel. New Haven: Yale University Press, 1979. Pp. 53–82.

———. "Avalokitesvara / Kouan-yin—exemple de transformation d'un dieu en déesse." *Cahiers d'Extrême-Asie* 2 (1986): pp. 17–80.

Strickmann, Michel. "The Consecration Sūtra: A Buddhist Book of Spells." In *Chinese Buddhist Apocrypha,* ed. Robert E. Buswell. Honolulu: University of Hawai'i Press, 1990. Pp. 75–118.

———. "Chinese Poetry and Prophecy: The Written Oracle in East Asia." Manuscript.

Su Jinren 蘇晉仁. "Liang Shi Huijiao ji qi Gaoseng zhuan" 梁釋慧皎及其《高僧傳》. *Shijie zongjiao yanjiu* 世界宗教研究 (1981.1): pp. 133–140.

Suwa, Yoshizumi 諏訪義純. "Chūgoku Bukkyō ni okeru saishoku shugi shisō no keisei ni kansuru kanken—Bukkyō denrai yori Ryōsho ni itaru jiki" 中国仏教の菜食主義思想の形成に関する管見—仏教傳來より梁初にいたる時期. *Nihon Bukkyō gakkai nenpō* 日本仏教学会年報 43 (March 1978): pp. 73–99.

Suzuki, Keizo 鈴木啓造. "Chūgoku ni okeru sōryo no shitei kankei ni tsuite" 中国における僧侶の師弟関係について. *Shikan* 史観 57.8 (March 1960): pp. 146–161.

Swain, Joseph. *The Hellenic Origins of Christian Asceticism.* New York: n.p., 1916.

Taira, Hidemichi 平秀道. "Shin-i shisō to Bukkyō kyōten" 讖緯思想と仏教経典. *Ryūkoku daigaku ronshū* 龍谷大学論集 347 (April 1954): pp. 123–141.

Takakusu, J. *A Record of the Buddhist Religion as Practiced in India and the Malay Archipelago.* London: Claredon Press, 1896.

Tambiah, Stanley. *Magic, Science, Religion and the Scope of Rationality.* Cambridge: Cambridge University Press, 1990.

Tanaka, Keishin 田中敬信. "Ryō kōsōden ni okeru shin-i" 梁高僧傳における神異. *Indogaku Bukkyōgaku kenkyū* 20. 1 (1972): pp. 291–293.

Tang, Yongtong 湯用彤. *Sui Tang fojiao shi gao* 隋唐佛教史稿. Beijing: Zhonghua shuju, 1982.

———. *Han Wai Liangjin Nanbeichao fojiaoshi* 漢魏兩晉南北朝佛教史. 1938. Reprint. Beijing: Zhonghua shuju, 1984.

Thomas, Keith. *Religion and the Decline of Magic.* New York: Charles Scribner's Sons, 1971.

Thompson, E. P. "Anthropology and the Discipline of Historical Context." *Midland History* 1. 3 (Spring 1972): pp. 41–55.

Todorov, Tzvetan. *The Fantastic: A Structural Approach to a Literary Genre.* 1970. English trans. Ithaca: Cornell University Press, 1973.

Thurman, Robert, trans. *The Holy Teaching of Vimalakīrti.* University Park: Pennsylvania State University Press, 1976.

Tsai, Kathryn Ann. *Lives of the Nuns: Biographies of Chinese Buddhist Nuns from the Fourth to Sixth Centuries.* Honolulu: University of Hawai'i Press, 1994.

Turner, Victor. "Religious Paradigms and Political Action: Thomas Becket at the Council of Northampton." In *Dramas, Fields, and Metaphors: Symbolic Action in Human Society.* Ithaca: Cornell University Press, 1974. Pp. 60–97.

Twitchett, Denis. "Problems of Chinese Biography." In *Confucian Personalities,* ed. Arthur Wright and Denis Twitchett. Stanford: Stanford University Press, 1962. Pp. 24–42.

———. *Printing and Publishing in Medieval China.* New York: Frederic Beil, 1983.

Ui, Hakuju 宇井伯壽. *Zenshūshi kenkyū* 禪宗史研究. 1935. Reprint. Tokyo: Iwanami shoten, 1966.

Van Gulik, R. H. *Sexual Life in Ancient China.* 1961. Reprint. Leiden: E. J. Brill, 1974.

Verellen, Franciscus. "Luo Gongyuan: Légende et culte d'un saint taoïste." *Journal Asiatique* 275. 3–4 (1987): pp. 282–332.

———. "Evidential Miracles in Support of Taoism: The Inversion of a Buddhist Apologetic Tradition in Late Tang China." *T'oung Pao* 78 (1992): pp. 217–263.

Wagner, Robin. "Buddhism, Biography and Power: A Study of Daoxuan's Continued Lives of Eminent Monks." Ph.D. dissertation, Harvard University, 1995.

Wang, Yao 王瑤. "Wenren yu jiu" 文人與酒. In *Zhonggu wenxueshi lun* 中古文學史論. Beijing: Beijing daxue chubanshe, 1986. Pp. 156–175.

Ward, Benedicta. *Miracles and the Medieval Mind: Theory, Record and Event 1000–1215.* Aldershot: Scolar Press, 1987.

Watson, Burton. *The Zen Teachings of Master Lin-chi.* Boston: Shambala, 1993.

———. *The Complete Works of Chuang Tzu.* New York: Columbia University Press, 1968.

Watters, Thomas. *On Yuan Chwang's Travels in India.* London: Royal Asiatic Society, 1904.

Wechsler, Howard. *Offerings of Jade and Silk: Ritual and Symbol in the Legitimation of the T'ang Dynasty.* New Haven: Yale University Press, 1985.

Weinstein, Donald, and Rudolph Bell. *Saints & Society: The Two Worlds of Western Christendom, 1000–1700.* Chicago: University of Chicago Press, 1982.

Weinstein, Stanley. *Buddhism Under the T'ang.* Cambridge: Cambridge University Press, 1987.

Welch, Holmes. *The Buddhist Revival in China.* Cambridge: Harvard University Press, 1968.

———. *The Practice of Chinese Buddhism 1900–1950*. 1967. Reprint. Cambridge: Harvard University Press, 1973.

Welter, Albert. *The Meaning of Myriad Good Deeds: A Study of Yung-ming Yen-shou and the Wan-shan t'ung-kuei chi*. New York: Peter Lang, 1993.

Wijayaratna, Mohan. *Buddhist Monastic Life According to the Texts of the Theravāda Tradition*. Cambridge: Cambridge University Press, 1990.

Woodward, Kenneth L. *Making Saints—Inside the Vatican: Who Become Saints, Who Do Not, and Why*. London: Chatto and Windus, 1990.

Wright, Arthur. "Fo-t'u-teng, A Biography." *Harvard Journal of Asiatic Studies* 11 (1948): pp. 321–371.

———. "Biography and Hagiography: Hui-chiao's *Lives of Eminent Monks*." In *Silver Jubilee Volume*. Kyoto University: Jimbun kagaku kenkyū-sho, 1954. Pp. 383–432.

———. *Buddhism in Chinese History*. Stanford: Stanford University Press, 1959.

Wright, Dale S. "The Discourse of Awakening: Rhetorical Practice in Classical Ch'an Buddhism." *Journal of the American Academy of Religion* 61. 1 (Spring 1993): pp. 23–40.

Xiao, Dengfu 蕭登福. *Han Wei Liuchao Fo Dao liang jiao zhi tiantang diyu shuo* 漢魏六朝佛道兩教之天堂地獄説. Taibei: Xuesheng shuju, 1989.

Xuyun. *Empty Cloud: The Autobiography of the Chinese Zen Master*. Trans. Charles Luk. Longmead: Element Books, 1988.

Yamazaki, Hiroshi 山崎宏. "Tō no Dōsen no kantsū ni tsuite" 唐の道宣の感通について. In *Tsukamoto Hakushi shōju kinen—Bukkyōshigaku ronshū* 塚本博士頌壽紀念—仏教史学論集. Tokyo: Tsukamoto hakushi shōjukinenkai, 1961: pp. 855–868.

Yampolsky, Philip. *The Platform Sutra of the Sixth Patriarch*. New York: Columbia University Press, 1967.

Yan, Gengwang 嚴耕望. "Tangren xiye shanlin siyuan zhi fengshang" 唐人習業山林寺院之風尚. In *Yan Gengwang shixue lunwen xuanji* 嚴耕望史学論文選集. Taibei: Lianjing chuban shiye, 1991. Pp. 271–316.

Yan, Shangwen 顏尚文. "Liang Wu Di "Huangdi pusa" linian di xingcheng ji zhengce de tuizhan" 梁武帝「皇帝菩薩」理念的形成及政策的推展. Ph.D. dissertation, Taiwan Normal University, 1989.

Yanagida, Seizan. "The 'Recorded Sayings' Texts of Chinese Ch'an Buddhism." Trans. John McRae. In *Early Ch'an in China and Tibet*, ed. Whalen Lai and Lewis Lancaster. Berkeley: University of Calfornia Press, 1983. Pp. 185–186.

Yang, Shoujing 楊守敬. *Riben fangshu zhi* 日本訪書志. Linsuyuan 鄰蘇園 edn, 1897.

Yasui, Kōsai 安井広済. "Nyūryōgakkyō niokeru nikushoku no kinshi" 入楞伽経における肉食の禁止. Ōtani gakuhō 大谷学報 43. 2 (December 1963): pp. 1–13.

Yasui, Kōzan 安居香山. "Kan-Gi Rikuchōjidai ni okeru toshin to Bukkyō—tokuni sōden o chūshin toshite" 漢魏六朝時代に於ける図讖と仏教—特に僧傳を中心として. In Tsukamoto hakushi shōju kinen—Bukkyōshigaku ronshū 塚本博士頌壽紀念—仏教史学論集. Tokyo: Tsukamoto hakushi shōjukinenkai, 1961. Pp. 855–868.

Yu, Anthony C. "'Rest, Rest, Perturbed Spirit!' Ghosts in Traditional Chinese Prose Fiction." Harvard Journal of Asiatic Studies 47. 2 (December 1987): pp. 397–434.

Yü, Chün-fang. "Ch'an Education in the Sung." In Neo-Confucian Education: The Formative Stage, ed. Wm. Theodore de Bary and John W. Chaffe. Berkeley: University of California Press, 1989. Pp. 57–104.

———. "P'u-t'o Shan: Pilgrimage and the Creation of the Chinese Potalaka." In Pilgrims and Sacred Sites in China, ed. Susan Naquin and Chün-fang Yü. Berkeley: University of California Press, 1992. Pp. 190–245.

Yü, Ying-shih. "Han." In Food in Chinese Culture, ed. K. C. Chang. New Haven: Yale University Press, 1977. Pp. 53–84.

Zheng, Yuqing 鄭郁卿. Gaoseng zhuan yanjiu 高僧傳研究. Taibei: Wenjin chubanshe, 1990.

Zhou, Shujia 周叔迦. "Hanzu sengfu kao lüe" 漢族僧服考略. In Zhou Shujia foxue lunzhu ji 周叔迦佛學論著集. Beijing: Zhonghua shuju, 1991. Pp. 718–725.

Zhou, Yutong 周子同. Zhongguo xuexiao zhidu 中國學校制度. Shanghai: Shangwu yinshuguan, 1933.

Zürcher, Erik. The Buddhist Conquest of China. Leiden: E. J. Brill, 1959.

———. "Perspectives in the Study of Chinese Buddhism." Journal of the Royal Asiatic Society 2 (1982): pp. 161–176.

———. "Buddhism and Education in T'ang Times." In Neo-Confucian Education: The Formative Stage, ed. Wm. Theodore de Bary and John W. Chaffee. Berkeley: University of California Press, 1980. Pp. 19–56.

———. "Han Buddhism and the Western Region." In Thought and Law in Qin and Han China, ed. W. L. Idema and E. Zürcher. Leiden: E. J. Brill, 1990.

———. "A New Look at the Earliest Chinese Buddhist Texts." In From Benares to Beijing: In Honour of Professor Jan Yün-hua, ed. Koichi Shinohara and Gregory Schopen. Oakville: Mosaic Press, 1991. Pp. 277–300.

Index

abhidharma, 116, 120, 121, 166 n. 235
Amitābha, 35, 39, 95, 102; paradise of, 5, 43, 56
Amoghavajra, 77, 80, 89
arts of calculation *(shushu)*, 79–80
asceticism: appeal of, 65; and chastity, 17–22, 140; Christian, 21; and clothing, 31–32; criticism of, 18, 65; and diet, 34, 35, 140; filial piety, 39; as ideal type, 14, 140; pre-Buddhist, 18; theories of, 65, 168 n. 269; and tricksters, 58–60. *See also* blood-writing; *dhūtāṅga*; mutilation
Aśoka, 36, 44
astrology, 80
Avalokiteśvara. *See* Guanyin

Bai Juyi, 20, 46, 124
Bai Xingjian, 20, 64
Ban Gu, 100
Baochang, 11
Baolin zhuan, 136
Begging, 33–34, 159 n. 101
Beidu, 51
Bianji, 20
Biographies of Eminent Monks (Gaoseng zhuan): compilation of, 6–7, 11; influence of, 50; intended audience of, 7, 54, 60; readership of, 7, 11–12, 68–69; sources for, 4, 10–11, 13, 19, 151 n. 31; structure of, 8–9, 14
Biographies of Famous Monks. See Mingseng zhuan
Biographies of Nuns (Biqiuni zhuan), 21, 24, 156 n. 28

blood-writing, 40–41, 49–50; criticism of, 46
Bodhidharma, 41
Bodhiruci, 87, 174 n. 113
bodhisattvas, 116, 127; as mediators, 103. *See also* Guanyin, Mañjuśrī
Book of Changes, 100–101
Brahmā, 78
Brief History of the Clergy (Sengshi lüe), 29, 33, 123
Brown, Peter, 65
Buddha: bodies of, 102. *See also* Śākyamuni
Buddhapāli, 67, 106, 175 n. 120, 179 n. 207
Buddhayaśas, 80, 115

calligraphy, 116–117, 141
Chan monks, 144; and encounter-dialogue, 133–134, 143; as ideal type, 130, 133–135, 141
chanting, 92, 166 n. 224; and meat-eating, 56
chastity: of laymen, 22, 156 n. 35; of nuns, 21. *See also* sex
Chengguan, 59, 72
Chengshi lun, 120
Chen Shou, 7
chives, 24
Chuji, 72
Chu sanzang jiji, 51, 83
clothing: and asceticism, 31–32; color of, 29; monastic regulations on, 29; purple robe, 31, 41; silk, 30, 32, 159 n. 90; the three monastic robes, 30

213

Consecration Scripture (Guanding jing), 77–78
Contemplation Scripture (Guan wuliangshou jing), 56
correlative thinking, 98–99

Danxia Tianran, 134
Daoan, 5, 8, 80, 114, 120, 122
Daoism, 113, 160 n. 119, 163 n. 166; and prophecy, 81; as rival of Buddhism, 108, 124, 155, 180 n. 224; and spells, 95; and supernormal powers, 71, 110
Daorong, 115
Daosheng, 123, 128–130
Daowen, 128
Daoxuan, 127; on asceticism, 34–35; biography of, 1–2, 4, 14, 59, 119, 151 n. 20; on bodies of a Buddha, 102; and compilation of *Further Biographies of Eminent Monks*, 5, 7, 12; on meat and wine, 57, 166 n. 228; on miracles, 99–100; on silk, 32; on spirits, 107–108; on supernormal powers, 72; on thaumaturgy, 68
Daoyuan, 136
debate, 123–127, 141
demons, 34, 82, 84, 96–97, 176 n. 144; and illness, 85
Dewoskin, Kenneth, 75
dhāraṇī, 88, 95, 174 n. 113; pillars, 89
Dharmaguptakavinaya. See *Si fen lü*
Dharmakāla, 80
Dharmakṣema (Tanwuchen), 85, 155 n. 21
dhūtāṅga, 34–35, 39, 141, 160 n. 106
Diamond Sūtra, 56, 91, 120
diet: eating only before noon, 34. See *also* meat; vegetarianism; wine
Dignāga, 124–125
divination, 72, 73, 77–82; hostility toward, 81; prohibitions against, 78; as rhetorical device, 80
Duan Chengshi, 45

education of monks, 118–123, 182 n. 25
Emei, 106
Empress Wu, 76
enlightenment, 3, 8, 129, 132, 133
Ennin, 92
ethics, 17
exegesis, 115–116

Famen Monastery, 35–37, 41, 44, 161 n. 123
Fanwang jing, 78, 162 n. 158

Fazang, 44
fengshui. See geomancy
filial piety: and asceticism, 39; and mutilation, 49–50, 164 n. 194; and vegetarianism, 23, 26
Flower Adornment Scripture (Avataṃsakasūtra), 105–106
fortune-telling. See divination
Fotucheng, 73–74, 84, 86, 88
Fotudeng. See Fotucheng
Fozu tongji, 94
Further Biographies of Eminent Monks: compilation of, 5, 7; praise for, 12; sources for, 10–11; structure of, 9, 100, 151 n. 28
Fu Yi, 61, 94

ganying. See resonance
Gao Pian, 27
Gaoseng zhuan. See *Biographies of Eminent Monks*
Gaozu, 62
garlic, 24, 156 n. 43
geomancy, 79, 142
ghosts. See spirits
Gibbon, Edward, 65
ginger, 24
gods. See spirits
Grand Master of Guangling, 54
Guangyi, 22, 120
Guanyin, 101, 103–106, 109, 171 n. 39, 178 nn. 187, 192; and spells, 87, 174 n. 108; and wine, 28
Guṇabhadra, 78, 85–86
Guṇavarman, 25

hagiography: constraints of, 62, 90, 112; and demands of narrative, 35; impact of, 144; interpretation of, 1–4, 67–69, 74, 129, 143, 149 n. 4, 152 n. 38. See also *Biographies of Eminent Monks; Further Biographies of Eminent Monks; Song Biographies of Eminent Monks*
Hall of the Patriarchs (Zu tang ji), 133, 136
Hanshan, 54, 118
Han Yu, 48
hell, 51, 56, 88, 128. See *also* netherworld
hermits, 112–113
Hongren, 134
Hongzhou School, 132
Housenghui, 98
Huainanzi, 98
Huaisu, 64, 117

Huang Tingjian, 13
Huanpu, 132
Huichi, 122
Huihong, 135, 137; criticism of *Biographies of Eminent Monks*, 12–14
Huiji (Yangshan), 41, 133
Huijiao: and compilation of *Biographies of Eminent Monks*, 4, 6, 7, 10; on language, 130–131; on miracles, 99; on mutilation, 163 n. 179; on suicide, 46, 163 n. 179; on thaumaturgy, 68, 70
Huike, 41
Huineng, 132–134, 143
Huiyuan, 22, 28, 88, 120, 123, 126
Hu Shih, 49, 65

immolation. *See* suicide

James, William, 65
Jiaoran, 46, 117
Jing'ai, 119
Jingxiu, 21, 24
Jīvaka, 84
Jiyin, 12
Jñānagupta, 174 n. 113
Jōjin, 12

Kaṣāya. *See* clothing
Korea: monks from, 22, 121. *See also* Silla
Kucha, 18, 32, 123
Kuiji, 59, 121, 124
Kumārajīva, 18–19, 87, 115, 120, 123

Lamotte, Étienne, 96
language: limitations of, 125, 131
Laṅkavatārasūtra, 157 n. 47
Laozi, 113, 124
Layman Pang, 133
Leach, Edmund, 103
leeks, 24
Lévy-Bruhl, Lucien, 110
Liang Biographies. See *Biographies of Eminent Monks*
Liang Wu Di, 25, 61, 124, 157 n. 61, 167 n. 248
Lingyi, 117
Linji, 133, 134
Linjian lu, 13
Lives of Nuns. See *Biographies of Nuns*
Lives of the Desert Fathers, 21
local cults, 108–109, 180 n. 223
logic, 124
Longxing biannian tonglun, 94
Lotus Sūtra, 40, 42, 43, 90, 92: and Guanyin, 104; and miracle tales, 12

magic, 82, 92, 93, 97, 110, 175 n. 130. *See also* thaumaturgy
Mahāsāṃghikavinaya (Mohe sengqi lü), 23
Mahīśāsakavinaya, 78
Maitreya, 102, 161 n. 130; chanting name of, 5; paradise of, 5
Mañjuśrī, 37, 41, 67–68, 105–107, 127, 130
martyrdom, 40; Christian, 42. *See also* sacrifice; suicide
Master Bundlegrass, 45
Mazu, 132
meat: and chanting, 56; and monks, 51–52, 64; renunciation of, 24; social significance of, 22
medicine, 173 n. 99
Medicine King, 38, 42–43
meditation, 34, 91, 119: as ascetic practice, 35; and miracles, 99; ridicule of, 134; and supernormal powers, 3, 70, 72
memorization, 114–115, 141
Ming Biographies of Eminent Monks (Ming gaoseng zhuan), 137
Mingseng zhuan, 4, 7, 10–11, 150 n. 6
miracles, 176 n. 150; Christian, 96–97; miraculous birth, 3, 99; and Śākyamuni, 102; and the supernatural, 96–97; tales of, 69, 74–75, 104, 152 n. 33
Mohe sengqi lü (Mahāsāṃghikavinaya), 23
monastic correspondence, 122–123
monastic income, 33
monastic libraries, 118
monastic regulations: on clothing, 29; criticism of, 133; on divination, 78; on meat, 23; on sex, 19; study of, 119; on suicide, 46–48; as system of practice, 17; on vegetarianism, 23–24; violation of, 18–19, 52, 62; on wine, 28
mutilation, 142; canonical sources for, 42–43; criticism of, 47–50; and filial piety, 49–50, 164 n. 194; of fingers, 21, 37, 41, 44, 48; of hands, 45; motivation for, 41, 42–45, 50; as offering, 41, 42, 48; official proscriptions against, 48–49; of penis, 22; as purification, 43–44; and relics, 36–37, 41, 43–45; reverence for, 46; ridicule of, 134

Nantuo, 52, 55, 62–63
Narendrayaśas, 87
Needham, Joseph, 97
netherworld, 27, 89, 91. *See also* hell

Nietzsche, Friedrich, 65
Nirvāṇa Sūtra, 24, 49, 128
*Notes on the Regulations in Four Divi-
    sions*, 34, 120
nuns, 52–53, 164 n. 188; and sex, 19, 20,
    21, 155 n. 18; and vegetarianism, 24

Ōmura, Seigai, 80
onions, 24, 156 n. 43
ordination, 114, 118, 182 n. 27
orthodoxy, 127–130
Owen, Stephen, 117

participation, 110
Peacock King Scripture, 84
Pei Xiu, 26, 131
*Perfection of Wisdom Scripture
    (Mahāprajñāpāramitā)*, 87, 174 n. 108
persecution of Buddhism: under Tai
    Wu Di, 19, 62; under Wuzong, 68, 76,
    93, 94
pilgrimage, 67, 105; under Zhou Wu Di,
    124
Pi Rixiu, 49–50
poetry, 117–118, 141
prophecy, 71–76, 140, 142
Puji, 72
Purui, 12
Puxian, 106

Qingxu, 171 n. 41
Qingzhu, 132

rain-making, 77, 85–86
Ratnamati, 80
*Record of Spiritual Resonance Associ-
    ated with the Three Jewels in China*,
    99, 102, 107
recorded sayings *(yulu)*, 132–135,
    185 n. 101
relics, 100, 161 n. 123: of the Buddha,
    35–37, 43–44, 48; of monks, 45; and
    mutilation, 36, 41; reverence for, 46
renunciation: of food, 22; of meat, 23–
    24; of social norms, 29; symbols of,
    16
resonance, 97–101; in pre-Buddhist
    China, 98, 100
Ricci, Matteo, 115

sacrifice: of body to animals and
    insects, 39; of body for others, 40. *See
    also* martyrdom; mutilation; suicide
Śākyamuni, 124; and miracles, 102
Samantabhadra, 106
Saṅghadeva, 121

scholarship: appeal of, 116; Chan
    attacks on, 131–135; as ideal type, 14,
    130, 141; in pre-Buddhist China,
    112–113
Sengqie, 110, 163 n. 170
Sengrui, 120–121
Sengshi lüe. See *Brief History of the
    Clergy*
Sengyai, 25, 43
Sengyou, 51
Sengzhao, 113
sermons, 119–121
sex: chastity, 17–22; Christian views on,
    19; in heaven, 19, 154 n. 14; illicit,
    19–20; monastic regulations on, 19;
    and monks, 52; social significance of,
    18
Shanwuwei. *See* Śubhakarasiṃha
Shide, 54
Shishuo xinyu, 101, 122, 125, 130,
    169 n. 12, 173 n. 99, 176 n. 132
shushu, 79–80
Si fen lü (Dharmaguptakavinaya), 23,
    78, 115, 120
Sifenlü bushan xingshi chao. See *Notes
    on the Regulations in Four Divisions*
Silla: monks from, 39, 72, 128
Sima Qian, 7, 100
*Solemnity Treatise (Mahāyānasūtrālaṃ-
    kāra)*, 47
*Song Biographies of Eminent Monks
    (Song gaoseng zhuan)*: and Chan, 13;
    compilation of, 6, 8, 134; criticism of,
    12–13, 135; praise for, 12; sources for
    10–11, 60; structure of, 9, 100
Song gaoseng zhuan. See *Song Biogra-
    phies of Eminent Monks*
sorcery, 81–82, 93, 97, 128, 144,
    176 n. 144
spells, 144; and demons, 84–85; in
    India, 83, 172 n. 81; and liturgy, 89,
    92; manuals of, 83–84, 89, 94, 141;
    in pre-Buddhist China, 82, 93; as
    rhetorical device, 87; scriptures as,
    90–92; and the state, 92–94; treat-
    ment of sickness with, 84; used to
    attain water, 85–86. See also
    dhāraṇī
spirits, 107–109, 141, 180 n. 219
Śrīmitra, 84, 94, 176 n. 132
Stein, Rolf, 108
Strickmann, Michel, 77–78
Śubhakarasiṃha, 1–2, 4, 59, 77, 89,
    166 n. 237
Sucaoshi, 45
Su E, 36

suicide, 142; of the Bodhisattva, 39; criticism of, 46–48; by fire, 37–39; monastic regulations on, 46–48; social pressures to commit, 45; and the pure-land, 43, 163 n. 166
Sun-kyŏng, 128
supernormal powers, 100, 176 n. 144; appeal of, 111; and meditation, 3, 70; of mind-reading, 71; as rhetorical device, 111; ridicule of, 134; of sight, 3; six basic types, 70, 140, 169 n. 12; and tricksters, 59–60

Taiping guangji, 59
Taizong, 8, 20, 94, 101
Tanjie, 5, 10
Tantrism, 166 n. 237
Tanwuchen (Dharmakṣema), 155 n. 21
thaumaturgy: as ideal type, 14, 140; and "participation," 110; and proselytism, 68; as rhetorical device, 111; techniques of 76–82, 140. *See also* divination; magic; rain-making; sorcery; spells; supernormal powers
Thomas, Keith, 76
transgression: justification for, 55–58; as rhetorical device, 55–56, 59. *See also* tricksters
transmission of the lamp *(Chuandeng lu),* 136–137; as genre, 132
Treatise on Consciousness Only, 121
tricksters, 52, 58–60, 63. *See also* transgression
Turner, Victor, 42, 141

Ŭisang, 22

Vajrabodhi, 77, 89
vegetarianism, 156 n. 43, 157 nn. 44, 50; as ascetic practice, 24, 34, 140; and filial piety, 23, 26; hostility towards, 27; among the laity, 25–27; and Liang Wu Di, 25; monastic regulations on, 23–24; and *Nirvāṇa Sūtra,* 24; in pre-Buddhist China, 22–23, 26, 157 n. 64; promotion of, 24–25, 55
Vimālakīrti, 55, 105, 113, 127, 130
vinaya. *See* monastic regulations

Wang Mi, 121
Wang Wei, 118, 152 n. 43
Wang Xun, 121
Wanhui, 73–74, 75, 81, 116
Welch, Holmes, 111
wine, 158 n. 71; as medicine, 65; monastic regulations on, 28; and

monks, 28, 52, 64, 140; social significance of, 28
women: and fortune-telling, 78; as source of defilement, 20, 21
Wŏn-ch'ŭk, 121
Wudeng huiyuan, 137
Wuran, 45, 67–69, 105
Wutai, 37–38, 41, 67, 105, 179 n. 205
Wu Zetian, 76

Xianzong, 36
Xichen, 41, 44
Xingzhi Jueshou, 13
Xiqian, 108
Xuanzang, 59, 72, 99, 121, 124
Xuanzong, 62, 77, 89, 93–94, 120
Xu gaoseng zhuan. See Further Biographies of Eminent Monks
Xuyun, 2–3

Yangshan Huiji, 41, 133
Yang Shoujing, 12
Yanshou, 153 n. 53, 164 n. 185
Yantou Huo, 13
Yaoshan, 133
Yijing, 16; on monastic clothing, 29–30, 32; on mutilation, 47; on suicide, 45, 47
yinming, 124
Yixing, 72, 171 n. 56
Yizong, 35
Yoga Treatise (Yogacaryabhūmiśāstra), 121, 166 n. 235
Yuankang, 30
yulu, 132–135, 185 n. 101
Yunmen, 13

Zanning: on begging, 33; on Chan, 131–132, 134–135; and compilation of *Song Biographies of Eminent Monks,* 6, 8, 59–60, 128, 134; on debate, 123; on demons, 95–96; on meat and wine, 58; on miracles, 100–101; on monastic clothing, 29–31; on mutilation, 47; on spirits, 107–108; on suicide, 44, 47; on supernormal powers, 71, 116
Zhang Heng, 17–18, 22
Zhan Ji, 18
Zhaoxian, 134
Zhaozhou Congshen, 134
Zhi Dun, 125, 126, 130
zhiguai, 69, 107, 150 n. 16, 169 nn. 5, 9
Zhijue. *See* Yanshou
Zhipan, 94
Zhixian, 132

Zhiyi, 85
Zhuangzi, 113, 120, 131
Zhuhong, 95
Zhu Xi, 137
Zizhi tongjian, 94

Zongmi, 131, 132, 144
Zürcher, Erik, 110
Zu tang ji (Hall of the Patriarchs), 133,
    136
Zuxiu, 94

About the Author

JOHN KIESCHNICK received a Ph.D. from Stanford University in 1995. After a year as a postdoctoral fellow at the Center for Chinese Studies, University of California, Berkeley, he took up his current position as an assistant researcher at the Institute of History and Philology, Academia Sinica in Taipei.

CPSIA information can be obtained
at www.ICGtesting.com
Printed in the USA
JSHW010051230722
28437JS00001B/5